NO DRUMS TO BEAT – NO FLAGS TO FLY

E B Parkes

MINERVA PRESS
LONDON
MIAMI   RIO DE JANEIRO   DELHI

First Published 2000 by
MINERVA PRESS
315–317 Regent Street
London W1R 7YB

Printed in Great Britain for Minerva Press

NO DRUMS TO BEAT – NO FLAGS TO FLY

To the men of 10 Platoon
who are no longer with us

No future left,
Nowhere to turn,
Just lying here
With vision blurred.
Knowing not
If day or night.
Living moving shadows
Through the mist they came.
My pain now gone,
Just a lifeless form,
They had won.
I could hear the drums
And see the flags,
My other life had just begun.

Contents

Foreword

In the aftermath of the Second World War, in the Far East with the Japanese Empire now at an end, the Europeans, having lost so much face, were finding it difficult re-establishing their pre-war powers. Now that the Japanese occupiers had been defeated and driven out, those once occupied were left with only one thought in mind – independence.

After years of suppression and injustices from the war, the people clamoured for home rule and self-determination.

At the time, the civil war in China had come to an end to leave the Communists the victors over the Chinese national armies, bringing with it communism, and the ideals which were to sweep the underprivileged Third World countries, and the fight against poverty and imperialism.

This quickly found followers in the countries with a large influx of Chinese immigrants, thus leading the dissidents to create unrest. From then on it was only a short step to open violence.

Soon countries like Indo-China, Korea and Malaya were in open combat with the communist guerrillas. Malaya at that time was a British protectorate and any defeat for Britain could prove disastrous for the recovery of the British economy.

Malaya, with its huge wealth of raw materials, had to play a large part in helping to pay the British war debt, and was to be protected at all costs.

It was in these circumstances that the British army found itself once more at war, fighting a vicious enemy, who asked for no quarter, and for whom no quarter was given.

This is the story of one particular platoon from one of the serving regiments, the Worcestershires. As part of 'D' Company, 10 Platoon were no better or worse than any other platoon. Made up of regulars and National Servicemen, a motley group of butchers, bakers and always the troublemakers, this is their story. I introduce you to 10 Platoon.

November 1996 – Visions

On this cold, wet and windy day. A day of remembrance. Standing there before a grey wet obelisk of granite. Pulling up my collar against the biting wind. Eyes, slow moving down the brass plaque. The raised tarnished letters forming unknown names to me.

Those names had altered history from two world wars, and the Korean conflict. But to my eyes the roll of honour was incomplete.

The cenotaph stone I stood before towered over the gathered crowd, paying homage to a bygone age. Fathers and sons who had given their lives.

My eyes, although on the plaque, were elsewhere. Looking into the past. The preacher's voice rambled onward about Queen and duty, as feet shuffled for warmth beneath the sea of umbrellas. The preacher's voice now tailing off into obscurity. My mind's eye stirring up visions of the past of some forty odd years ago. Was it really that long ago?

Visions of young boys sprang to mind. Young, eager and full of life. The sons of some of those here today. Come to give thanks to those that had given their all, never to realise their dreams. Never to return home. To die violently beside empty guns.

Those that had died at the hands of women, others from dreadful mistakes. Over the years, those that returned, some passing on, leaving a mere handful.

The brass plaque never knew these men. Never honoured them. They too died, only in those days it was for King and country. Unknown boys who died like men. My eyes filled with tears as I write this story as a tribute to lost friends with whom I shared a great adventure, and comradeship, lasting to this day. This then is their story.

February 1950 – To be a Soldier

That day I stepped down from the coach and crossing over in a flurry of snow, carrying a battered old suitcase, I joined the others who had also received their calling up papers to report to Whittington barracks. We followed in the footsteps behind a straight, upright looking Corporal, who lead us towards a Victorian two-storey building which was to become our home for the next twelve weeks, and for some the start of purgatory. Leaving our suitcases on our chosen beds in the cold barrack room, we were then taken to the quartermaster's stores. Here they issued us with blankets and oversized clothes. The swapping and changing that followed were the start of some hilarious scenes before most ended up with a better fit.

As ironing and bulling our kit took up most evenings, a stolen half hour down at the Church Army canteen was most welcome, where an egg and chip supper, costing only a few pence, filled our growling stomachs.

During the day the army cooks would offer us two choices, either undercooked or overcooked food. But after a day's training this looked good to a hungry man. Each day was drill day. In the snow and rain we marched and counter marched, stamping and turning in unison, in the cold snap of the winter mornings, bringing steam rising from the labours of the marching men to hover like a cloud as we were drilled.

There were days when we were marched down to the rifle range, lying prone in the mud. We sighted and fired at targets some distance away where a small waving figure was seen to either register a hit or miss. A waving disc showed a hit on the target front, pointing to where you had entered.

Somehow, during this time, I found myself in the boxing team. This had its advantages. Besides getting away with chores, we were treated to free drinks after the contest, as well as meals down at the Church Army. There were times, however, when we were too sore to eat. And on one occasion my hands were so swollen, I couldn't even hold the knife and fork.

Basic training had now finished, and we found ourselves in the snowy mountains of North Wales, learning to live with live ammunition being fired above our heads as we crawled beneath barbed wire. They called it battle experience. After one Saturday night out, down in nearby Port Madoc, a near riot developed between the local teenagers and the platoon. This brought a swift rebuke from the people of North Wales, asking for a ban on all future Midland regiments being trained there. Alas, like all good things, it had to end.

The training now complete meant the platoon would receive their regimental cap badge. This was a reef knot, surmounted by a royal crown, meaning I was a member of the South Staffordshire Regiment.

My kitbag was now stencilled with my name, number and overseas destination, which was Hong Kong. This was what I had been waiting for – an exotic beach, on a far away island in the sun. Shouldering our kitbags, we boarded the troopship, *Empire Fowey*, at Southampton. At last the waiting was over, as the ship's bullhorn blasted out the last call for those going ashore, and the gangplanks were lifted. As the waving crowd of onlookers gazed from the quay, a shudder ran through the ship as the massive engines began to turn the screws. Below our feet the deck trembled, as we entered the sea lanes of the English Channel. The sea swell lifted the bow of the ship high into the air. The engines pushed us forwards as we left the white chalk cliffs in our wake fading to a dark smudge. We headed out to the open sea.

From the portholes singing was heard as the bow broke through the heavy waves. Without realising it at the time, some of the singers would never return home. Our whole world, in the following days, was to change drastically.

June 1950 – The Card Players

It was on a sultry night in June that the real story began as the night skies were blotted out by the overhanging trees of the rubber plantation. Slight murmurs were coming from below within the bivouacs, sounds belonging to a weary platoon. In the darkness a muffled cough disturbed the sleepers, bringing a slight movement from the men, before settling down once more.

Almost immediately I awoke startled. Quickly sitting upright, I caught my head on the canvas roof of the two-man tent. Awaking in such darkness only added to the trauma I felt at that moment. Then, trying to use my ears as eyes and adjusting my breathing, I listened for the sound that had woken me.

Holding my breath, I heard the hum of a mosquito drawn like a magnet by the salty sweat covering my face. As the humming stopped I felt the slight hypodermic needle prick of its blood-sucking mouth pierce my skin. I instinctively brought my hand sweeping upwards in a vain attempt to kill the irritating menace.

The sound that had awoken me earlier was heard again, only this time it was followed by a succession of bangs and flashes which could be seen from the open-ended basher (the nickname we gave the two-man tents). As the short burst of gunfire ended my companion sat bolt upright.

'What's all the bloody noise going on, Ebee? What's all the bloody fuss about?'

Trying to keep as calm as possible, I answered in a low voice, 'Shh, keep still and quiet, there's something going on in the village.'

As if answering my companion's question for me, the gunfire erupted once more. Echoing through the darkness came the sound of crashing wood and human screams, bringing with it a cold sense of fear of not knowing what was happening. Then everything fell silent. Hardly daring to move, our rifles in our hands, we sat ready. Still tired, we dozed through the rest of the night, till daybreak.

That day 'D' Company, an infantry company of the 1st Battalion of the Worcestershire Regiment, had camped at a derelict rubber planter's mansion known as Tenang. This was far from the main road in the southern state of Johore, which was fighting for its life against communist guerrillas.

Earlier that morning we had been ferried by company lorries down the narrow, dusty dirt tracks, to our destination. At first we treated the journey as a joke as we bounced along. But by the time we arrived, we all felt sick and sore. Shouldering our packs and holding our short rations, we turned to see the lorries disappear in a cloud of dust the way we had come.

Carrying our packs and trailing our rifles, balanced in our right hands, we moved from the dirt track into the overgrown rubber. The Tamil labourers had neglected the rubber for months. Intimidated by the roving gangs of Commies for working for the rubber planters and afraid to venture into the rubber, their livelihood was threatened. It was acting on this information that had brought us here. We pushed firmly ahead, following the one in front, Indian file fashion. Hardly stopping or talking we travelled all day. As night fell we moved up closer to the one ahead. It was quite easy to lose one's way so we kept close, at times treading on the heels of the man in front. We lost all sense of time with eyes aching as we peered into the darkness, avoiding whipping branches as best we could.

It was a little after seven in the evening that we had stopped. The darkness made it difficult to clear a space in order to erect a basher. The basher was made from a poncho thrown over a straight cut branch, held at each end by a cleft in a forked stick, and pushed firmly into the ground. The hanging edges of the poncho pulled out tightly sideways and staked into the ground. This made an excellent waterproof shelter. Meanwhile another poncho was unrolled and laid beneath as a groundsheet. When finished it made a two-man tent, roughly three feet in height. Although cramped for space we were at least dry. At the rear of the basher we placed our packs which doubled up as pillows.

We erected the bashers in a circle. This served to give us all-round firepower against surprise attack. Heapy and myself crawled inside. By now we were ready to kill for a smoke, but couldn't, because to do so would risk exposing our position in the dark.

In low voices we spoke of home. We found out by chatting that we lived only a few miles apart. We had even been dancing at the same dance hall but had never met socially.

With the air full of buzzing mosquitoes, we pulled up our collars and rolled down our sleeves. Although we felt most uncomfortable in the stifling heat, it was far better than catching malaria. With my bush hat the last thing to be pulled down over my face, our tired bodies had soon fallen asleep, until woken by the gunfire and flashes.

A tug on my boot brought me to my senses. At the entrance of the basher, in the semi-darkness, was Corporal Cole. He was crouched down and still shaking my leg, whispering to both of us, 'Come on you bastards, wake up, it's stand to!'

Then he pissed off to wake some other unfortunate bastard in the nearby basher.

Turning to give Heapy, who had quietly dozed off again, a dig in the ribs, we crawled in the half light through the open-fronted basher and stopped just a few feet beyond, lying prone and quiet, our rifles pointing ahead of us in readiness for any dawn attack.

When dawn finally broke the word came to stand down. Returning to the basher, we broke open the rations. It was over a cold breakfast that we learned what had happened during the night. The shooting had occurred down at the village, which was hidden from view by the surrounding trees some hundred yards down the red track from where we lay. We sat and ate cheese and biscuits, washed down with a mess tin of water poured earlier from a water bottle which had been boiled on a metal fret found amongst the rations. This was to become known as the Tommy cooker. I watched Heapy carefully pour in enough tea for both of us, then the sachets of sugar and finally the milk.

From nowhere the ants and flies would appear, settling on the surface of the tea. The leafy ground soon came alive with ants, scurrying away with crumbs and grains of sugar back to their nests. Before I drank the tea I lifted the mess tin to my lips and blew the wildlife away. Then, once clear, I drank the tea as if they were never there, just like any Sunday picnic. It didn't take us long to find out that to have a smoke very often helped to fill empty stomachs as well as steady nerves.

Hearing someone coming we turned round to see Sergeant Cushion coming over towards us.

'Leave what you're doing and follow me. There's something I want you to do.'

Without further explanation he turned to the nearby basher where Gowey and Hutch sat.

'And you two come along as well. Leave your things where they are, just bring your rifles.'

He turned as he spoke to move away towards a dusty track. Standing up I threw the remaining dregs of tea from my mess tin onto the ground, before popping it back into my pack, and followed after the striding Sergeant down the rain rutted track, with the other three falling in behind. We began to wonder where we were going. Looking ahead we could see the thatched roofs of some village hidden from where we were camped by overgrown bushes. Sheltered beneath coconut and date trees, the village looked peaceful enough. However, in front of one of the larger shacks a crowd had gathered. They jostled to view something on the ground. Getting closer we pushed our way through. Lying in the dust we saw the blood-soaked body of a man clad in a filthy vest, stained trousers and some well worn bumpers on his feet (a kind of training shoe). A cap, bearing the red star of communism on the peak, lay as if thrown on the dead man's chest. This was my first encounter with the enemy and I didn't like it one bit. The only friends the dead man had right now were the flies, who were never choosy, as they buzzed and sucked the congealed, treacle-like blood.

Just beyond were three steps leading up to a porch. Here, deep in conversation with the headman of the village, was our own platoon officer, Lieutenant Bury. The Lieutenant let it be known that his name should be pronounced Bewery. He was a man who had aspirations for a quick promotion, volunteering his platoon for any dirty job no matter how dangerous.

Still following the Platoon Sergeant, the three of us went around to the rear of the shack, leaving the villagers chanting and gesticulating out the front, pouring out their feelings on the lifeless corpse. Moving round the back of the shack, we ducked under clothes lines that stretched across the unkempt yard. The lines were tied between large coconut trees that had broken coconut husks scattered beneath them. They sagged under the weight of the blankets, airing out in the early morning sun.

Suddenly from nowhere we were surrounded by snarling dogs kept by the villagers used to keep down the vermin. We drew our sharp machetes to defend ourselves, waving them in front of the pack warning them not to come any nearer. The snarling dogs took heed and slowly pulled back, tails between their legs, before turning and slinking away, sending hens that were clucking and pecking into the air, feathers flying in all directions. It was during this scene that we first encountered the bodies. One was directly below a window. He apparently had come crashing through wooden shutters and was somehow still precariously hanging on broken rusty hinges. Lying in a crumpled heap, a third body lay some yards to the front. He had been shot, but afterwards it seemed he had tried to get up and had got to his knees but then had collapsed and died. He lay there amongst the cultivated patch of pineapples as if praying, on his lifeless knees.

With the sun high in the heavens beating down on us relentlessly, we subconsciously used our bush hats to wipe away the dusty sweat as we awaited orders from the Sergeant. With the toe of his boot the Sergeant turned over the first body onto its back, commenting as he did so, 'That's the way I like to see 'em!'

The disturbed flies hummed angrily from the dark bloodstained chest. We could see he had taken a full magazine burst from a Sten gun. It was this that had awoken Heapy and me in the middle of the night. Swatting at the flies as they tried to land on our faces, after the tantalising salt, the Sergeant said, 'You two pick this one up, and the others grab the one in the garden patch and carry them around to the front of the shack with the other one.'

As he spoke he turned and disappeared around the shack side, leaving the four of us chorusing after him, 'Okay Sarge.'

As both of us bent down, Heapy commented, 'What a bloody mess, I wonder if his mother knew he was out last night?'

Slinging our rifles over our shoulders we picked up the body. I grabbed the ankles and Heapy the head by the shoulders. Half-carrying half-dragging we struggled round to the front, heaving and grunting as we went. We placed the body in the dust next to the one already there.

We could hear the other two cursing over the third body. The taller of the two, a guy called Gowey, a slow-moving man and at times rather an awkward cuss, shouted at the smaller man called Hutch who was constantly dropping the legs of the dead man, 'Pick the bloody body up and hold it. Do you want him to walk round on his own?'

The heavy body was causing the slighter built Hutch some trouble in holding it steady. He groaned back at his larger companion, who was waiting for Hutch to grab a hold.

'Why couldn't he have been shot through the front window instead of the back? He would have saved us all this bother.'

This was a typical remark from Hutch, who was now shuffling along with Gowey walking backwards holding the legs. As they came to where the other two bodies lay they let the body go, causing the head to hit the ground with a bump.

The three Chinese must have felt perfectly safe as they sat playing cards in the paraffin lit room of the shack that night. Smoking and drinking they had sat unperturbed as the Lieutenant and the others had crept onto the porch, before bursting in on the surprised card players and firing from the hip as the Commies tried desperately to escape. Two dived through the closed shutters at the back of the shack. One ran towards the firing guns before crashing through the door, the forward rush taking him down the steps where he eventually came to a stop.

Standing close to the bodies, the excited crowd of rubber tappers jeered and poked their former tormentors bodies in a show of false bravado, knowing for the time being they were safe.

While this was going on the Sergeant came over and told the four of us to search the inside of the building. Once inside we found blood spattered on the rush carpet leading to the window. Under the blankets of the two beds made from rough wood and criss-crossed rope, we found two rifles and a shotgun along with a bandoleer of shot gun cartridges. A third firearm was on the floor where it had fallen from beneath the window, where it had once hung. A deck of well thumbed playing cards lay scattered about the room and an empty bottle that had once held whisky and some drinking cups were beneath the overturned table. In addition we found the two missing caps with red stars above the peak.

Carrying out the guns we noticed the crowd slowly beginning to disperse, the men in their black shorts and vests following the women in their once highly clean colourful sarongs now stained by the sticky latex of spilt rubber resin. Their earnings from trees emptied into containers carried on their backs every day, other than for buying food, were worn as gold around their necks and armlets. They grinned at us through their gold teeth, trusting no one, not even the banks.

Still on the porch the headman denied any knowledge of the Communists. Frightened of reprisals, he joined the other villagers casting wary eyes as they looked on.

Further up the track, through a dust cloud, came our transport bouncing and lurching before grinding to a stop. We loaded on the bodies and with most of the villagers now in their shacks, we strode along after the lorries, followed once more by the snarling dogs.

Packing up our gear we struck camp, and with guns slung on our shoulders we marched on to the track before clambering aboard the waiting lorries. There we sat, on either side of the corpses, occupying the centre of the truck. Our sole thoughts now were on what was for dinner back at camp. Personally I could have eaten a horse. The trucks continued rumbling down the tracks, making the red dust blow into a cloud behind the wheels and caking the dust onto our sweaty faces. We ducked as the swaying vehicle lurched too close to the overhanging branches. We held on to our hats as the branches caught the men in the back of the lorry, scratching faces and arms as well as ripping shirts. The bumping and lurching threatened to throw us from the rear of the wagon.

Before long we were climbing the sloping hill which lead us into Tenang camp. We passed the guard tent, and stopping with a sudden jerk, sent those on the back sprawling forward. This brought a stream of abuse from the already knackered men.

We jumped down and slipped off the packs and rifles, before

laying them on the ground. Next we lifted the bodies from the lorry feet first and dragged them and lay them down besides the guard tent. From somewhere a couple of ponchos were found to cover the bodies until their removal. While all this was happening the rest of the platoon was handing in their grenades and extra ammunition. The grenades were defused and boxed, leaving us with much lighter pouches, especially myself as my gun, the EY, fired the platoon's grenades as well as bullets.

Leaving the ammunition to be carried by others to the ammo tent, we trooped over to our tent lines, passing as we did the officers' quarters which was once the pride of some rich planter and now needing a coat of paint and refurbishment. Opposite, three rows of tents stood close together. Each row had two tents, two tents for each platoon: 10, 11 and 12. The tired men of 10 Platoon limped into the first two tents. Finding my bed under which I threw my packs, I flopped down on the mattress. The light breeze blowing through the rolled back tent walls felt good. Still lying down I undid my ammo bandoleer from around my waist. Then bending over the side of my bed, I placed the ammo on my pack, almost falling off the bed in the process. At the same time Heapy shouted over, throwing a fag towards me, 'Catch Ebee. I'm too knackered to bring it over to you.'

My reaction was to catch it in my left hand and light it as I undid my jungle boots. I had eased off the socks that I had worn for two days and boy it felt great as I massaged my feet.

I stripped off the sweat stained, and rather smelly clothes, kicking them under the bed till next wash. Then I opened the locker at the foot of the bed and took out a towel, some soap and talc. I stood up to wrap the white towel around my naked waist. This brought a few wolf whistles from the men. I showed them what I thought of them by giving them the V sign. Slipping my feet into my leather army boots, I shuffled passed the beds asking, 'Anyone for tennis?'

I did a little hop and swing at an imaginary ball and as I did so the towel slipped, causing a response from the laughing Heapy, 'I like your racket you've got there!'

Half-running in my loose boots, dodging the socks thrown at me, I passed the dinning room. With the tent walls rolled back you could see amongst the shadows the rows of empty tables and benches, and at the far end the serving tables from where the cooks dished out the food to forty or so men per sitting. From the outside kitchens the smell of chips wafted through the air. My taste buds started to stir and I licked my lips. At the back of the cookhouse sat three squaddies on fatigues, peeling potatoes for the chips and plopping the peeled spuds into a galvanised bath.

Hearing footsteps behind me I hurried to get a shower. The noisy generator told me the shower was now working. I made a dash for the last few yards, my boots clumping up and down on my feet as I went and I threw my towel on a hook near the top of the galvanised walls. Once inside, I turned the shower tap fully on. In the first few seconds the cold water made me gasp and I caught my breath as I cooled down. Then the cascading water washed the smell of sweat and dust of the last few days away. The cool water, which was pumped from a nearby stream below the camp, felt like pure heaven.

Then the others arrived. Big Gowey had finished ahead of us and had dried himself down. And rolling up his towel into a lengthy rope he swished it at the unsuspecting naked bathers. His victims jumped and shouted as the rolled up towel landed on their naked behinds. Partly skating on the wet concrete, two of us grabbed hold of him. As he struggled we dragged him unceremoniously, shouting and cursing, back under the shower. And there we held him while someone gave him a taste of his own medicine.

The horseplay over we dried ourselves and made our way back to the tent lines where we dressed in a pair of black shorts, grey socks and army boots. While waiting for dinner the men made their beds. The mosquito nets, hanging from the canvas roof with the ends tucked neatly under the mattress, made us feel like pieces of meat beneath a meat fly cover.

From the dinning room the clanging of a steel wheel was the signal dinner was ready. This brought a mad rush from the men, all eager to be first in the queue. Grabbing mess tins we hurried to the dinning hall and formed a queue, tapping impatiently on the white platter mugs issued when we joined the army. Mine, like so many others, had long since gone, broken in transit or merely knocked off a table somewhere along the line. The queue began to shuffle forward as the cook placed the last tray of chips onto the serving table. Then as the queue moved down, the cook duly ladled out a portion of chips into the outstretched mess tins. As the queue continued to move the next server plonked a sorry looking egg onto my chips. Staring at the rubber looking egg, the cook caught my eye, then gave me this advice, 'You either eat it, or play with it. You please yourself!'

At the end of the table was a box of apples. This was the sweet of the day. With my free hand holding the smaller of the mess tins, I dipped it into a bucket of steaming tea. With the mess tin dripping with tea I turned round and looked for a place to sit, if possible, by the rolled back tent walls. Then I heard my name called.

'Over here Ebee, I've kept you a place,' a grinning Heapy shouted, waving to attract my eye. With little room elsewhere I walked over to him and sat down on the wooden bench. I nodded a thanks and looked down into the mess tin.

'What's the chips like, Heapy?'

He responded with, 'I think the eggs are made out of that latex stuff.'

With my knife and fork at the ready I started to dig into the meal. The rubber egg was cold, the yolk solid like a flat pebble you would find on a beach. Only the chips had that familiar taste of what mother used to fry. The thick noggin of bread had rather a currant look about it. On closer inspection, the blackcurrants had legs and bodies. The flour from which the bread was made was infested with ants. As this was all we had to eat, we had no choice. Swilling it down with the still hot tea had the effect of making me sweat even more.

Back in the tent sitting on the edge of the bed, crunching the apple and half-listening to the chatter and laughter of the others, a head poked through the tent entrance. It belonged to Sergeant Cushion. I was thinking to myself what an appropriate name he had, with the attitude he had and the way he turned up at the oddest moments, he should be stuffed without a doubt. His pencil thin moustache couldn't hide his smiling mouth as he announced, as if breaking up a party and enjoying it, 'When the dinning room's empty after lunch, the Lieutenant wants you all over there for a briefing on the jungle do's and don'ts. So don't skive off!'

Straightening up he turned and strode over to the next tent up the line where the rest of the platoon slept, to repeat what he had told us. I thought to myself, sod off and leave us alone. Then he passed the entrance once again on his way back to the office.

July 1950 – Camp Life

Half the platoon was already there when Heapy and myself entered the mess. The dining room benches faced a blackboard, with some memos already chalked on. The dining room filled quite quickly, with the men pushing past those on the front benches to sit on a table behind. Everybody seemed to be talking at the same time. Smoke was rising from the cigarettes to form a blue haze swirling above our heads, before being pulled out into the bright sunlight in waft-like waves.

By this time the full compliment of 10 Platoon were already present and waiting patiently for the appearance of Lieutenant Bury, and the Sergeant, who were way over the parade ground. The bungalow door opened and out they came. Stubbing out the cigarettes on the dirt floor, we came to attention as the Officer came ducking under the low eves of the canvas roof. His first words were, 'At ease men. Those with cigarettes may smoke.'

Removing his officers' peak hat, he wiped the inside before placing it on the table. He retained his silver capped cane with which he struck the open palm of his left hand from time to time, as if enforcing home his words. I removed my own bush hat, crumpling it slightly in my hand, then wiped away the sweat from my face as it slowly trickled down from my forehead from the overcrowded tent and the smoke.

The eyes of the officer wandered over the young men under his command, a mixture of factory workers, builders and shop-keepers who were now National Servicemen. He gazed at us, not in disdain but with a look that seemed to say, 'Would they do?' The old adage came to my mind: 'You are only as good as your commanders!'

Clearing his throat in the dry air the Lieutenant began with, 'This is the first opportunity we have had to get together. So I would like to introduce myself. My name is Second Lieutenant Bury, and like you I have only been over here a short time. Within the next few days we shall be going out into the jungle for the very first time. A few simple tips and words now will prove invaluable. Last night for instance was a prime example of everything going to plan. It also showed the plantation workers we can protect them.'

The Lieutenant turned to the blackboard. 'There will be times when we shall be carrying our own dead back like those Commies out there, ready to be taken by the ration trucks into Segamat to be laid out on display on the forecourt of the police station waiting to be identified by relatives or friends and later to be claimed for burial.'

Everyone was now hanging on to every word the officer spoke.

'Before we go out you will be issued with rations. A box of seven-day rations will be given to you to be shared with a partner. Keep to that partner. Get to know each other's habits. A good bond between the platoon is essential. These rations will be divided equally between each pair.'

My thoughts of a partner had already been made. Heapy and me. What a team I thought, as I listened to the Lieutenant.

'Food will not be the only thing you will be carrying. There will also be guns and ammunition, as well as extra magazines for the Bren gun.'

His tapping stick, falling on his palm, emphasised the words he was speaking.

'Then there's the water, your poncho capes, a change of socks. It all adds to the weight and only you will be carrying it. Over rough terrain, in the sweltering heat and heavy rain. So keep the pack down to bare essentials. Are there any questions you would like to ask me?'

Looking around the sea of faces, the Sergeant rose from the table where he sat and spoke. 'Come on, answer the Lieutenant. There must be something someone wants to know!'

A buzz went round the room as the men muttered to one another. From somewhere near the centre an arm shot up, and silenced the room as we peered to see who it was. We quickly recognised the speaker as Corporal Cole, a quietly spoken man who suggested, 'Sir, instead of everybody cooking individually how about taking out a communal pot. Say a large biscuit tin with a bit of wire to carry it, and to hang it over just one fire instead of several. Each man could contribute a tin at meal times.'

The officer pondered on the idea, then finally answered, 'That sounds a good idea, Corporal. See what you can do.'

With one asking a question there were soon others. Then the officer asked for a leading scout. The chosen man was Batey, a short stocky guy, who had led yesterday's patrol. This was one position I didn't care to have.

Meanwhile other questions were being asked, one being, 'What if we run out of ammunition or food?'

The Lieutenant replied, 'Another good question. I'm glad you reminded me. It's one I should have mentioned earlier. We shall be supplied by airdrop. An Army Dakota plane will parachute all our needs to us.' He paused. 'That's if weather permits of course. Does anyone else have any questions?'

Looking round and seeing no more raised hands the Lieutenant turned to the Sergeant, and with his free hand picked up his peaked hat. Seeing this the Sergeant brought the platoon to attention. The Lieutenant then touched his hat with his cane, turned and bent under the tent flaps before striding towards the office.

Born in Malvern and educated at a private school, the Lieutenant had left to join Sandhurst, the officers training school. He had passed out to find himself a Platoon Commander of a fighting force in Malaya. The army was now his career.

Once the officer had gone the Sergeant told us to sit back down. The air was stifling under the canvas.

'Before you all go there are a few things I would like to add. In your kit you will find some waterproof wallets. These are not for money, but handy for cigarettes and matches. In the humidity over here everything goes green and damp if not kept in tins. So keep these in the wallets. Also keep a new razor blade in your hatband. You may find it useful in case you get snakebite. And above all else keep quiet when we are out there. Sound carries a long way, and we don't want to tell them where we are.' He spoke with his eyes as well as his mouth, to impress upon us to listen, to what was being said. He continued, 'Sound in the jungle echoes for miles. When you've finished with empty tins, bury them along with any other visual signs of camp life we might leave behind.

When you pack your rations, pack evenly. Remember you have to carry them and we don't want any sore backs.'

What he said made sense. The game we played had no room for mistakes. Any made might cost a life.

'Don't pack unwanted articles such as shaving kit. Beards out there help to combat against mosquitoes biting. No books and especially no booze.' He emphasised the last sentence.

'Right you can all fall out now but remember what I've said.'

With the sound of benches and tables being pushed to one side I left the tent, to walk right into the full glare of the afternoon sun.

Having made our beds the men sat reading while some got out their pens to answer their mail from back home. A few cleaned their rifles out of boredom. Leaning forward from where I sat, I stretched out for the tin of fifty cigarettes that sat unopened on the locker at the foot of the bed. I lit one and then lay back onto my pillow watching the smoke drift lazily upwards. Even with the walls rolled back the air was motionless. Not a breath of breeze anywhere.

It was now three weeks since we were landed on Singapore Island having been told two days earlier while still aboard the troopship *Empire Fowey* that thirteen of us from the Staffords were being transferred to the Worcester Regiment. It gave us little time to get kitted out when once ashore in jungle green. Everything was green. Green uniform, green boots, green underwear, and even green guns.

After spending a few days at Nee-Soon Barracks, we were sent up country in Northern Malaya to a camp in Kedah called Sungi-Patani. It was about this time I got my nickname. On one particular pay parade, hearing my name, I came to attention and stepped forward for my pay. Having received my pay the Sergeant called me over, as he had done with the others, asking me for my full name. I replied by giving him my initials first and my surname last, saying, 'E B Parkes, Sergeant.'

'Ebee, Ebee. What sort of name is that? I've never heard of that one before.'

Amid laughter I explained to the Sergeant, but from then onward I became Ebee to all and sundry.

Two weeks later we were on the move again to where we are

now, Tenang, the nearest town of any size being Segamat. Feeling as if I had just shut my eyes, the cookhouse call came clanging to tell us teatime was here and to come and get it. Not fully awake I swung my legs off the bed and sat for several seconds as I regained my composure. Then gathering my hat and mess tins followed on after the others. Upon reaching the mess tent I found we had a salad for tea. Eggs, lettuce, tomatoes, cucumber and the dreaded Spam. I half ate the salad before pushing it away from me and began eating my sweet, which was tinned pears. We had a second choice as a drink tonight. Besides tea there was lemon squash. During the meal there was much talking and guessing as to when and where we would be going out.

Night closed about us. The petrol generator was switched on. The bulbs flickered for several seconds as the power surge stabilised and finally settled down. The tent walls were rolled back for the night, so as not to leave any easy targets for anyone lurking beyond the barbed wire perimeter. Guards patrolled along the perimeter, at intervals, for any such event.

My tea finished, I stood up, collected my mess tins and scraped the remains of the salad outside into the bin. Alongside the bin was a galvanised bath of hot water into which I plunged the mess tins, giving them a quick rinse then a shake to get rid of the excess water.

Later, as I lay in bed, I listened to the lads down at the Char Wallah's drinking beer and occasionally laughing from hearing a bawdy joke. I could hear the humming of the mosquitoes, as they searched for a meal in the never-ending heat. I started wondering what tomorrow would bring. Gradually the noise from the beer tent subsided as the drinkers left for bed. The lights dimmed as the generator began to splutter to a stop leaving only the chirping crickets rubbing their legs together in an incessant hum. A few beds creaked as the occupants tried to settle for the night.

Feeling as if I had just closed my eyes and gone to bed, the morning call left me yawning as I pushed away the mosquito net. I sat there for a few seconds and slowly came to my senses, then dressed in a dazed state with eyes half shut. I collected my towel and shaving kit and joined the others in the wash house. Using cracked mirrors and cold water we scrapped and scratched at the stubble with well worn razor blades. A toilet roll was placed above the washing trough and was frequently used for plasters on the inevitable nicks and cuts.

After breakfast we had our daily parade, and we quickly formed ranks of threes. 10 Platoon were the only ones on parade as 12 Platoon had quietly moved out in the early hours. This meant 10 Platoon taking over all camp duties. We were stood at attention. Sergeant Cushion stood out in front, facing the platoon, and there we waited for the appearance of the Company Commander, a Major Hall. Finally he appeared followed closely by our own officer. The Sergeant brought the men to attention once again, then turned to salute the officers who then returned the compliment. The OC proceeded to inspect the paraded men walking along the ranks looking us up and down and stopping occasionally and picking out minor faults, such as your hair's too long, get it cut. Perhaps a button unfastened or even missing.

Following on the heels of the Major was the Sergeant, who would glare at the unfortunate soldier. The soldier knew he could expect a dirty job at the end of the parade. With the inspection over the Major would return to the front of the parade, and as he did so two Corporals came round with the daily malaria and salt tablets. They too walked along the ranks and handed each soldier one of each. As soon as I was given mine I unscrewed the cap of my water bottle, which I had brought with me, popped the tablets into my mouth and washed them down with the now warm water.

Once we had been given our various jobs for the day, four of us trooped over to the stores to draw out shovels and a boring tool. We had been given the unenviable task of digging latrines. Carrying the heavy borer with me was Heapy who had also been honoured with the chore. His wavy hair was now showing the first tints of grey and he had a square jaw that gave him a look of determination. It wasn't a job I would have chosen on such a warm day. Come to think of it, it wasn't a job I would have chosen period. Carrying the tools we moved through the tent lines to someway beyond where the wooden sheds stood. We dropped the tools on the ground and chose a spot near the huts. This was so we could use the extracted soil to fill and cover the old, and almost filled, shit houses.

We began turning the borer in the starter hole. Two people were holding the borer upright and turning it, withdrawing it from time to time to empty the bucket attached to the screwing end as we got deeper and deeper.

With the first hole dug to a depth of around ten feet, we lay down for a rest and a quick smoke only to hear a voice bellow out from between the tent lines, 'Up on your feet!' The owner of the voice was the Sergeant. 'If the officer sees you he'll be asking me if you are on your holidays.'

It was at times like these I felt like a convict. Stripped to the waist handling a heavy borer, and in the midday sun. The rising temperature was making the stench rise from the overfilled holes of the latrines, and this was having an effect on the Sergeant, so he left.

Covering our mouths and noses with our handkerchiefs to try to nullify the powerful smells, we finally finished. We pushed the first hut over so the four of us could carry it over and cover the newly dug hole, and reeled backwards at what we saw: the writhing mass of maggots and swarms of flies, as they flew from the hatching larvae. The used assorted paper lying below moved with the crawling maggots. We quickly covered the unsightly mess with soil from the nearby holes, then left the holes to settle.

Having completed the job, we were now covered by a layer of dust and sweat, and slowly walked back to the stores to return the tools. On the way back we met the Sergeant who told us to go and get a shower. We did this gladly. Washing away the smells we knew it would be weeks before the huts were moved again.

August 1950 – The Paddy Field

'Wakey wakey, let's be having you!'

The voice broke through my subconscious sleep as I raised my eyebrows and half-opened one eyelid. The face that starred at me now was also the owner of the voice, Sergeant Cushion. His face looked as though it were made up of tiny squares as I looked at him through the mosquito net. Then he was gone, only to be heard a few seconds later repeating the same words to the occupants of the next tent.

After breakfast came morning parade, where Heapy, Hutch and some lad named Pouney were given cookhouse fatigues. I myself was given guard duties and this meant that I pretty much had the day to myself, unless something unlikely turned up. Lunchtime came and passed, the day slowly passing by as the ration trucks arrived back from Segamat. All available men were roped in to help unload the supplies. I helped unload bags of spuds, nets of onions, carrots, crates of lettuce and tomatoes for salads. By far the most interesting were the boxes of Australian rations. These boxes were marked in stencilled letters, the date boxed and for how many. Each box was a week's ration for two men. Our information was that Australian rations were far, far better than British ones, in that they had more variety.

In addition to the rations, the trucks also brought the mail, a good morale booster at any time. Sometime later, during the afternoon, the mail call brought the men together. The mail had been sorted out into the different platoons, and 10 Platoon's was called out in alphabetical order. We all listened expectantly for our names to be called by Corporal Cole.

'Private Heap, there's two for you. Private Hutchinson, there's one for you. Private Parkes?'

'Over here Corporal,' I blurted out.

He searched the sea of faces till he found me holding out my hand above those in front of me. Getting that warm feeling of hearing from home, I made my way over to the tent. I sat inside and smoked while I read the news from home.

We were now dressed and shaved and carrying our rifles, as we made our way down to the dining tent for an early tea. Early tea was laid on for the guard and we sat down to sausage, potatoes and cabbage, and two halves of tinned pears for sweet. This left us with just enough time for a few puffs of a cigarette before guard mount.

With the ceremony of guard mounting over, Gowey and I drew first stint on guard. We walked in opposite directions to cross over at the far side of the camp about twenty minutes later. Gradually the light began to fade and the generator was started up, but we could still see those having tea in the dining tent. The general hubbub of camp life went on as we patrolled beneath the trees, but eventually with dinner over the mess tent fell quiet.

Those first two hours passed slowly with just the moon for company and the occasional meet with Gowey. We changed over with the next two on guard and went to find our supper. The cook had already been and left the night's feast of cheese and onion, and a half-bucket of luke warm cocoa, under a towel. By the light of a hurricane lamp and half asleep, I ate my supper. Then afterwards, on one of the beds made available to guards, I fell asleep with my collar turned up, sleeves rolled down and my bush hat over my eyes.

Being dismissed from guard duty early next morning also meant a walk past the dining tent as the cooks prepared breakfast. As I approached, a strong smell of bacon wafted by, filling the coolest part of the day's air. As I continued to walk I saw right in front of me cardboard ration boxes stacked three boxes high. My first thoughts were of 'going out'. Quickening my step I hurried into the tent where the others were still asleep. Unable to contain the news to myself I awoke the sleeping Heapy, whose grunts and groans at being shaken brought the others fully awake. They soon told me the news could have waited.

I changed out of my trousers and into shorts, and with my towel tucked under my arm I ambled over to the shower block. The only ones inside were those who had also been on guard. Over a breakfast of bacon and a skimmer, called an egg, the talk centred on the ration boxes. We tried to prophesy when and where we were going.

Once breakfast and the parade were over, the platoon was tasked with opening the boxes. Given one box between two we quickly opened it with a long machete, and emptied the contents onto the ground. Kneeling beside the tins we counted them out. With twenty tins apiece, and of various sizes, we carefully packed the green haversacks. There was tinned milk, tea, sugar, bacon, sausage, beans etc. There was even toilet paper. Once we had packed the tins and made sure that no tins were sticking in our backs, we carried the backpacks over to our tents, and began sorting and packing our personal needs. Not that there was much room as the packs were nearly full now. In the side pockets of the pack would be the mess tins. In the other, a change of socks, also some ciggies and water purifying tablets. The tablets allowed us to make use of the streams while on patrol.

Our medical orderly was Hutch, who carried the daily salt and malaria tablets. He also carried morphine injections in throwaway syringes, a strong pain-killing drug. This was along with other medical essentials he carried on his side in a small satchel.

On my jungle green webbing belt were placed my ammo packs. Also hung there were my machete, bayonet and water bottle filled with fresh water. Below my pack was slung a tightly rolled poncho cape. In the band around my bush hat was a new Gillette razor blade, still in the paper. As the Sergeant said, it could come in useful if bitten by a snake. A quick cut between the two fang marks, a tourniquet around the arm or leg, whichever the case may be, could save you from a painful death. After a cobra bite however, only a prayer might help. From the Char Wallah's I bought three fifty tins of fags and a couple of boxes of matches. I bet my life I would forget something. I smiled as I thought to myself that it was as if we were packing to go away on our holidays.

Just after lunch 11 Platoon came in through the gates. They had just completed a two-week patrol, and looked dishevelled, unshaven and a few were sporting ripped uniforms. A more knackered bunch you never did see. The Sergeant brought the men to a halt as their officer, a Lieutenant Richards but known as

Chico, gave the Sergeant orders to carry on and sloped off to his quarters. Collecting the grenades and the extra Bren magazines, the Sergeant and his Corporals defused the primed grenades, before boxing them. They then got two men to carry the collected ammunition over to the armoury before dismissing the platoon.

11 Platoon's return meant 10 Platoon going out much earlier than expected. After dinner we were told to change into jungle greens with sleeves rolled down. Sleeves rolled down were a precaution that had little effect. The mosquitoes still bit through the clothing. We hadn't long to wait before the Sergeant told us to get kitted up and be outside in five minutes. We slipped on our now heavy packs, picked up our rifles and set off for the parade ground. Those with Brens and automatic weapons followed suit after a quick check that nothing had been left behind.

We lined up in threes as the Corporals, Coley and Nodder, nicknamed from the way he held his head, handed out grenades. Only this time we were handed an entirely new grenade. Instead of exploding shrapnel, these would burn phosphorous on explosion and smoke – useful for laying down a smoke screen.

Darkness was now upon us as we waited for the Lieutenant. He soon appeared at the door of his quarters, talking to the Sergeant asking if everything and everyone was ready to move on out. As soon as he was assured that it was, we broke rank and formed an Indian file. Leading us tonight for the first time was Hank. He came from Stoke, known as the Potteries back home. He was rather short and stocky with red hair, and characteristic freckles. With his Australian made Owen gun tucked beneath his arm, and the index finger of his right hand closed over the trigger, this cocky little man led the way past the guard tent, then through the entrance and down the track. Following just a few yards behind Hank were two riflemen, and behind them the Lieutenant. After him the Sergeant, followed closely by the wireless operator. The wireless operator was a Greek named Drakopolis, or Drak for short. He carried the eighty-eighty wireless set, its aerial waving side to side surmounted by a small rectangular flag on top, which jigged up and down at the slightest movement. Next came big Gowey with the Bren gun, then more riflemen.

I could be found about halfway down the line, and behind me

was Heapy. He called himself my number two on the EY rifle. This was a standing joke between the two of us. It was a position made up solely to keep us together, and so far we had got away with it.

Up front the sound of the stewpot, well actually a biscuit tin used as a stewpot and part of our everyday lives, could be heard bumping into something hard. This resulted in a low voice up ahead to say, 'Keep that bloody thing quiet!'

It sounded ominously like the Sergeant's voice.

The night air filled with mosquitoes that were making meals out of us. You could feel the bloody pests on your neck and face. It was at about this point that I caught my foot on a root or something and nearly fell. I swore under my breath and cursed at the darkness. The pack straps were beginning to cut into the flesh of my shoulders. Putting my thumbs beneath the straps and easing the pack further onto my shoulders every few minutes eased the pain, but only for a short while. All I could hear now was the crump crump of rubber soled jungle boots on the bone hard track. The breeze began to strike up and rustle faintly through the trees on either side of us. The silhouettes of the trees gave the surroundings a haunting feeling. You were half-expecting the earth to explode into a shower of light, your imagination running riot as your eyes tried to pierce the inky blackness of the night.

We lost all sense of time and direction in the moonless night. Then we began to get the strange feeling we were veering to our right and about to leave the track. The hard feeling beneath our feet gave way to a softer tread as well as the soft swish of knee high grass against the rubber boots. As we moved slowly into the enveloping blackness, only the movement of the shadow before me kept me on course to wherever we were going.

From the front came a whispered message we were crossing some railway lines. Were these the same lines we had seen from the ration trucks some days earlier? Moving carefully up the embankment I felt with my feet, until one foot caught the rail. I then lifted my foot higher and stepped over the unseen rails.

Out of the darkness a large shape loomed over to my left. This proved to be a thatched roofed shelter used by train passengers. It soon disappeared into the gloom. Meanwhile Hank the leading scout had found a track, though it was more by luck than judgement, and the going from now on was a little easier. Just then we were ordered to close up. Then we knew why. We had left the knee grass behind and were entering some thick under-growth, known as berlooker, that skirted the jungle edges. The weight of our packs was beginning to tell, and what with the pack and humidity and pushing our way through, our strength was soon sapped. The order to stop came none too soon.

I slipped off my pack with a sigh of relief, and began to move my shoulders in a circular motion. Then sinking onto my pack with my elbows propping me up, my thoughts turned to the sheer pleasure a cigarette would give me right this minute. Unbuckling my webbing belt and leaving it to fall around my waist, I took the water bottle from the pouch. I unscrewed the cap and gently shook the bottle in a circular motion, as if it were a double brandy. I put the neck of the bottle to my lips and drank the warm liquid. It seemed to have no effect on my thirst, hardly quenching the palate as the water trickled down my throat.

Stretching full length and using my pack as a pillow I settled down for the night. Or at least as best I could. I pulled my hat over my eyes. It was as if I'd switched off a light bulb. Having been on guard last night and after this night's little stroll, I felt totally exhausted.

Dawn was a misty affair and made the clothes feel damp. Heapy woke me in a quiet voice, asking, 'Have you had a good night, Ebee?'

With my back feeling as though I'd just broken it I answered, 'Yeah. The beer was a bit warm but the cabaret was great.'

Laughing at seeing the funny side of the joke he said, 'I stayed in all night. You could have sent for me.'

We broke off our mythical conversation upon hearing from the front that we should have a cold breakfast before moving on. I turned to Heapy to see whether he wanted cheese or jam on his biscuits, as he rummaged through his pack for the Tommy cooker.

'Cheese, Ebee,' was the reply.

From out of his pack he brought the cooker and opened a tin

of flammable tablets. He took out one of the tablets and placed it in the centre of the cooker. Once lit it became an efficient little cooker. Meanwhile I began pouring water from my bottle into a mess tin, then balanced it on the cooker. We ate the crunchy cheese biscuits as we waited for the water to boil, then poured in the tea from a freshly opened tin, and Heapy began stirring it with a broken stick. At the same time ants scurried about, carrying off crumbs of biscuit. The empty cheese tin was a seething mass of red foraging ants and then the red devils started biting us as we brushed them away from the tea.

We were just about finished when the call to move on came through. We buried the empty tins beside the track before shouldering our packs on still sore shoulders.

The patrol continued, breaking every hour on the hour for ten minutes. Enough for a smoke and no more. We stumbled along, keeping to the track all morning. The ground was littered with twigs and broken branches, but the narrow trail looked well used.

On one break as we were taking a swig of water, we heard the sound of gunfire. Instinct made us throw ourselves to the ground. Through the undergrowth the figure of Corporal Cole came gasping, blurting out, 'The front section have hit an enemy patrol that was coming across an old paddy field.'

Rising as one the rest of us ran, bent double, as shots clipped through the bushes towards the front of the patrol some fifty yards ahead. Even without packs, which we had left when we first heard the shots, running in this heat and carrying guns was hard work. With pounding hearts we came out on the edge of a bank, to gaze on what looked more like a swamp than a paddy field, stretching for nearly two hundred yards across and covered in slimly rotten trees. This was where the Commies were caught. Picking their way over from one rotten log to another, they were now fast disappearing on the opposite side and into the undergrowth and leaving in their wake a few scattered dead, lying half-submerged in the mud. Before we knew what we were doing we half-plunged into the muddy, waist-deep glue.

Firing rapidly from the hip at the fleeing Communists, bullets were scything through the tall trees known as lalang. Trying to make headway through the stagnant slime, with the mud hampering our movements, we were soon in the same position as the Communists were only moments earlier.

Dragging ourselves out of the mud on the slippery bank, we turned to look back and were relieved to see we had crossed without losing a single man, or even getting any wounded. Still covered in the foul smelling slime, those getting out first made for the undergrowth, where the Communists were last seen heading to make sure they had gone. Those of us left behind stood in the blistering sun baking and drying the foul smelling mud to our skin and clothes. The flies began to buzz around our heads. Having to endure it was unbearable.

Lieutenant Bury, by now jubilant at having such an early success, was delighted with the results. He ordered six of us to recover the bodies from the swamp, and take them to the far side. Getting over to this side was bad enough. But to go back and drag a heavy body, one only dreaded the thought.

I gave my rifle to Heapy to carry and again waded up to my waist in the churned up quagmire. I began to push and struggle towards the first body, slumped where he had fallen, over a rotting stump of a tree. The task required two of us and the only married man in the platoon, Bill Weaver, who partnered me gave out a shout as we neared the body.

'This one's still breathing over here!'

At this the Sergeant called back without any hesitation, 'Don't take any chances. Shoot him.'

Weaver raised his Sten gun, pulled back the bolt and with an well aimed burst shot the limp body. The body jerked as the bullets struck home. Lifting the bodies to partially free them from the mud, we began dragging and shoving them over the large tree trunks, their heads banging against them as we roughly handled them with their dead eyes glaring at us. As we paused for a breather we could see their faces. They were all young Chinese. No cause or ideas like theirs were worth ending up like this for.

On reaching the other side, Weaver scrambled up the bank, his lower half a glistening mass of slime. He began to pull the body up by the arms as I lifted and pushed until the body was clear. I dragged myself out and rolled over onto my side, gasping for air. From nearby there came a splash as the last body was pulled clear by Hank and Gowey.

Weaver was now searching the body of the one he had pulled clear for watches or rings. On the left hand was an expensive looking ring. Probably stolen on a previous raid on some unprotected village. With the others on their way back, he couldn't risk anyone seeing him remove the ring, so he produced a knife and duly cut the little finger off. He got his ring and the finger got brown as it was tossed in the mud.

By dragging the bodies feet first we had gradually worked and rolled the blood-spattered vests upward on the bodies. This left visible the gaping wounds and the holes left by the bullets. They had the appearance of being poked into the flesh by a large sharp pencil.

One Commie had lost his false teeth, which must have fallen out somewhere in the swamp. We gazed at the bodies lying on the side of the bank. The crawling flies began inspecting every nook and cranny of the remains of those young lives forfeited in a cruel ending.

On the far bank the returning front section began to appear from the thick undergrowth. This meant the Communists had fled without offering any resistance, back to their jungle lair. They struggled across the green matted surface, opening up new paths as they waded through and leaving a criss-cross pattern over the slimy surface. They had retrieved the Commie's weapons from where they fell. As they reached our bank we gave them a hand to get out and some dropped to their knees after their exertions.

While they recovered, the rest of us – six in all – cut down and trimmed three strong branches to make poles for carrying back the bodies. We then tied the hands and feet together using the toggle ropes which we had brought with us. We then threaded the poles between the tied wrists and feet, the same way that natives carried their live or dead animals to market. It was a crude but simple method of transport.

Soon afterwards we started the long trek back to Tenang. With the poles resting on our tender and sore shoulders, the bodies swung from left to right to the rhythm of our walk. The sightless face of a Commie starred blindly into my face. The congealed blood had almost clotted on his vest in the full-blown heat of the day. After a while the continuous jerking movement of the pole on my raw shoulders was more than I could bear and I called on Weaver at the front end to stop.

'Weaver, will you put the pole down. Only it's rubbing my shoulder like hell.'

We laid the pole and body on the ground before I reached for my hat and drew it across my face, which was now covered in sweat. Then I folded it up into a pad and placed it on the sore shoulder, before asking Weaver if he was ready to continue on our weary way.

It seemed as if we had trudged on for hours this way and we began to stop more frequently. The sun beat down relentlessly with the low trees offering very little shade. I was becoming oblivious to the pain in my shoulders.

By now we were getting our hand signals together and instead of turning to those behind to tell them what was going on up front, we simply put together a few simple hand signs which made it easier to communicate, and was certainly quieter.

Townsend, carrying an Owen gun, was now leading scout giving Hank a well earned rest. When he signalled to stop by raising his hand shoulder-high this was repeated down the line until all had got the message. Giving out a sigh of relief I lowered the pole on the side of the track. Heapy closed up behind me and slipped off his pack and two rifles, one of which was mine. Orders from the front had told us we had stopped for a meal. No fires. Only Tommy cookers to be used.

This brought a response from Heapy. 'That old biscuit tin will never be used. It was a waste of effort bringing it.'

Just as he finished talking, he nodded past me. On turning round and looking in the direction he had nodded, I saw the rest of the patrol resting. I also saw the Lieutenant walk over to Drak, the wireless operator. A few moments elapsed as they spoke, before the wireless operator donned the earphones and made a call to base. Talking into the microphone, Drak relayed the message given to him by the officer. Then holding only half the earphone to his left ear, the officer spoke into the mouthpiece. He had made arrangements to enter camp after nightfall, as this was the time we were expected back. A password for recognition was given, to be exchanged with the guard on arrival. Handing the earphones to the operator, he stood up and ambled over to where his pack lay beside the track.

I asked Heapy if he fancied sausages. He answered with a nod and I started busying myself by finding and opening a tin of sausages. Once opened I found a skinless, triangular shape of sausage meat. I placed it in a mess tin with a knob of marge, and putting it onto the already lit Tommy cooker, proceeded to fry. Breaking a twig from a bush next to him, Heapy carefully turned the browning bangers as they sizzled. Somewhere down the track the smell of bacon filled the air. The sausage was now cooked and carefully shared out by rolling half the sausage from one mess tin to another. We ate the sausage with our fingers and drank hot tea between mouthfuls, as the Corporals lay wrapped in ponchos beside us and out of the sun. We kicked at the empty tins that brought the flies once more to torment us.

Finishing the meal we rinsed the mess tins out before burying the old cans in a shallow hole. It was uncanny how you could stop in any place, and within minutes it was swarming with ants.

Collecting our gear together we changed places. Those that had carried the guns now carried the dead. The poles were lifted and at once the feeding flies buzzed crazily at being disturbed. I began to wave my hat, as they descended, in order to disperse them.

Starting back with the knowledge that we could all be sleeping in our own beds tonight gave us that extra lift in our step. Still wary we were still in bandit country in late afternoon, we emerged in the lalang grass. This stretched out towards the railway tracks, where only a few hours earlier we had crossed in total darkness. Even now the light began to fade as the sun sank behind the distant trees, outlined on the far hills where Tenang lay.

Walking through the lalang brought other bugs to bite and irritate us as the long grass swished against our boots. We all hoped we could reach the dirt track before nightfall. God only knew how we would cope carrying the corpses over the lalang and broken ground. By the time we had crossed the railway tracks, darkness was upon us but at least we were nearer the road. Eventually we moved on to the road and although in darkness, we made good progress. We approached with caution as we neared the camp.

The guard, having heard us, threw out his challenge, 'Who goes there? Friend or foe?'

Townsend, the leading scout, exchanged passwords with the guard. On hearing the password the guard ordered the platoon to come forward. Those with the poles made for the side of the guard tent, and laid the bodies down. A few words of relief were heard and from somewhere an old blanket was found to cover the bodies until morning.

Somehow, after taking a shower, we managed to get to bed only to wake the next morning painfully with stiffness from the previous day's efforts. My shoulders were very badly bruised and red. I sat on the edge of the bed and reached down for my boots. I gave them a tap to dislodge any unwelcome guests, which may have crawled in during the night, before putting them on. Beside the bed was my pile of stinking clothes. I rolled them up and tied them in a bundle before putting my name and number on a piece of paper. They would be sent down to the dhobi wallah's in Segamat to be washed. I had been so tired the previous night that I couldn't remember getting in between the sheets.

I was walking across to the dining room, when from the corner of my eye I saw a quickly moving shape. My reactions were sharp and I swiftly moved away from a bad tempered monkey, the company's mascot. He was tethered by a long piece of webbing around his waist to a tree. Anyone coming within range would either be bitten or clawed. He had been bought by one of the regulars, a Ben Elkins, from Sungi-Patani, probably from a street trader. Only Ben could handle the wild beast, taming it with a dead snake knowing that monkeys feared snakes. 'Clem' had been a victim himself some weeks earlier. Attacking someone once too often during the night, the victim had almost hacked to death poor old Clem with a machete. Ben though had sewn the badly gashed monkey's injuries and had saved the poor creature's life.

September 1950 – You will Fight or Die

The truck drivers left the dining room early after breakfast. They left with two guards to each truck. The lead vehicle already had the bodies loaded onboard, while the second lorry had our dirty washing, labelled 10 Platoon.

With the patrol coming back early, we were not finished for the day though our successes were fast getting the platoon a reputation of being a search and destroy group. So we sat and waited, reading our mail with backpacks at the ready. It would take only minutes to be either marching or loaded onto wagons and back out on patrol. Maybe that was it. We were waiting for the trucks to come back from Segamat.

Fatigues were done. The cookhouse vegetables were ready for cooking, the showers hosed down, the area cleared of litter. With only the mail to look forward to the trucks could be heard returning way before they reached the camp. The armed guard standing behind the driver's cab gave a wave to the waiting men before jumping down over the sides.

With orders to unload we dropped the tailgate. Two climbed aboard each truck and began passing crates of onions, cabbage, sacks of potatoes, etc., into the arms of those on the ground.

Stepping from the office, just as the stores were finished being unloaded, walked Corporal Cole carrying the all-important mail. For me the mail seemed more special. My call-up papers had come only a few months after my father's death. This meant me having to leave my mother in a time of grief, and having to cope without her son. Shouting out our names the Corporal came to the last letter. I stood there waiting for my name to be called, only to be disappointed this time around. I felt miserable. Not receiving any mail before going out to finish the patrol meant that my next mail would be a week or more old before I would receive it.

As the night drew on we learned the patrol would continue in the early hours, but in a different area. We slept in full uniform until almost four o'clock in the morning until being woken quietly to parade outside.

Patrolling and ambushing the tracks for that week went very peacefully. We did however manage to use the cooking pot, and found it very useful cooking the communal stew. Doing it this way saved us the worry of what to choose to eat.

Seven days later we returned wearily back to camp, our food just about gone. Feeling hungry and wanting a shower, we stripped off our clothes, and hobbled over to the showers, with just a towel and loose boots. We entered the showers in threes and stood under the rose, too tired for horseplay.

We were now showered and shaved and feeling fresh. Sitting down to a fish and chip dinner soon solved the problem of being hungry. That night there was no scraping the leftovers into the bin. The plates hardly needed rinsing.

Like any night of the week, the only place to go was a short walk down to the Char Wallah's, for a drink of tea which was an art in itself to see made as he poured the tea from one jug to another. Either that or a bottle of Tiger beer or even a fizzy drink.

Standing behind a table, as if it were a bar, the Char Wallah was serving the early birds. The table was wet from the dripping water off the bottles which were kept in cold bath water.

The tall, lean, dark-skinned Indian had a contract with the army to sell, on isolated camps, alcohol, tobacco and cigarettes. He also cut and sold sandwiches which he called 'banjos'. Cheese, cheese and tomatoes, fried eggs. If you wanted biscuits, he sold packets of four.

Most of the lads had their drinks, sandwiches and ciggies on credit. The Char Wallah kept a tally on each man, by writing down the goods that they had in a book. Come pay day the Char Wallah would wait with his book open. A few argued with him as to the amount they owed. There were those who used the protesters' names for free beer. All in all it was best to pay when you could, with cash. When all was said and done, it was the only place we had.

I handed over a red ten-dollar note for a cold beer and a cheese banjo, pocketed the change and sauntered over to a table where the other platoon members were talking. About women, naturally. Eating and drinking, laughing and singing. A story here, a joke there, as the flitting shadows around the naked light bulb brought the night fliers to life. The larger moths competed with the mosquitoes as they flew in circles, creating a Chinese shadow theatre on the canvas roof.

The tables, laden with bottles of Carlsberg and Anchor beers, began to get knocked over the merrier the men got. This brought the Char Wallah round from behind his table, his arms waving, to calm the situation down a little.

Leaving the smoke-laden atmosphere of the tent just before lights out, I felt more relaxed than I had been for days. Here we could let off steam, talk as loud as you wanted, and smoke when you pleased. The complete opposite to when you were on patrol where only 'Adam's ale' was to be found.

With arms round each other's shoulders, we swayed and staggered to our tent lines before wishing one and all goodnight. Finding my bed I stripped down to just my bare essentials. It was much cooler once you were under the mosquito net to sleep in the humidity of the night.

Then there was the hubbub of the washhouse, the noise of the running water and first one then another asking to borrow your razor or soap, telling you they had run out or even the excuse, 'I've left it on the bed.'

I heard a familiar voice behind me as I reached for the mirror, 'Leave it there Ebee, old buddy!'

That could be only one person. Heapy. He was one of the last up, and was grinning from ear to ear, his eyes half-shut.

Halfway across the parade square, way over from the gate, the guard was heard shouting, '*Brinti, Brinti!* Stop, I said stop.'

Speaking in both Malayan and English the guard was holding back a crowd of hysterical Chinese and Tamil rubber tappers. From the guard tent the remainder of the guard appeared and joined the lonely guard on the gate.

Separated by the barbed wire surrounding the camp, shouting and waving their arms in near panic, a crowd had gathered. They took some consoling from the guard to keep the noise down so as to hear their grievances. The disturbance soon brought the officer of the day over. With the majority of officers out with the other platoons, those left in the camp had to double up their duties. 10 Platoon's Lieutenant Bury crossed quickly over from the mess to find out what all the noise and fuss was about so early in the morning.

Waving for them to keep quiet he listened to one and then another. He found out their grievances were caused by last night's raid on the nearby plantation owned village. Being easily accessible to raids from the Communists and having a quick getaway if need be, a group of six heavily armed Chinese had raided their homes. Moving from shack to shack, harassing and beating the occupants up, both Chinese and Tamils had been systematically beaten and robbed. Ransacking their belongings as they searched for valuables and with no money or jewellery found, they had filled bag after bag with tinned food and non-perishable goods. Before they retreated back to their jungle camp they had rounded up the young men, choosing the strongest, and a Chinese girl. They had threatened the villagers with reprisals if they exposed them to the military. With their unwilling abductees carrying the booty, later to be indoctrinated in the ways of communism, and hopefully to fight for the cause, the raiders had returned to the jungle.

The rubber owners, for cheap but hard-working labourers, had employed those who had been abducted. During the mayhem the ones who had been beaten proceeded to show us their badly bruised bodies, split lips and blackened eyes. We tried to calm them down by saying, 'We will see what we can do. Search the area and try and find out where they have taken your sons and daughter.'

They eventually made their way back to their near deserted village, still chanting out the names of their children. With both 11 and 12 Platoons already committed to patrols, 10 Platoon had the only available men for this emergency. Almost immediately we were told to get changed and need only bring our weapons and water bottle, a few toggle ropes and our machetes.

Losing no time at all we were quickly outside, Hank going to the front and taking up the lead scout's position. With the Sergeant giving the signal to move at a quick pace, we left. Falling in behind us was a handful of villagers. This left only skeleton forces to 'hold the fort' back at camp.

Moving in the direction the villagers had given us, we passed the neat little rows of shacks. The smoke from the outside fires was rising almost vertically in the calm of the day. We caught the smells of oriental cooking as well as the smells of the barking dogs, chickens and pigs. Their way of life, which was very much different from our own, was now in chaos.

The track left by the abductors seemed too easy to be true. They were either careless or supremely confident. Moving quickly we came to the railway. Suddenly Hank raised his hand and brought the patrol to a stop. The Lieutenant and the Sergeant went forward to where Hank was stooping down. On the ground, lying face down was the young Chinese girl. Catching hold of the shoulder Hank turned the body over. Hank stepped quickly back and turned away, clenching his teeth.

Blood from a gaping wound covered the slashed throat. Fresh blood on top of dried which had stained the clothing. The crude slashing of the neck had severed most of the jugular. As if that wasn't enough, they had also stabbed her in the chest and neck. With the head and blood came the inevitable flies and beneath the body lay a pool of blood where ants scurried in confusion, having such an abundance of food.

Women from the village were let through the cordon of arms. Immediately seeing the body, they fell on top wailing and gesticulating to the heavens, seeing their loved one struck down in cold blood.

Leaving them to make their own arrangements to move the body we pressed on, wondering how many more we were going to find this way.

Behind us we left the railway and pushed through the same lalang, where only a few weeks earlier we had clashed on the open paddy field. Was this the same gang we had hit so hard?

Striding under the relentless sun's heat, the lalang let loose the basking flies and made us increase our pace so as to reach the shade and protection of the overgrown thickets, and entwining creepers.

I unfastened my water bottle from my pouch, unscrewed the cap and drank as I walked. The effect was almost immediate. The sweat was pouring from my body and my shirt was open to the waist and clinging to my skin like a wet rag.

We heard from the front the sound of hacking, and we came to a grinding halt knowing we had lost the scent. The trail was dead. The hacking continued as we tried to find a way through the dense undergrowth. Slowly but surely we moved on, passing the cut-down branches and creepers and stumbling over the cut shoots.

Keeping a wary eye open for whipping branches, those in front pushed forward. The scratching thorns ripped at clothes and tore flesh. I prayed we would find the trail soon.

I was trailing my gun blindly following in the footsteps of the man ahead. Then I realised he was crossing his arms above his head, relating back to his followers there was a track ahead. We had stumbled on the one lost earlier. This was to be made clear a few moments later. Murmurs came back down the line saying we had found one more body.

The information coming down the line was a bit sketchy, saying he was found hanged but little else. Leaving those around me I began sidling up to where the body was seen hanging. Well away from the trackside it was only the broken down undergrowth that made Hank feel suspicious, conduct a small search and make the discovery. Otherwise he may have hung there for decades before being found.

Keeping well away from the track, this gang of vicious thugs, so-called freedom fighters but nothing more than a gang of murderers, had failed in their efforts to convert the man to fight for their cause.

Under and around the tree stood the Lieutenant and the Sergeant with the first section. Above them, swinging back and forth in a half circle, was one of the young Chinese, his arms pinioned high up between the shoulders and head lying to one side. A large knot was visible as the body turned. Made from a clothesline the pressure from the rope forced the eyes to bulge from their sockets and the tongue was forced between the yellow teeth in a grotesque manner.

Those around the tree seemed uncertain what to do. They seemed more interested in the flag hanging limply above the staring corpse. Through the folds of the flag the Hammer and Sickle could clearly be seen, and it was this that made those below suspicious. There seemed to be something more than just a hanging flag.

Hutch, who was lighter and more agile than most, was helped into the tree. He carefully took his time, as if searching for something. Then excited shouted to those below, 'I've found a cigarette tin, jammed in a fork!'

The Sergeant immediately piped up, 'Careful what you do. Is there any string tied to it?'

Hutch took his time before answering, 'Yes, Sarge.'

With this the Sergeant called again, 'Hold the string. Don't pull it, whatever you do. And cut the string before anything else.'

Hutch gently cut the string and prized the fag tin from the fork and off the branch, thus releasing a very ingenious booby trap. Quick and simple to apply but deadly to those standing below – a crude but effective trap.

Passing the fag tin to someone on the ground, Hutch – still in the tree – cut the rope holding the suspended body which crumpled on hitting the ground. He was the last of the abductees we were to find.

Although the search continued until dusk, the others, if not dead, would be press-ganged into serving their new masters to face a life or death struggle.

We began to make our way back with the men from the village carrying the body on a pole following up the rear. We passed once more the spot where the murdered woman was earlier found. The blood stains were now a dry mat where her lifeblood had drained away. Abused and then killed to gratify animals. This was nothing short of barbaric.

By the time we reached camp the blue skies had turned to a dark clear night. The mess hall lights could be seen where the rolled tent walls had been carelessly left open. We crossed to the line of tents, where once inside we placed our weapons in the gun racks. After a hasty wash we collected our mess tins, and although late had our dinner.

Back in the tent we settled for a night of playing cards. Sitting on the bed and around it. Using the centre to hold the pot, the game of poker began. The stakes began rising from a few cents to a dollar and the losers began dropping out with the words, 'That's me done.'

Those returning from the Char Wallah's asked who was winning. As they undressed for bed and as 'lights out' drew near the game ended.

'Lights out in five minutes!' the Sergeant said. The chugging generator stopped. Then darkness.

October and November 1950 – The Man with Two Heads

The day we were introduced to the new trackers was like stepping back in time. They came from a little known place called Sarawak, on the West Coast of Borneo, from a tribe of forest people.

They were a pagan tribe of headhunters in the past known as Hebans and reputed to be the world's best trackers. They had heavily tattooed faces and bodies. Their ears were disfigured by tribal customs such as cutting their ear lobes and inserting wooden pegs and ornate pebbles. These elongated the lobes to reach the shoulders. Around their necks hung a skin pouch rolled in linen, with lucky charms and holding some ancestral hair or bone. Others wore a brave enemy's bone. They believed that it would ward off evil spirits. Even ward off bullets.

They spoke in pidgin English, missing out the connecting words that clipped the sentences down to a minimum. A Heban was assigned to each of the platoons. Luang, the elder of the Hebans, and the assumed leader, was assigned to 10 Platoon to take over where dogs had shown indifferent results.

Given their own tent and food, they at first kept to themselves and cooked over open fires in woks. Their concoctions of meal heavily laced with curry gave off highly spiced aromas.

When introduced it was like shaking a water pump handle for several minutes. Although their hands looked hard and leathery, they were quite soft.

Headhunters. The thought conjured up a nightmare beyond belief. Before the Second World War the custom of these people of taking human heads from opposing warrior tribes was still in practice, along with the old black art of shrinking heads. Then the war had come and the Japanese slowly and surely stamped out this evil practice to leave only magic and potions.

We learned that Luang's son, named Rawang, was 12 Platoon's

tracker. We heard stories of his encounters with the Japs, and how one encounter had ended painfully. He was still bearing the scars where the Japanese, when he paddled too close to one of their gunboats moored on the river near the village, had shot him in the leg and thigh.

Blue skies began to change to racing dark clouds. Then grey heavy clouds that brought the rains. The monsoon season was upon us changing open areas to giant lakes, and rivers to swollen torrents. The heavy rainfall ground all operations to a halt. Fortunately the Commies, like us, were also bogged down by the weather.

The heavy rains were to lash down for days, blocking roads into town. The floods created havoc in the low-lying villages where livestock and cultivated fields were swept away. Bloated cattle, pigs and chickens floated downstream, to join other drowned creatures too weak from hunger to fight the fast flowing currents. Snakes slithered through the clouded waters making any movement by boat or wading highly dangerous. Only the very brave or desperate were tempted to try. Insects clung to floating debris off the trees as they fought for survival.

At HQ as the rivers rose, sandbags were hastily filled as they waited for the nearby river to burst its banks. Throughout the region the only way to travel was by boat or raft. The rafts were poled along, laden with crates of chickens and pigs that had survived, coconuts picked perilously in the rain, and small amounts of vegetables from where the flood had not yet reached. They paddled their produce, however small, to the town market where perishables were quickly sold.

On ration days when we ventured forth only the high wheel-bases of our vehicles kept the engines above the water level. The drivers had to use all their skill and knowledge of the area to try and keep the vehicles on the hidden roads. The crossing of the bridge into Segamat was hair-raising to say the least.

Holding on to the sides of the steel trucks, with ponchos draped around our shoulders, we shielded ourselves from the driving rain. Bush hats dripped water into our eyes, blurring the vision. We felt generally miserable.

We drove through the town centre past those who had dared

to venture out, some beneath umbrellas, some in shop entrances. We noticed their expressionless eyes and unsmiling faces as we passed.

We were soon loaded with the rations. Boxes of this and bags of that. Then we went to collect the mail from the quartermaster's stores. As soon as we were loaded we climbed over the rations, and sat wedged between the boxes and the sides of the lorry. We got underway and, although a harrowing experience, we arrived safely back at Tenang.

After weeks of heavy rains the end was in sight. Gradually the rivers began to subside, draining the roads and fields back into the rivers and leaving flies, bloated bodies and mud everywhere.

The first patrol was terrible. We were in ankle-deep mud, which made sucking and gurgling noises as we struggled along. Slipping and tumbling the air was thick with bad language as we cursed every step. The bodies rotting in the sun seemed to move. Then on closer inspection we saw that it was maggots. Deep in the jungle we came across the carcass of an elephant. A full-grown male lying on its side. The skin was stretched over the huge bones. The eye sockets were empty and the once strong tusks hung loosely in the upper jaw of the skull. Slipping on the treacherous mud had brought this massive body down and unable to regain its feet it had simply died. A few days from now even the skeleton would be gone as the wild animals and insects took turns to dispose of the body. Leaving the heavy smell of death we continued on our way.

Pushing through the wet undergrowth, Luang, now established as our tracker, turned towards Hank with fingers over his lips. Hank nodded that he understood and they both stopped in their tracks. Along the track in front came the sound of leaves and twigs cracking under foot. Movement.

Suddenly before us stood a Commie, equally shocked at meeting someone in such a remote area. With both parties surprised, no one moved for a second or so until the Sergeant knocked both Luang and Hank sideways and in one movement brought his Owen gun on target. He fired one burst from the hip as the Commie was bringing his own gun to bear. Standing momentarily in a rather startled fashion, as if to say, you've shot me, he pitched face downwards and lay still.

Getting up quickly Luang and Hank moved forward searching the track up ahead for any more surprises. Finding and hearing nothing they returned to find the Sergeant going through the clothing of the dead man. He turned out a few notes and coins and scraps of paper, then turned his attention to the knapsack about his shoulders. He handed the sack to the Lieutenant, coming to the conclusion the dead man was a courier, a sort of postman between Communist groups in the area.

The knapsack contained letters, some food and a packet of cigarettes. Throwing out the cooked rice the Lieutenant kept the knapsack and contents for later translation by the intelligence section.

The Chinese courier had caught the burst chest high. Death was instant. A few yards further past the body lay his hat never to grace his head again. It was covered in the dark red blood we were now used to seeing. Examining the shotgun he carried we found that it was cocked. A few more seconds and it could easily have been one of us lying there.

From the body we stripped a bandoleer of shotgun cartridges and laid it alongside the shotgun.

We buried the man in a hole already prepared for us by the fall of a tree, now rotting with its roots fully exposed. Dragging the body over to the hole, we threw in the corpse, pushing it down with our boots. Then with the sides of our boots we pushed in the soil before finally throwing his hat in. We shouldered our packs and left the lonely grave without a prayer or comment.

After a two week long patrol we returned to camp, without finding the enemy camp where the dead courier was either going to or from. The documents that he carried proved very informative. The intelligence boys wanted more however. They wanted the identification of the body and only the body would prove that.

So, three days later and the platoons out in the general area were searching for a fallen rotten tree Among thousands of trees. As if by some strange miracle, we did find the tree. However this was no guarantee of finding the body. It may well have been dragged away by some wild animal, a tiger perhaps.

With Luang as our head tracker we at least had a man of the

forest and by some unknown way Luang did find the exact tree. Parading himself around the tree, his thumbs stuck between his ammo pouches, in pidgin English and with a broad grin he said, 'Me find. Me find. Me very good tracker.'

You had to give the old devil his due. He knew his stuff all right.

Undisturbed by the animals, the ground was still covered by branches we had laid on top with the roots pointing down like fingers, saying here he lies.

Two members of the squad drew their machetes and knelt beside the grave, beneath the overhanging roots. They began to dig and scrape the topsoil away, stopping to tie handkerchiefs over their mouths, as the smell of the decomposing body rose. As the body became visible the putrid smell of death made those around the hole turn round and vomit.

Scraping the dark rich soil the amateur gravediggers unearthed the head first. There was movement within the scalp, which seemed to make the hair ripple. Gowey, being more adventurous on such occasions, lifted the heaving scalp with the aid of a stick, and exposed a writhing mass of maggots, wriggling, squirming maggots. Heapy who was a little further back rummaged in his backpack until he found what he was searching for. It was a buzz bomb. A spray for killing mosquitoes. Breaking the top off made the capsule fizz in a fine spray. Lifting the scalp again he sprayed the inside of the skull using a circular motion. Wriggling violently the maggots died, making the gruesome task less unbearable as they began to uncover the rest of the body.

By now the head and shoulders were pulled above the ground. One of the diggers brushed the clinging soil away from the man's eyes using a handful of leaves.

Some of the men began to mutter, 'How the hell are we going to carry such a stink? And will it get worse every day?'

Lieutenant Bury had the answer all along. Knowing the head was the only part needed for identification, he turned to Luang and asked him if he would cut the head from the body.

With tight lips he nodded yes and began to draw his native parang – a sword – from its split bamboo scabbard bound with copper wire. He stepped astride the body and brought the parang way above his head. For a second or two he seemed to meditate. His eyes fixed firmly on where to cut. Then the parang came down with a swish, cutting through the sinews and spinal bone. He then changed his stance. Again eyes fixed. The parang poised above once more. Then swish, as the blade descended, slicing through the opposite side. The head rolled from the torso. Bending down, Luang lifted the head high for all to see his handiwork, turning the head round by the hair.

It was at times like these you realised how little emotion was shown, no matter how horrendous the situation may be. We emptied the maggots from the head and dashed some water, from a bottle, over the face. Heapy drew out the waterproof green wallet from his pouch. These were used when fording rivers to keep essentials dry such as cigarettes and matches.

Gingerly lifting the head by the black hair, Heapy lowered it into the now empty pouch. Tying the top tightly, he had been chosen to carry the head back. The head weighed about twelve pounds, and was a considerable weight to carry, especially knowing what it was. Macabre, to say the least.

We covered the headless torso first with soil and then branches, and shouldering our packs we made good the remaining hours of daylight.

Walking along with Heapy in front of me, I couldn't get the picture out of my mind of Luang standing over the body. It was as if he was doing a ritual ceremony back home in Sarawak, an event which the victor would perform on his opponent. First shrinking the head in sand, before hanging it up in the tribal hut.

Unconcerned Heapy strode on. The smell was now contained in the bag. A sudden thought came to me: that's the only man I know with two heads.

Night came. The evening meal of stew finished, we washed out our mess tins in a nearby stream, and refilled our water bottles. We bedded down for the night. It was then that Heapy had the bright idea of carrying the head down to the stream. Tying it and staking it to the bank, the head sank to the bed of the stream, moving slightly in the currents. There was no one more grateful than me to see the grotesque and evil head taken from where we were about to sleep.

Halfway through the night a tugging on my boot told me it was my turn on guard. I left the snoring Heapy in the blackness of the basher. Feeling tired I listened to some animals further upstream splashing as they stumbled in the darkness. The camp slept peacefully on.

At the end of my guard – referred to in military speak as stag – I crept to the nearest basher. Feeling for the leg, and gently tugging its owner awake, I pressed the illuminated watch face into his palm and left him in the dark. I crawled back to where Heapy was and lay down beside him. He was still unconsciously scratching but was too tired to remain awake.

Waking from an uncomfortable night's sleep I sat up itching, as did Heapy. We were covered in red spots and bite marks. We had erected the basher on a nest of elephant fleas! With the red mite still on our clothes, we stripped off and shook our trousers and tunic, to the laughter of the onlookers, as we stood naked as a robin.

After a breakfast of bacon and beans we broke camp. Heapy retrieved the soaking head and repacked it in his backpack. With any luck we would be sleeping in our own beds tonight.

It was almost an hour after we broke camp, when a 'splat splat' heralded the start of a deluge. Rivulets turned into torrents, and we were soon fording streams and wading across in the teeming downpour.

We scanned the muddy ground for the first signs of the dreaded leeches, when a rustling made me turn quickly. There scampering away in the sodden undergrowth was a full-grown golden armadillo, a rare anteater with powerful front claws, shaped for digging rather than running, long snout and equally long tongue, and a plated iron-hard skin for protection. This enabled it to endure the bite from its favourite food – ants or termites. The armadillo didn't know how lucky it was to escape the local villagers. An animal such as this was a rare delicacy, seldom caught.

Well into the afternoon, soaked and bedraggled, we found the waiting trucks as we trudged down the muddy track that was once the road. Like drowned rats we climbed aboard the trucks. Our clothes hung on the slim frames of our bodies as the water dripped from them. The short journey back to camp was miserable and uneventful.

Once back we ambled back to the tent lines. As we were already wet there seemed little point in rushing. Inside we stripped off and nearly rubbed ourselves raw with clean dry towels. Once dried and changed and with a long awaited cigarette between my lips I began to feel human again.

Finding an empty ration box, Heapy unwrapped the waterproof wallet and took out the head. He then placed the head on the wooden crate. From somewhere a camera was found which prompted Hutch to come out with a comment, which although funny, made some sort of sense, I suppose.

'He can't have his photo taken with his hair looking like that. Anyone got a comb and some hair cream?'

There and then the hair was combed and groomed. The head's sightless eyes were partly open as the camera's flash lit up the tent. Shortly afterwards the Sergeant entered the tent and retrieved the head, to be taken away for identification. Personally I was glad to see the back of it. Whoever he was alive, his face would give me nightmares at a later date in revenge.

December 1950 – The Man with the Blue Chin

Reading the detail board outside the office, we noticed there was a request for volunteers to join the regiment police. Anyone interested was to contact the platoon officer to see if they could be released from patrol duties. A Jeff Taylor, also from 'D' Company, was thinking about applying for the post. Forwarding my name for selection I was slightly resented by some of the platoon. But I had had enough. I wanted out. Although I regarded all coppers in the past as another breed of mankind, I was prepared to become one of them. Anything to get away from the hell that most patrols were. Though not popular the police job at least promised the offer of a dry, regular bed and little danger of getting killed. With this in mind I forgot about what the job entailed and went ahead.

Close to the camp we had built a rough rifle range, where on odd occasions a platoon would go down for practice. Below the range, which stood on the side of a hill, ran a road that ran through the surrounding rubber plantation. I was now on one of these occasions lying down facing the target, a playing card with the ace of spades.

'A dollar you don't hit it, Ebee,' someone shouted.

Just as I squeezed off the shot, a puff of dirt beyond the target told me before I even examined the card that I had missed. Turning sideways I gazed at the grinning faces, but no one owned up, and no one said you owe me a dollar. It had been said only to put me off my shot and it had worked.

Before the shoot we had all agreed to put a dollar each into the kitty to be won by the first one to dot the ace. A couple of shots had already clipped the edge but not a full hit. Hard, but not impossible to do.

Taking turns the next marksman was the sentry. I went over to relieve him so he could take his shot, and stood there silently smoking, half-expecting a cheer to go up, signalling a winner.

From where I stood on the hill, although surrounded by thick bush, I still had a clear view of the winding track that led past the road which led to our camp.

Several minutes had now passed and the only thing I was expecting was a winning shout, when from between the trees, dust began to rise. And from behind it the first of three army lorries. Above the cab of the first truck, cradling a Bren stood the gunner. Upon hearing the rifle fire for the first time the gunner quickly scanned the area. Sensing he was going to open fire in our direction, my instincts told me to warn the others on the range, who were currently unaware of the impending danger. I shouted out, 'Get down. Get down. They're going to fire!'

Looking puzzled as I waved my arms they soon realised something was wrong. At that moment the Bren gunner opened fire raking the hillside and ripping through young trees to my front. Following the burst those on the backs of the trucks were now jumping clear scattering into the bush below me. The scene was now set for a bloody skirmish. Shouting at the top of my voice, I yelled, 'Stop firing. Stop firing. It's your own men!'

I continued to shout, but someone below me must have heard because next I heard a shout, 'Cease fire. Cease fire everybody. It's the men from 'D' Company. Hold your fire.'

With caution I stood up waving my rifle. Those on the trucks had genuinely thought they were being attacked from ambush positions. The Sergeant who was with us went down the hill to have a word. He returned a few moments later and informed us they were from 'B' Company. He also told us that there would be an enquiry into why they were in 'D' Company's area without our knowledge.

We collected the box of ammunition from the range. We never did find a winner that day. That night however, down at the Char Wallah's, the first drink came out of the kitty.

I had all but forgotten about the request for the police post when it came through. I had been accepted. I packed my kitbags and accepted a frosty goodbye from my friends. Feeling like a rat deserting a sinking ship, I kept asking myself, Why can't you cope with the bad things? They have to.

I boarded the lorry that was to take me to Segamat, wondering as we rolled over the down bridge if I had done the right thing.

The dust lifted into a cloud as we entered the market centre.

People busied themselves around the open-air market. Buyers plucked chickens from the numerous crates and haggled over prices. Tethered goats chewed at the woven baskets. Seller and buyer both argued and bartered for the best price, as the goods lay strewn at the feet of the traders.

Progress was slow through the centre, as we weaved our way honking the horns and waiting for the road ahead to clear. We eventually left the powerful smell of the market behind us and headed on to open road, before finally reaching HQ.

The camp was split into two by the main road. On one side was headquarters, while on the other the newly formed 'A' Coy (company), yet to do its first patrol. Behind the camp, overlooking the hill, was Segamat's university.

We turned off the road and into HQ, passing the red and white halt poles. Just inside the gate was the regimental police post, a thatched roofed bungalow with a path between well kept gardens which lead to the guardhouse door. Shouldering our kitbags, Taylor, the other volunteer, and myself walked up to the door covered on both sides by giant sunflowers. We knocked on the door, resulting in a gruff voice answering, 'Enter.'

On entering we were confronted by four beds against a wall. In the centre of the room was a table and four chairs. Under the window, behind a polished desk, sat the Provost Sergeant. He had a large red face and boasted a bushy moustache and his barrel of a chest with arms and body sported tattoos from around the world where he had evidently been. He looked up from the papers he was reading and glanced at each of us in turn before asking, 'Which one of you is Parkes?'

Answering as I stood to attention, 'I am Parkes, Sergeant.'

'Hmmm! And why do you want to join the regimental police?' he asked scratching his smooth chin thoughtfully.

Having anticipated he might ask this, I already had an answer. And whether I remained here or jumped back on the wagon to return to Niyor now depended on that answer. I had gone through this over and over again in my mind. Trying hard not to sound like a parrot or as if I was reciting from a book, I cleared my throat and answered, 'I feel that I have something to offer in the way of how to enforce army rules, while at the same time the initiative and conviction to carry my actions through.'

There, I'd said it. And without making a pig's ear of it. Glancing upwards I said a silent thanks.

Tapping his fingers together the Sergeant rocked gently forwards and backwards on the chair's two back legs, before asking the same question to Taylor, this time adding some sarcasm.

'And why do you want to join? For an easy time no doubt. Well you might find it more demanding if you stay.'

Without hesitation Taylor answered back, 'No Sergeant. I have great respect for army discipline.'

Taylor rumbled on some more in the same vein as I had. But had we said the right words to convince the old fox? The Sergeant stood up and walked over to the closed door opposite. With his back to the pair of us, he said in his gritty voice, 'My name's Sergeant Golden. And in there is the holding room, at present empty. I want to see it full.'

We looked past his broad back to see six empty beds. Folded on each bedspring were three biscuit mattresses, topped by wooden pillows. A wooden locker lay at the foot of each bed. The unbarred windows seemed out of place. Prisoners would find it easy if they wanted to escape. All they had to do was jump through the open window. One drawback though. Where would they go? Home was eight thousand miles away. By sea or land.

Without having to say as much, we knew the Sergeant had given us the job, on a month's probation. The 1950 Christmas period was just a fortnight away. So what better time was there than now to break in two new rookies? Partnered by the senior NCO over the following days, we learnt some of the duties we were expected to carry out. These included supervising offenders and confining them to barracks. We also had to find them jobs, the more menial the better. I was told the cookhouse was a favourite punishment imposed. There was the cleaning of scores of greasy pans and scouring out waste bins. Then there was the scrubbing of office floors. What better time for the offenders to think of their wayward ways.

Town patrol at night was the one I liked doing the best. The places classed as 'out of bounds' to all other ranks did not apply to the police. Segamat, like any other large town, had its own red light district in the backstreets. Soldiers visited the brothels and prostitutes, mostly on pay-day and at weekends. There were nights of brawling in the bars. Disputes between the shopkeepers and the bartering soldiers got out of hand. Squabbles between the locals we left well alone. Our job was strictly military only.

With the holding room getting full most weekends, the following Mondays were a busy day for the commanding officer. Hearing cases from the weekend's exploits, he would sentence the offenders either to loss of pay, being confined to barracks, or both. The more serious cases were sentenced to the glass house, at Kluang's military prison, personally somewhere I didn't want to see.

The run up to Christmas meant an increase in drunken sprees in the town, generally ending with broken up bars and some of the soldiers needing hospital treatment. The soldiers usually ended up paying for the damage and finishing the night in the holding room.

There were those who were hard habitual drinkers who were bent on becoming our regular customers. In the holding room at that moment was one such person named Charlie Bannister. A well built man he was decent enough when sober, but a devil when drunk. And his present crime was being drunk, and he was sentenced to fourteen days loss of pay and fourteen days confined in the holding room. Serious, but not serious enough to send him to the military stockade at Kluang.

Bannister had what was referred to in the army as a blue chin. No matter how many times he shaved, he was left looking as though he hadn't. No matter how hard he tried, he still had a blue chin. This got him into frequent trouble when going on parade. The inspecting officer continually harassed the poor man for not having shaven.

Feeling a little more than sorry for the man I gave him the odd cigarette when the others went for a meal and left me in charge. I found an old pair of chest expanders left behind by a previous visitor. Charlie asked if he could borrow them, and soon became obsessed with his physical fitness. He would stretch the expanders in all directions, but at least it served two purposes. It kept him quiet and helped to kill time as well.

Christmas morning came and the hard gritty voice of the Provost Sergeant could be heard growling out, 'Wakey, wakey. Let's be having you up.'

This came on top of a very hectic Christmas Eve. Downtown the locals saw how the educated English held up the Christmas calendar in their drunken state which often ended in brawls.

Waving a bottle of Bells scotch whisky, the tottering Provost Sergeant had every intention of getting us all drunk before breakfast. He filled outstretched mugs with liberal helpings. And sitting on the edge of our beds, rubbing our eyes, we sipped the festive drink while giving each other Christmas greetings.

Later, with towel and soap beneath my arm, I made my way over to the deserted wash house. Everyone it seemed was still in bed. Today being Christmas was a time when all army regulations were turned upside down. The officers would serve dinner to the ranks in the mess hall, and turned a blind eye to most things, including comments. This custom went back many years in the British army.

I was enjoying the comforts of the empty wash house. Instead of the usual fighting for a place to wash, I shaved that morning at a leisurely pace. Finishing, I rolled up my shaving kit and soap into my towel fully intending to enjoy a good Christmas.

Back in the guardroom we finished off the rest of the Bells whisky before going down to the dining room for breakfast. The whole place had been transformed by paper decorations and coloured balloons. Even at this early stage beer bottles lay everywhere as people got into party mood.

The cooks that morning had done us proud with a full English breakfast. Looking around the room there were those who were the worse for drink, and would probably end up spending the day in bed.

With breakfast over we stood outside, rather at a loose end with not having anything to do, other than drink ourselves silly. Then Taylor said, 'Fancy going down to the church, Ebee? And do a bit of relenting of your sins.'

Feeling slightly merrier and free from regimental armbands that said I was police, I answered, 'Why not. And when we come out, what's stopping us having a drink then?'

Segamat town was only a few minutes' walk from the camp. The white building of the church stood near the railway station. Standing in the arched doorway a Chinese clergyman shook each hand as they entered the cool hall. The congregation quickly began filling the pews. They came together from different faiths. Christmas united multiracial marriages, Buddhists and Muslims alike.

The patterned tile floor of the aisle led the way to the altar, mounted by brass candlesticks on either side of the highly polished cross. Above and beyond this a stained glass window depicted the Last Supper, with each disciple with oriental features. This was how they saw religion. We sat near the back, amongst the mixture of races, as the service began. First with a carol, then the Christmas story told in a simple way, and understood by all. Prayers were offered for a more peaceful 1951. Amen to that. The service ended with children lighting candles.

We were soon outside once more in the humidity of the day. It wasn't exactly like back home, where the snow and ice gave Christmas that feeling we all knew. How I wish I were there right this minute.

With dollars burning a hole in the lining of our pockets we soon found a suitable bar. High in the ceiling a large fan whirled round, cooling the air considerably. Behind the bar was a red-faced fat Chinese man, who stood grinning. Behind him the well stocked shelves had a fine selection of spirits and beers. A box of King Edward cigars lay open beside the brass cash till.

I stood facing the barman and without turning I asked Taylor, who by now had selected a table below the fan, 'What's your pleasure, a whisky, or maybe a beer, or whatever takes your fancy.'

The barman was waiting to take my order as Taylor leaned forward and pointed to a bottle marked Jack Daniels.

'I'll try some of that whisky there. Yes, that's the bottle.'

The barman's hand hovered over the square shaped bottle before he took out the cork and poured out two liberal helpings. I paid the man and gently carried over the whisky, along with the bottle under my arm, and placed the glasses down on the table.

We summoned the barman, who we called Charlie, to bring

over the box of cigars. He also brought over a dish of salted peanuts and placed them invitingly in the centre of the table. Holding the box of King Edwards open the Chinaman looked on as we selected a good cigar each. Lighting the cigars with a cough then smoking and drinking, we proceeded to get pissed with the minimum of effort.

All about us on the walls, playing possum, were fly-eating lizards. They would stay perfectly still until an unsuspecting fly landed too close. The long flickering tongue would dart with amazing speed for its meal. Only the rolling of the skin over the eye gave any sign of pleasure from this immobile reptile.

Taylor began flicking the peanuts at the wall lizards. On occasion he hit one, causing it to dart away across the whitewashed wall. As it escaped it discarded its tail. The wriggling nerves of the tail left the lizard's attacker bewildered at the escape method used.

Through the swirling cigar smoke, the clock high on the wall showed twelve o'clock. With lunch back at camp at one o'clock I muttered to Taylor, 'Just one more drink for the road and we'll go, otherwise we'll miss out on lunch.'

Getting up I held the chair to steady myself, before walking to the toilet, down the passage beyond the bar. Turning into the toilet, I found instead a hole in the ground where the toilet should have been with two footprints on either side of the hole. Working it out I stood astride the hole, whistling and looking downwards.

Back at the table I sat down heavily. Like myself, Taylor was drunk. Having pushed away the last drink, the barman hurried from behind the bar to usher both of us into the street. With arms wrapped around each other's shoulders, we sang and lurched from one side of the road to the other. The townspeople were wary as we stumbled along. Children stopped playing to watch our antics, and began mimicking and laughing at us. The irony of the situation was we couldn't arrest ourselves for being so drunk. The moral of the story therefore has been who guards the guards?

Somehow we managed to arrive back at camp. There we were standing at the bottom of the path, leading to the door of the open guardhouse. In my present state the path seemed to move and swerve. I closed one eye and stretched out my arms. I then tried to aim my body at the open door. I staggered up the path and slammed straight into the doorframe, then bounced off with arms flailing. In an effort to regain my balance I stumbled sideways. I was rolling over in my drunken state among the towering sunflowers, trying to regain my footing, when from behind me standing on the office balcony overlooking the road stood a figure whose voice boomed out, 'Get that bloody man out of that garden, before he damn wrecks the place. He's a menace in that state. Get him inside quick!'

The voice belonged to the Regimental Sergeant Major. Lying on my back, gazing upwards, I gave him a wave and shouting back from the flattened flowerbed said, 'I'm a steamroller, look.'

Gazing at the flattened flowerbed, with a stupid grin on my face, the RSM muttered something under his breath and stamped away. Had it been any other time bar Christmas and I would have been facing charges of misconduct. My last memories of Christmas for that year were of being lifted from the flowerbed, carried to my bed and being thrown roughly onto it. Over the next day or so any fluid I drank turned to alcohol. My head was full of tiny hammers all banging away. I was full of apathy.

Recovering from my escapades I found myself buttoning on the RP (Regimental Police) armband above the elbow, adjusting the gun holster on my waist and pulling the peaked cap low over my eyes. With Taylor also ready we stepped out to patrol the fleshpots of Segamat's pleasure areas.

We carried walkie-talkies for getting in touch with base, for backup or transport if necessary. We had one torch each for the dark alleyways and the old policeman's friend the truncheon used for equalising the odds in bar room brawls. We climbed into the fifteen hundred to be dropped off where the most popular bars were and the music was the loudest.

Outside on the streets only a few people stirred. The lonely taxi-trike owners waited in the cab seats for the solitary fares that came their way as a soldier, worse for drink, wanted a lift back to camp.

Shops stayed open late lit by their own lamps. Passing away the boredom and watched by others, the 'click-click' of the Mah-jong counters became lost in the darkness. We sauntered past the dentist to find him asleep in the open fronted shop, lying there in his dentist chair.

We made calls on the out-of-bounds brothels and other places of low life. One such place was down a dark alley. Our torches picked out the dumped rubbish. The dark shape of a dog yelped as I kicked a tin can towards it. The foul smell was on a par with the seedier sort of life found here. At the end of the alley was a set of dimly lit stairs, the red light giving the area its name and notoriety. Situated behind the shops, the brothel's only access was down this dark alley. A thieves' paradise waiting for an unsuspecting victim. We climbed the stairs to find gauze covering the open door.

This led into a dingy rundown hotel. Standing behind a counter, a grubby furtive figure of an old wrinkled up Chinaman took money from a young looking man. He placed the money in a quickly filling tin box. The younger man turned to take his place in the forming queue of men. Some stood smoking, others leaned patiently against the wooden walls of the hall. A door opposite seemed to hold their attention more than the others.

As we stood there talking to the desk clerk, we noticed every twenty minutes a man would come out of the room and one of the waiting men would enter. From the adjoining room a giggle was heard.

Turning to the old Chinese we asked for the keys. Shaking his head and then his hands he said, 'No, no, no one's in there. No one, Johnny.'

Taylor and I looked at one another, and coming to the same way of thinking, went over to the door. Putting our shoulder to the flimsy door, the bolt splintered off from the inside. The door swung open to reveal a man on the edge of the bed, hastily pulling up his trousers while a young Chinese girl of around eighteen stood opposite, naked with her back and elbows on a set of wooden draws, the only furniture besides the bed in the room.

There was no sign of embarrassment on her smiling face, her firm young breasts pouting straight at us. Her man friend or client soon dressed and left in a hurry.

Moving from the room we saw the desk clerk gesticulating and waving his arms as he tried to keep the waiting clients quiet. He shouted at us in a pleading voice, 'No soldier. No soldier. Please go away.'

Shoving past the old pimp, because that's what he was, we left the uneasy queue of men shuffling as they waited their turn with the girl.

Patrolling around the smoke-filled and noisy bars we gave the drinkers an occasional glance. This had the desired effect on them and kept the night free from trouble. With this done we found a quiet bar out of the way and enjoyed a cool beer and a smoke.

Then more out of curiosity than anything else we returned to the brothel we had visited earlier. It was now quiet and looked even shabbier now that the corridors were empty. The door to the young prostitute's room was ajar. We pushed open the door and there she was, lying on her back, legs apart and showing her red and white polka dot panties. It was as if her legs were too sore to close. Then again twenty or more men was a lotta lotta loving. Hearing us enter the room she glanced up at both of us. I turned and hurriedly left the room with the words, 'Not tonight Josephine, sorry.'

Accidents in the army were bound to happen when you were around firearms. These turned ugly and often final. This particular accident was more unexpected than usual as it came from a kind gesture which quickly turned into a tragedy.

Returning from one of the first patrols, 'A' Coy from the opposite side of the road from HQ came in weary and low. Moments later came a shot and the next thing we knew they were bringing a body of a young boy into the holding room. The body was placed on one of the empty beds, before being transferred to Kluang for a post-mortem. It had been wrapped in a poncho cape so as not to upset the onlookers.

Following on behind the stretchered body came the upset Sergeant, totally distraught, to report the accident to the Provost Captain. We were standing in the background as the details of the shooting were given. With a shaking of the head and a quiet voice the Sergeant gave his version.

'The platoon had just come in, and someone had asked for a smoke. Without thinking I threw an open packet on the table. Those that smoked pushed forward, reaching over the table for a cigarette. Then it happened. A shot went off. It was several seconds before anyone spoke.'

He stopped to gather his composure. Going through the ordeal all over again, before continuing.

'From the far side of the table Private Whittaker said he had been hit in the stomach. There on the table, a cocked Owen gun had accidentally been triggered by someone reaching for a smoke. We laid him on the bed but he died within minutes. It was too late to do anything for him.'

Looking devastated the Sergeant finished his statement. The Provost Captain thought for a few moments, before replying to the visibly upset Sergeant in a supportive manner.

'Unfortunate. Very unfortunate. But you can't hold yourself responsible for such an accident. There will have to be an enquiry. In the meantime try to carry on. Everyone shares in such a tragedy as this one. That will be all Sergeant. Carry on.'

Saluting, the Sergeant turned on his heel leaving the officer to make the arrangements for transferring the body. It would be taken to Kluang morgue and from there to the military cemetery in Singapore for burial.

On that day a burial party from 'A' Company would be there to represent the Whittaker family. A photograph taken after the ceremony showed the headstone and the epitaph. Here lies Private Whittaker aged eighteen years. Had died for King and Country. The real story never to be known by his family. Perhaps it was better this way.

Next morning after CO's orders, while taking down the names of those to report for jankers (the name given for extra duties), I was to see for the first time since his release Charlie Bannister, now back with his platoon and a member of the quick response squad on twenty-four hours standby. The idea was thought up to combat bus ambushes and lorry attacks. Charlie was a member of an eight-man squad. An armoured Dingo, a small armoured car carrying twin Vickers guns, was also detailed to go along with the squad on any emergencies. It was the last time I would see Charlie alive.

A wireless message from the local police station brought the newly formed rapid response group into action. The message was a lorry transporting raw latex rubber had been stopped and set on fire by Communists lying in wait beside the track leading to the main road on the far side of Segamat.

Hearing the call the duty officer appeared on the balcony directly above the waiting squad and gave directions to the driver and with horns blaring they sped into town. Warning people to clear the way, the squad swept through the crowds and over the bridge they thundered, where they saw, above the trees, a thick black pall of smoke rising as the highly inflammable toxic rubber burnt. They turned to where the road led to the burning truck and bounced on the rutted track, slowing as they approached to stop short of the blazing inferno. The blackened tree had wilted from the intense heat. The ruptured storage tank and spillage had burnt around and beneath the lorry and from time to time small explosions rocked the truck, making the surroundings barely visible in an otherwise bright and sunny day.

Taking it slowly the armoured Dingo passed beyond the blazing scene. The Sergeant sitting in the turret shielded his face from the fierce heat behind the twin Vickers machine guns. Jumping from the car the men quickly formed some sort of order walking behind the Dingo, their eyes searching the billowing smoke and the strangely quiet surrounds.

Then, without warning, from both sides of the road came a withering fire. From the ditches and trees the unseen Commies sprung the trap on the exposed squad with everything they possessed – semi-machine guns, shotguns and rifle fire – raking the surprised men from end to end and hitting each one several times over. Without a shot being fired in return the men were sent spinning as the terrible firepower took its toll. Meanwhile the armoured Dingo was some way ahead and trying desperately to turn about on the confined track, knowing if it left the road there was a good chance of getting bogged down in the softer soil and ditches and leaving itself a sitting target. At last it extracted itself and with the hatch down tight drove into the centre of the firing, returning fire from its heavier calibre guns and emptying the magazines before reversing to reload. Appearing above the turret the Sergeant exchanged the magazines before slamming down the hatch once more and going in again and firing short bursts, this time at individual targets.

Figures in grey uniforms scrambled away as their position was exposed by the heavier calibre bullets smashing through the trees and bringing down branches and young trees. Eardrums were singing from the piercing noise as it made the head spin and the senses reel.

When it seemed there was a withdrawal from the attacking force, a faint cry could be heard coming from the prone figures lying wounded and dying alongside the burning truck. At least there was someone alive.

The weak voice called out again. Although badly wounded the will to live was still strong.

'Help me. Oh God help me. Don't leave me here to die like this. Somebody please please help me.'

The voice petered away. It may have been his last moment. We shall never know.

Without any thoughts for his own safety the Sergeant leaped down from the Dingo turret and began to run forward to his trapped men. He was cut down in a hail of fire and fell some yards short from his men, to join them in death. No man hath greater love than to lay down his own life, so others may live.

This left only the Dingo driver. Closing the hatch he reversed some way down the track. He was in a bad state of shock. Using the wireless was the only hope of help. Calling for backup he was told to keep clear of the ambush, and only observe. He would be joined by forces within minutes. Through the slit hole above the steering wheel he kept watch, hearing only bullets strike the armoured plate. Being told to stay put, he waited peering through the sight.

Suddenly from the trees and ditches rose women onto the road carrying in their hands knives and machetes to stand over those who were still alive. In a frantic frenzy of shouting, madness descended on the gory scene. The women, waving their heads and machetes, proceeded to stab and slash the dying helpless soldiers. Occasionally an arm went upwards from the wounded men in an attempt to fend away a descending blade as it cut through bone and sinew. The madness subsided as the last one died.

Bending over the bodies the women searched the blood-soaked clothes, picking over the corpses like carrion crows before retreating carrying away weapons and bandoleers full of ammunition, grenades and any other useful equipment. Joining their comrades they melted into the rubber and then the undergrowth to go back to their camp deep in the jungle, leaving behind a burning lorry and strewn bodies in their wake.

Back at HQ the message was received with stunned disbelief as the driver gave an eyewitness account of the scene. Meanwhile a relief platoon was quickly put together, and in a short time, two steel-sided lorries were underway carrying nearly forty armed troops through the Segamat streets, leaving clouds of dust everywhere in a bid to save time.

The wheels thundered over the bridge, forcing those on the back to hang on for grim life. Then someone shouted and pointed to a column of smoke rising from above the greenery to our right. We could see black smoke stretching across the blue sky, as the acrid smell of burning rubber reached our senses. Then without warning or slowing down we swung into the rubber. The men slid from side to side as the trucks lurched. Ahead the lone Dingo driver waited.

We came to a skidding halt within a few feet of the almost burnt out container lorry. Instantly those on the back jumped down and took up defensive positions. Through the thick smouldering smoke of the rubber the Dingo could be seen. The head of the driver poked through the turret. Although badly shaken, he managed to indicate that the Commies had withdrawn.

On hearing this the officer in charge gave the order to advance with caution. Moving beside the smouldering truck they soon found the sickening sight. Utter barbarism. Bodies were cut to pieces with the blood hardly beginning to dry. Gaping wounds lay open to the bone. Unrecognisable to those who knew them, only their dog tags would prove who the dead were. The flies were becoming more active now with so much blood around.

Small explosions from the tyres on the truck made us aware we were still in a volatile area. Then a shout came from one of the searchers.

'Over here. Look what I've found. A photograph.'

There on the chest of one of the bodies was a photograph of a head which I had witnessed myself being beheaded. Was this the

Communists' way of revenge? Was this the cause of the women's barbaric behaviour? There was no ready answer.

Unknown to me at the time was that one of the bodies was Charlie's. For once his blue chin went unnoticed.

The grim task of collecting the bodies had begun. Some of the carriers knew the victims. They were their buddies. Many had started their army careers at the same time and had formed a bond of high friendship. Seeing their friends like this brought out that feeling they had for each other.

Only a skeleton of the burnt out truck remained. Void of tyres, the chassis lay almost on the ground, the cab a blackened shell. There was an occasional 'pfffftt' as a spurt of air rose from a pocket of trapped gases.

The driver of the burnt out rubber truck was never found, his fate a complete mystery. Even to this day the photo of the severed head, found on the soldier's chest is an unpleasant memory in 'D' Company's records.

January 1951 – Night School

My probation period as an RP was now up and I stood before the Provost Sergeant, my kitbag packed and by my side. I listened to my list of faults and failings as they were read from the paper the Sergeant held.

'You show signs of weakness in your dealings with the detainees. Issuing warnings, when arrests should have been made. And not firm enough with those on fatigues and those confined to barracks. I have no alternative but to send you back to your company as unsatisfactory for the post. You are dismissed.'

I had certainly botched this job up. Why on earth he didn't come straight out with it and say I was not a big enough bastard for the job, I didn't know. You probably had to take lessons to become one. I'll never know. Taylor had passed the probation period, but I didn't feel any resentment towards him.

I picked up my kitbag and felt down because I couldn't hold the job down. But on the other hand I admitted to myself the job wasn't really to my taste. Anyway the rest had done me good. I felt fitter and healthier than when I first came from Tenang.

I now had to face the platoon as a rejected misfit. I would have to prove myself all over again. The one thing I didn't want was resentment from those I liked. That would be like putting a bullet in my head. I walked over to the transport pool and waited for the arrival of the supply trucks from Tenang. I didn't have to wait long before the dust cloud heralded their arrival. They swung in through the gates and pulled up alongside the warehouse stores. Leaving my kitbag for a moment I reported to the convoy NCO. He accepted my report and told me to help with the supplies.

With the last bag of spuds and the last box loaded onboard, I heaved my kitbag onto the truck, using the rear tyre as a lift. Then seeing the NCO get into the cab, I climbed up the lorry's sideboard and scrambled over the bags of vegetables and dragged my rifle and kit behind me, before settling down amongst the onions and spuds for the ride back to Tenang.

I was too busy thinking of what lay ahead of me to realise we had passed through the town and rumbled over the bridge. It wasn't until the driver dropped into a low gear on the rough dirt road, leading up to the hill to the camp, that I realised where we were.

Holding my kitbag in one hand and the rifle by the strap I swung my leg over the steel side and felt with my boot for the back wheel. Eventually finding it I stood on it and lowered myself to the ground. Leaving the unloading to the others I grabbed my things and walked over to the familiar office to report back. I knocked on the door and a voice from within said, 'Enter.'

I stepped inside and saw, sitting behind the desk, 10 Platoon's Sergeant Cushion. I placed my kitbag on the floor beside me and waited for some form of witticism from him. When he finally looked up and saw me, he folded his arms at the back of his head and leaning back in his chair said, 'The prodigal has returned back to 10 Platoon. Well, well, well. Erm, do you think you've done roamin'?'

'Yes, Sergeant,' I answered the only way I could.

'All right then. Go and find a bed. You know where to go.'

He brought down his hands to continue with what he was doing before being interrupted. I grabbed my kitbag and left the office.

'Thanks, Sergeant.'

From the office I made for the 10 Platoon lines, passing Clem the monkey who bared his teeth and growled. His wicked eyes showing he was still a wild beast at heart. I muttered under my breath, 'You evil bastard!'

It was Poncho the dog that was the first to welcome me back. His wagging tail told me he still remembered. He jumped about me as I patted his head and then he followed on behind, sniffing at my heals. Upon reaching the tent I ducked under the flaps. The barking dog had announced my presence and return to the platoon. Seeing who I was, a chorus of voices struck up, 'Ebee's back. We said you'd never make a copper.'

To me, that statement said all I wanted to hear. There was no resentment. The feelings I had of being left out in the cold were gone completely.

Dropping my kit onto the spare bed the questions began to flow between us. The one question was how was Christmas. My version brought a few laughs. However, their Christmas had been different. As first one, then another told me.

'We spent Christmas in the jungle. On a night when we should be merry, we sat around a fire and sang a few carols. That night we didn't much care about communism. We threw caution to the wind.'

It was a night when ill feeling was forgiven, and peace reigned. At least for a little while.

I still hadn't unpacked when the lunch gong began clanging. Searching near the top of my kitbag I found my old mess tins. Yes, I had gone from eating off a platter and was now back to tins. I then joined the others in the queue. We ate and talked while we sat. The food was pretty much the same. It was the appearance of the Sergeant that made us stop what we were doing.

'I want everybody outside the office at two o'clock. Be there and tell the others.'

By others he meant those that had already eaten and left. The Sergeant left us wondering what it was all about.

Outside the office we stood talking and smoking, all twenty-six of us, waiting and watching every time the office door opened. Then the Sergeant walked out carrying a round object which looked like a lifebelt with a short rubber hose. Attached to the hose was a funny looking revolver. He placed it on the ground in front of the platoon. Only a few had seen this weapon before. It was a flame-thrower.

Gathering round, the Sergeant proceeded to give us a quick instructive lecture on the rudiments and uses of the flame-thrower. Each one of us would need to understand how to use it. He then showed us how it was filled with a highly inflammable petroleum jelly. He ended with, 'Always keep the filling clear of naked flames. The reason I'm showing you this flame-thrower is we may be using it tonight on an ambush. I want everybody ready. Just bring your rifles, ammunition and water bottles.'

'Where we going, Sergeant?' Batey piped up, speaking for everybody there.

'We are going to night school, where the last few nights the Commies have shot the place up.'

Leaving the Corporals to fill in the gaps, and to choose a man to carry and use the flame-thrower, the Sergeant disappeared into the office.

Examining the weapon, we found the weight and bulkiness was the main problem. It was a no goer for jungle fighting where quickness and agility meant a lighter weapon. A weapon such as a flame-thrower would be too cumbersome.

Kitted out for just the one night the patrol left on the hour before dusk on foot. Any transport would certainly give the game away. Leaving the camp behind we were soon swallowed up by the darkness which closed around us. The slight breeze felt like a warm breath on our faces. We were in for a sticky night in more ways than one.

We gave the school a wide birth as we approached. Behind a sandbagged pillar box besides the entrance, the voices of the police were heard. They had set up a roadblock to check traffic movements which seemed to intimidate the Commies who attacked it from time to time, last night being the latest.

We moved quietly past and down a track to the side already chosen which led past the school. A little way past we climbed a small rise. Behind the school and to our left was a swamp and to our right was the track where we set the ambush. We were hoping to catch the Commies between the school and ourselves. This meant they could only run left into the swamp or right and meet the flame-thrower. The idea was we would lay down a wall of flame, making a complete box, then slam the door shut. Wham! Squashing the flies inside.

We settled down to make ourselves as comfortable as possible under the circumstances. The mosquitoes began to rise en masse from the swamp and play havoc as the night wore on.

Nine o'clock came and went. Then ten o'clock. Through the night the minutes ticked by. It was at just about the time we had given up, when the first shot was fired. Followed by another. With the whine of bullets going overhead, mixed with tracer, the position was soon made out. They were coming from the rear. We were trapped in between by our own making. We had laid the ambush too close to the school. All we could do now was lie there till dawn, or wait for the Commies to end their attack. A lull came, then once more the attack continued from a different position as they tried to lure the police out. Knowing them they would be safely behind the sandbags.

Then as suddenly as it had started it stopped. Being bitten all night and lying low the end came as a welcomed relief. Dawn came with the mist rising from the damp ground as well as the swamp. We rose and after a few stretches made our way down the small rise. Marching on to the road the police looked surprised as we went past. They never knew we were there in the ambush position. Strung out along the road, in our green uniforms, we marched along like going for a stroll in the park in the cool of the early morning sunshine.

Further on up the road we came to a horseshoe-shaped quarry beside the road. It had been cut deep into the grey stone bank and excavated for road repairs but now abandoned.

In the quietness of the morning the Sergeant stopped to give us a demonstration of the flame-thrower. Slipping the canister on his back he pointed the revolver towards the surrounding rocks and fired. Like the squealing of a pig the far side of the quarry erupted in flame and smoke. The air was a mixture of petrol fumes and black acrid smoke. The intense heat and flame made it a horrifying weapon if you were on the receiving end. We could see now why it had been brought along. Besides making escape impossible, the targets shown up brightly in the flames would be like shooting ducks in a barrel.

With the blackened quarry now far behind us we enjoyed the early morning stroll and caught sight of a farmer as he flicked a slow moving bullock with an old bamboo cane on the way to market.

Rumours were abound we were moving. Onboard the supply trucks from Segamat came a number of crates. And the presence of the three platoons staying in meant something was afoot.

During morning parade the platoons were allocated different jobs. Some were to load the stores while others were to load the cookhouse stores and mess hall tables and benches into the crates provided. All tents would be taken down and beds and bed linen crated along with personalised kit, and loaded aboard the lorries.

Everything was still very hush hush. Everyone was guessing where we were going. The only place not mentioned was home. More trucks began to arrive from Segamat to transport the accumulated stores. With everything loaded bare patches stood where the camp had been. We were leaving a lot of bad memories behind us.

Occupying every available space we could find the overloaded trucks began moving forward. Smoke from the Char Wallah's tent billowed into the air as we slowly bumped along through the camp entrance for the last time.

From where I sat, high above the kitbags, I could see clearly the smoke and flames rising from his old bed. The mattress was well alight. And from within the mattress, trying to escape, black bed bugs came teeming out. They seemed to crackle and pop as the flames reached them. A shudder ran through me when I remembered how we ate sandwiches made up by his hands. The dirty bastard.

Round every bend in the road we lurched. Each bend and hole in the road threatened to throw us from our perches. Once on the main road the smoother conditions made the ride into Segamat much more comfortable.

Instead of going to HQ we were taken to the railway goods terminal. In the siding were two engines. The first engine was coupled to a lowloader on which was chained an armoured car fairly bristling with guns behind a searchlight. This train travelled ahead of another. Its task was to make sure the track ahead was clear and safe, and indeed still there. The Communists had a way of blowing up the track and bridge crossings.

Other companies of the Worcesters also loaded their stores that night onto specially chartered trains. Now exhausted by the efforts of our own loading, we boarded the train. The decoy train stood on the main line, its searchlight swinging from right to left as we were shunted onto the main line ourselves. That night we travelled some two hundred miles south down to Singapore to a transit camp on the island.

Over the next few days rumours were rife as to our next destination. We knew for a fact that the war in Korea was going badly wrong for the United Nations forces. A move from the heat of the jungle to the frozen climate in the northern atmosphere was too much for the top brass to ask us to do, especially those that had given their all over the last twelve months.

Then all of a sudden the fortunes of the Korean War changed. The rushing here and there stopped. Standing on a sandy parade ground, with the sand flies crawling around our ears and tormenting us, we waited for the commanding officer to read a document he held before him. Reading the letter he said, 'Being the nearest combat troops to Korea...'

Those first words shocked me right down to my boots. With not an ounce of fat between us how on earth could we keep warm in sub degree temperatures, and in a battle zone? But my fears were not founded, as the commanding officer went on to explain.

'We have been taken out of combat to reinforce the beleaguered American and United Nations forces. However, the Home Office in London has overruled this and we will be returning up country in a day or so. But not to the Segamat area.'

Relieved to hear what was said, our move may have turned out for the better as the officer continued.

'Our new area is still to be designated. Your own platoon officers will keep you informed of any further developments.'

After being fell out, and partaking in a lot of scratching, we sat on our beds smoking and arguing whether or not we were lucky getting out of going to Korea. The future in Malaya wasn't too bright either.

Stripped to our waists, with the sweat dripping down our bodies, we carried the heavy ammunition boxes from the lorries over to the freight vans in the sidings. Back and forth we went stopping occasionally for a drink from a container.

Hutch was in front of me carrying a box of mortars and whistling a none-melodious tune – when suddenly he stumbled over the rails. The box slipped from his shoulders as if in slow motion and down it went in a deathly silence, hitting the floor and making a dent in the hard concrete. My eyes shut as I anticipated what would happen next. The seconds ticked away as we waited for the following explosion, which would have caused a chain reaction as explosion after explosion would have ripped half of

Singapore apart. I visualised the trains, the freighters and lorries half-filled with explosives being blown to pieces along with perhaps thousands of people.

As the seconds turned into minutes I bent down and slowly righted the box of mortars. Opening the catch that held the lid, I saw that although displaced, the bombs had remained intact. A huge sigh of relief went up, as well as the words they called Hutch.

Back at camp that night the Sergeant told us we were going back up country in the next twenty-four hours. Upon hearing this, four or five of us went down into the village near the barracks. The village of Nee-Soon, although small, was well known.

Enjoying the last taste of freedom we might have for the next few months, we visited the bars and then partly drunk visited the local tattooist. Before I knew it I had a tiger's head on my forearm, and I was murmuring like a child. I wonder what my mother would think?

In the early hours we boarded the train. Then, more by chance than favour, we were detailed to guard the regimental colours in the rear carriage. I climbed up the steps with my rifle behind a Corporal and five Privates, to see some old wooden box lying down the centre of the coach. Lying like a long coffin were the colours which we were to guard for the journey back to wherever we were going. I got the feeling we were standing over a dead man, or rather the ghosts of the past. The colours weren't just made of cloth, more like a holy shroud that held the shadows of the past. Within its folds a monument of glory.

February 1951 – The Swimming Pool

Have you ever been on a train and listened to the wheels sounding out a message? Going clickety-click clickety-click. They were beginning to sound like the wheels were having their hypnotic effect, and I tried to sleep with my head resting against the open window of the carriage.

As we cut through the jungle we could see the ghostly silhouettes of the trees. Shadows were added to the scene as clouds passed over the moon. The stars seemed much nearer here than back home. We were downwind from the locomotive and the smell of oil drifted along with the smoke from the old straining engine.

The train continued to thunder through the towns and villages that lay beside the track. The coaches were swaying and sending me into a fitful sleep, knowing that at any moment the train could be heading for a smash, either derailed or hit by gunfire.

Hours later the train began to slow down and then eventually stopped. On a board that was ill lit I just managed to make out the name, Kluang. No, not Kluang! But it was. We had returned to square one. Amidst the shouting and shunting the railway workers, with the aid of the Sikh stationmaster, managed to get the train into the sidings.

The road transport was already there waiting for us. Still dark, the trucks used their headlights to assist us in the unloading. The contents of the freight vans were written on the side in chalk. We slid open the side doors on the freight wagons and, finding the crates that contained the tents, we began to manhandle them onto the trucks.

We were again stripped to the waist in the warm night. The unloading began in earnest. As soon as each vehicle was loaded the engine would rev up and, with a guard to ride as shotgun on the rear, off they would disappear into the night, deliver their cargo to various company camps, then return for more supplies: beds, bed linen, office equipment, cookhouse utensils, everything that was needed to run a camp. The station was a hive of activity as the empty lorries returned several times for their next load.

It was sometime after five o'clock in the morning when the last stick and tent pole was loaded and with eyes half-shut we left the sidings. Holding on to the swaying trucks we passed through the sleeping town, which was blissfully unaware that a train carrying close on a thousand troops had passed by to secure some sort of future for them.

We continued south for approximately five miles before turning into a track when the supplies bounced around. In the dark, unseen branches brushed over the lorries but by keeping low among the supplies we avoided the whiplash as the movement released the branches forward.

Coming up on our left was what we thought was our new camp, only to find that it had been claimed by 'B' Company some time earlier. We travelled down the track for another half an hour and it seemed that we would never arrive, when someone said, 'There's a light up ahead.'

Sure enough a village appeared on our left. A few twinkling lights shone through the wood slats of the shacks that were dotted about there. There were fires lit ready for the day's work, glowing in the half-light of the dawn.

We passed through the village and on its edge we saw an open-sided factory which, we learned later was where they turned the rubber latex into compact sheets. Just beyond the factory was 'D' Company.

In dawn's light we could make out tents already erected. In the centre and a little to the rear sat a derelict bungalow. The former plantation owner had once occupied it before being driven out by the Communists. This was now to be commandeered by the officers as living quarters.

We climbed down from the trucks, and with daylight just about to break we were told to rest for a few hours where we could. We managed to find a pile of blankets and soon fell asleep completely shattered.

For me morning broke with someone giving me a kick. Opening my eyes I peered over the blankets to find those around us sipping tea. I gave Heapy a nudge in the kidneys. This soon brought him alive. In next to no time I had borrowed two tin mugs and was on my way to the makeshift cookhouse, where the cook stood beside a hastily cut pile of sandwiches of corned beef and cheese. Carrying the tea and chewing on corned beef I ambled over to where the others sat and sat on an upturned box lying nearby.

As I ate I took in my new surroundings. The whole place was on a slight slope moving down from the empty bungalow which had been stripped of everything of value. Close by there were old overgrown tennis courts though the old nets and posts had long gone. At the bottom of the slope ran a bubbling stream.

During the next few hours we worked like roustabouts on a circus, raising tents, setting up lights, digging holes and knocking in tent pegs. The Sergeant found work for idle hands. First to go up was the cookhouse, next came the mess hall tent and the tent lines. Everyone was busy carrying benches, tables, beds, etc.

With this done we went in search of our kitbags. Out of the hundred piles we eventually found them but only after a twenty minute search and a lot of sore backs from all that bending.

Shouldering my kitbag I made my way with the others, to 10 Platoon's tent lines near the bungalow. We saw Clem tethered there. He was as wild as ever having spent last night in a box. His water dish was turned upside down.

Hardly having time to settle we were ordered to erect the showers. A generator would pump water up from the stream through pipes to showers. The generator would also supply power for the lighting to the cookhouse and bungalow as well as the tent lines. Beyond the stream the road could be seen weaving among the trees, the red soil of the track standing out clearly against the background.

Over the following days, with morning parade and chores completed, we would go down to the stream where, once permission had been granted, we began to widen it with trenching tools we managed to get hold of. The result was a place to go swimming and on most afternoons we would go skinny-dipping. Like crazed Irish banshees we went howling from the banks, diving and splashing. It provided a way of letting off steam and pent-up tension. The officers turned a blind eye so long as we made sure a guard was posted on watch near the swimmers with an Owen gun at all times. Besides the relaxation it provided, it gave the non-swimmers the opportunity to learn and to build up confidence.

One afternoon as we walked back up the slope we were met by the Sergeant, who greeted us with, 'There's an early tea laid on for you. Be ready to move out sometime after dark. Bring only your rifle and ammo.'

By six o'clock the night had descended and under cover of darkness we slipped silently out of camp.

Trudging along we passed the rubber factory. The dark shapes of the rollers used for turning the fluid latex into a more manageable state were now silent all except for the dripping water heard splashing onto the concrete floor. The Tamil labourers had long since gone back to their villages.

Moving on ahead we came to Niyor village which was home of the multiracial workforce of planters. From within the sound of an old wind-up record player churned out a Chinese melody, filling the night air. To my ears it sounded as if their instruments, like Chinese life in general, was out of tune. Their bland expressionless faces showed no sign of grief or happiness like death masks.

We carried on past unseen. On this occasion not even the dogs picked up our presence. Eventually the music became fainter and once more the darkness enveloped the village leaving us with only the sound of our boots for company. Well, that wasn't strictly true. The stinging mosquitoes and other insects landed on our unsuspecting faces resulting in swift action from us and often sudden death for the insects.

We now moved from the track and into the knee-deep lalang grass. With the trees no longer overhead, the darkness lifted to reveal the night sky. The ribbon of the Milky Way stretched across the heavens and shooting stars arced across the vast sky before disappearing beyond the horizon.

Most patrols began without any explanations. A quick 'Get ready' was usually all the warning we got. Tonight was no exception. With 11 and 12 Platoon now out on patrol this was to be the start of a new practice for platoons left at base camp. Carrying an extra bandoleer of ammunition around our waists, we would go down to the railroad tracks before breaking into two groups. One group would face down the track while the second group would face in the opposite direction.

Lying down alongside the track the Bren gunner would aim at an imaginary target, some way in front in the darkness, and would open fire in short bursts. As he did so a rifleman, kneeling beside him, would be firing single shots in the same direction, straight down the tracks and aiming low, trying to follow the tracers. The glowing tracer bullet arced in the gloom. In flight like a bird it gave the gunman information whether he was firing high or low. The other group was doing the same thing, only in the opposite direction. As my turn came round I knelt on the sharp granite chippings which held the sleepers. The sharp chippings dug into my knee. I took aim down the dark track and pulled the trigger. The recoil felt like a hammer blow to my shoulder as the butt was forced backwards. Again I pulled the trigger, only this time I held the weapon more firmly into my shoulder. I emptied the full clip of ten rounds before changing places with big Gowey, who was waiting for his shot.

Both groups continued firing covering nearly two miles of track between us. The theory was to prevent Commies interfering with the rails, either by displacement or by blowing them up. We knew they used the night-time as cover for their actions then during the day ambushed the derailed trains, shooting and looting the unfortunate passengers as many tried to flee the wreckage. Survivors were killed indiscriminately, women and children alike. These butchers of the jungle would show no mercy or favour. This was their way – the way of the beast. We never found out if this ever stopped the Communists or not although we never had a crash or part derailment in our area.

Guards would travel on the ration trucks on the once a week trip to Kluang for fresh supplies and mail. Although dangerous, it broke the boredom. Aboard the trucks we would sit with our backs to the steel sides. The Corporal would sit next to the driver in the cab whilst we were in the red dust thrown up by the wheels which made us cough and splutter. We bounced along, holding on for all we were worth. We sometimes thought the driver aimed for the holes. To communicate we would have to shout above the roaring engines to be heard. The bouncing distorted and blurred the words as they came out of our mouths.

'To thinnk weee pa-ad goo-od mon-eey foo-r ri-dees like thi-ss b-ackk homee.'

I laughed at the way Heapy spoke. Passing over a cigarette I replied, 'Enj-oy i-it wh-ile yoou ca-an.'

Lighting the cigarette was equally awkward. The lit match danced up and down before my eyes. We also kept a watchful eye open for low branches every time we hit a bump.

Going this route we would be passing 'B' Company's lines. They were our nearest neighbours some five miles down the track from Niyor village. As we approached their camp perimeter those near to the barbed wire waved and shouted, friends of ours from the time of basic training on first joining the army.

Once past we settled down once more knowing the main road was not far away. Once we reached the metalled road the ride became smoother but it wasn't until we reached Kluang that our bodies began to calm down from the violent shaking.

Kluang was also the home of the Ghurka regiment which was part of the same brigade as the Worcesters. As the truck ran up the hill we saw the Ghurka guard standing to attention beside a sentry box. He wore a starched green uniform and highly polished boots topped by the Ghurka's world-famous hat, cocked slightly to one side from the left. Hanging from his webbing belt was the equally famous Ghurka kukri. His shoulder flashes, like our own, were a crossed kukri and bayonet on a vivid red background.

The Ghurkas came from a tiny principality in northern India. Nepal had been friends and allies of the British for one hundred years or more. The Ghurka was a tough and dependable fighter and fearless unto death in any theatre of war.

We passed trucks from 'C' Company that had already been and loaded their stores and were now on their way back to camp. Stationed at Labis they had also had their fair share of trouble and grief.

We turned into the enclosed motor pool and supply depot. Parked in the centre of the compound stood the regiment's Dingo armoured cars as well as fifteen hundredweight pick-up vehicles. It was one of these that attracted our attention, as it was badly damaged on the driver's side. Moving among the vehicles the army mechanics, stripped to the waist with oil smeared over hands and face, worked on repairs, some half-hidden beneath bonnets, others with legs sticking out from underneath lorries. Everywhere the sound of tinkering could be heard and now and then a curse was uttered as a spanner slipped or a nut got cross threaded.

Heapy jumped over the tailboard, which he unlatched and let drop. Corporal Cole jumped down from the cab and told us to unload the laundry while he himself delivered the company's mail and collected the incoming mail from home. Under the quarter-master's nose we loaded the stores that were already laid out for the company. Along with Townsend, Hank and Batey we loaded the potatoes and cabbages, seven days' ration boxes and boxes of eggs and bacon and other sundries.

After a quick cuppa we went rambling round the compound looking under bonnets and having a general chit-chat. Coming to the badly damaged fifteen hundredweight we could see the driver's side had taken the full brunt of something. Finding a mechanic on a nearby vehicle I asked, 'What happened here then? It's a bit of a mess.'

Rubbing his hands on a bit of oily rag the mechanic looked up from under the bonnet answering, 'That's the pick-up the driver from 'B' Company got killed in. The wheel came off the driver's side throwing the driver under the stub axle. The axle went straight through the stomach. A bit of a messy job if you ask me.'

This was the first we knew of the tragedy. Being stuck out in the middle of nowhere we were the last to hear any news.

Seeing Corporal Cole returning with the mailbag I said a quick cheerio to the motor mechanic and made my way back to the lorry. One last stop at the dhobi wallah's for the fresh laundry then we climbed over the sacks and boxes and made ourselves as comfortable as possible and placed our rifles on our laps with a wave and a word, 'See you next time.'

The driver put it into first gear and slowly drove through the compound gates. We passed the sentry then drove through the town. The townspeople, Chinese and Malayan alike, gave us casual glances. Their solemn faces gave away nothing of their feelings towards us. They just carried on bartering over some article of goods. Only the children made their feelings known as they stopped playing and waved and giggled. Even the dogs seemed intent on having their say as they ran barking and snapping after the wheels.

Outside the town we were forced to the edge of the road by huge logging lorries carting giant trees to the sawmills. They were a variety of redwood exported all over the world and used in the construction of houses and furniture. Dust rose from the almost threadbare tyres making us cough and choke. It was to take several minutes for them to clear. Then they were gone and we pulled back onto the road once more.

From our vantage point up on the sacks we could see the paddy fields on either side of the road. In straw hats, shaped like cooking woks, the farmers and their families waded through the mud with their black trousers rolled up. Following behind them was a bullock drawn plough. They had the back-breaking job of planting out new rice seedlings for the coming summer crop. The dazzling sun reflected off the waters – a peaceful sight in a troubled land.

The flat fields of water soon turned to acres of rubber as we entered the plantation. We were now the leading truck in the convoy and it was our turn to leave the choking dust for those behind to eat. As we scanned the trees for signs of movement, the lorry began slowing as we approached a procession. It was a funeral. Leading the group was a team of bell-ringers and behind them a group with brass gongs striking them with small hammers as they walked. The funeral party was colourful, dressed in red and blue silks and wearing the black mandarin hats. A section carried banners written in Chinese of cryptic messages bearing the name and the status he had reached in life. At the centre of the cortege, behind the banners, four bearers carried the casket on wooden poles bedecked with exotic flowers.

We again drew to the side of the track and allowed the procession to continue past. The cemetery lay some way ahead where a temple and a Buddhist monk waited.

The tinkling bells and the melancholy gong faded as we continued on our way. Once the trucks were unloaded the cooks busied themselves checking the supplies before stowing them away. This left us time to shower and change before the evening meal which tonight was curried lamb and boiled rice. Afterwards we had a walk down to the new Char Wallah's. (The previous one had been sacked after the bed bug affair.)

I leaned over the counter and grabbed a bottle of Carlsberg floating in the galvanised bath of cold water. The Char Wallah already had his black book open at my name. Signing, I turned to see who was there and seeing a card school I walked over to the table. Five card stud poker was the game and eyes stared. First at the cards, then to each other looking for a response or expression as they rose the ante – or stakes – on the table. It was a game of bluff as much as actually having the cards. Cigarettes drooped from lips as the smoke rose above the player's heads. Some threw in hands as the nerves gave way only to shout and curse when they saw the winning hand turned over and knowing they could have beaten it if only they had kept their nerve and cards. If only.

I crossed over to a much quieter table where Hank and Hutch were having a casual chat. I listened as they spoke of weekends down at the old Paly, a drink in a milk bar and some lass to take home afterwards in the cool summer nights with not a care in the world. Why in the world did I want to see the exotic East? In future I would count my blessings.

Towards the end of the night the merrymakers drifted back towards their cots, a few cursing as they tripped over the tent's guy ropes. The generator spluttered to a stop and everyone was now asleep.

Chores were finished early and, having had permission, we trooped our way down to the swimming hole. Slightly overgrown on the banks through lack of use, the swimming area was virtually clear. We tossed a coin to see who would be the first to guard us. Gowey was the loser and sauntered away with the Owen gun under his arm mouthing obscenities at having lost the toss, while the rest of us began jumping into the cool running stream.

Being so hot and overheated the initial impact with the cold water made me catch my breath. The pool was overcrowded so normal swimming was out of the question. I came up gasping for my first breath when in jumped Breezy from the bank and landed on my back. The blow sent me back under the water. I broke the surface lashing out in anger with my fist and caught the unfortunate Breezy full in the face. Next thing arguing and fighting broke out as tempers were frayed. The others were now cheering the fight as we slugged it out splashing and tumbling everywhere. The fight ended when we had both had enough and were exhausted.

I relieved Townsend with aches to my jaw and ear, as well as spitting blood from a cut lip. I squatted on my haunches and pondered on my foolishness at starting the fight with one of my own platoon members.

Amongst other things in the seven days' rations were fish in oil and plenty of hard tack biscuits – things we didn't have any appetite for. On occasions when we had enough cans saved we exchanged them with the Niyor villagers for beer and cigarettes. Every time they saw us they would ask, 'Have you any more fish, Johnny? Any more biscuits, Johnny?'

This often brought questioning stares from the officers should they overhear the question. Whenever this happened though a quick word and a push from the old rifle often did the trick.

Most of our patrols were routine. However this particular one seemed to ring warning bells as the rations were not just handed out to us, but also to 11 Platoon as well. We had been expecting to go out at a moment's notice but for two platoons to go out together was exceptional.

The rations were packed away with the usual thoroughness. The foot powder was additional to what we usually packed. Wearing boots for long periods caused foot rot as not being able to dry your feet out after days marching across swampy water caused the feet to sweat. Your feet would then look white and bloodless and the skin easily peeled away leaving holes which then turned to sores. However with a liberal sprinkling of powder and a vigorous rub, the colour and feeling quickly returned. The alternative to this would be crippled feet.

We were waiting to board the truck. In the semi-darkness I could see Drak, the wireless operator, stood before me. Through the gloom appeared Sergeant Cushion. He carried the blackened stewpot and seeing me handed it over with the words, 'Catch hold of this.' And half-joking saying, 'And try to keep it from banging like a drum.'

As he walked away I murmured, 'You bastard you.'

Heapy started laughing behind me on hearing what I had said. I turned to look at him in the dark.

'And you... you prat...' I broke off the sentence as this only made him laugh even more.

Drak was having some trouble boarding with the radio being so heavy so we helped him by pushing and shoving from the rear. The stewpot was also causing me problems. Halfway on the truck my footing slipped and I skinned my shin. I let out a string of four letter words. Then in a rage I threw the pot clanging into the back. This brought a rebuke from the darkness, 'Keep quiet back there.'

Then more in anger than anything else I leapt onto the truck in one go.

Moving out in low gear we passed the twinkling lights of the village. We were talking in whispers and peering into the dark as the truck's lights made shadows. That night we were led by an armoured Dingo. With the twin Vickers uncovered, we were more than a match for any ambush we may have encountered that night.

Over the next few weeks the patrol would prove to be a torrid time for the two tough platoons and we would need every ounce of strength and tenacity.

At long last the convoy reached the road. With the headlights now full on we gathered speed. As we were causing our own breeze we held on to our hats enjoying the coolness that came with it.

The roads at this time of night were completely deserted. Passing the odd shack on the roadside we could see the paraffin lamps blinking through the slats and blanket-covered windows. Their lives would be in their own hands should the Commies visit them, something we had witnessed in the past.

In the darkness we could see the leading Dingo picked out by the following truck lights begin to slow down. Silhouetted shadows of buildings rose beside the road. This place was well known by those on supply duties. It was the notorious town of Labis in the state of Johore, a place known for terrorist activities.

Beneath paraffin lamps hanging from the walls sat the villagers talking and playing their favourite pastime, mah-jong. A few shops stayed open for that last little bit of business. You could see the shops' shutters leaning against the side walls as their owners swept out the day's dust onto the street. The time was now a little after ten o'clock.

Barking dogs leapt to their feet snarling and growling, angry at being disturbed from a leisurely doze. At the far end of the village the lead vehicle turned right onto yet another bumpy track. Ahead were the lights of 'B' Company camp. Under generator lights men moved about as they too made ready for the patrol.

The convoy finally came to a stop. The cab door swung open and out stepped Sergeant Cushion. He made his way to the back, giving out orders. 'Stay on the trucks until I find out where we're going.' He moved out into the shadows leaving those on the back wondering what was happening and what lay in store for us.

Lights were now shining everywhere as the generator in the background continued to chug away. I turned towards Heapy, who was never far away, to find him sleeping. He didn't even know we had arrived. Giving his foot a kick he awoke with a start. He peered at his surroundings asking, 'Where am I? What's up, Ebee, what's this place?'

'Pissin' sleeping again! You'd better wake up before you're left on the truck,' was my reply.

Footsteps were approaching. And on looking behind me I saw Corporal Cole coming towards us telling us where to go.

'Okay, chaps. Off the trucks, bring your kit and follow me,' he called out so that everyone could hear.

Carrying our packs, and me with my blackened pot, we got down from the tailboard, fell in and followed the Corporal.

We were walking towards the light of open tents which had been erected hastily and were devoid of beds. Tarpaulin sheets had covered the ground. They were normally used for covering supplies and sometimes lorries but tonight they were a ground-sheet.

Holding open the tent flap the Corporal said, 'Make yourselves as comfortable as you can. It's only for a short night. Oh, there's tea if anybody wants one down at the cookhouse.'

As he left us we rummaged through our packs in search of mess tins. In a nearby tent Corporal Chadwick of 11 Platoon, a short stocky guy and a regular with the regiment, was giving the same information to his men.

We placed our packs along the wall of the tent, giving us a fairly good idea which one was ours. Looking around the tent the thought crossed my mind that with everybody in the same tent there wouldn't be a fat lot of room to lie down.

I pulled the mug from my water bottle and following in Heapy's footsteps, ducked under the tent flaps and headed towards the cookhouse at the end of the path. Once inside we joined the long queue and I thought tomorrow there would be twice as many for breakfast though I would be at the front and not the back where I was now.

Dipping the mug into the bucket and letting the drips fall back we made our way outside into the cooler night air where we found a couple of boxes. We sat down under the night sky. The Milky Way stood out like a midnight rainbow and the night was cool and pleasant. What was the saying? The lull before the storm. I lit my fag and in between puffs drank the tea.

'Heapy,' I said as I stared upwards, 'I've a bad feeling about this patrol. A bad, bad feeling.'

We threw the dregs from our mugs onto the ground before slowly walking back to the tent. Pushing aside the tent flaps we could see a few of the others had returned. Stepping over their outstretched legs to where our packs lay, we put our mugs away before sprawling out. I lay with one hand beneath my head watching as the tent flap went up from time to time as the others rolled in. Some had found the Char Wallah's and were still drinking from the bottles they had bought. They knew drinking back at the lines was forbidden.

Someone said they fancied an 'Egg Banjo' and a voice started rendering a song, 'What a wonderful sight was 'C' Company at night.'

At which point everybody shouted, 'Put a sock in it somebody, for God's sake!'

After a few more jokes and wisecracks we heard, 'Lights out in five minutes. Get some sleep.'

The generator spluttered. The lights dimmed and then we were in total darkness in a strange camp. Lying so close together the air became stifling and clammy, as the men tried to settle in the uncomfortable conditions.

An early morning call, around five o'clock, brought the restless night to a grateful end. Thinking of last night's long queues I grabbed my mess tin and made a hasty exit, clambering over legs as I went. Running in the dark towards the lighted cookhouse I tried to overtake those in front. My eyes were unaccustomed to the dark though and I went running wide. I was actually passing them when suddenly the ground beneath my feet cut away. I felt myself fall before a terrific jolt ended the fall. In a world of darkness and momentarily stunned but unhurt, I found myself at the bottom of a concrete monsoon ditch, some six feet deep. Feeling badly shaken I scrambled up the concrete sides and staggered over to the cookhouse to join a queue even longer than the night before.

My appetite had almost gone from the severe shaking and I hardly noticed the bacon and beans the server placed in my outstretched mess tin. Carrying my mug of tea still dazed and feeling slightly sick, I glanced around the packed mess hall and seeing Heapy I limped over. I pushed in between the tightly sitting group upon which Heapy looked up at the intruder.

'Where have you been? I've looked everywhere. I even kept you a place in the queue. You said last night that you would be early,' he said, questioning me.

Don't ask. Just don't ask. You'd never believe me in a thousand years, I thought.

Back in the tent we slipped on the heavy packs and walked down to the waiting trucks whose engines were already revving. The early morning sun lifted the heavy mist, and found us sitting bunched up on the trucks, as we drove away from the camp.

We drove through the town of Labis. Hard to believe a sleepy little town like this could have such a history of violence and notoriety and on such a small island. Death seemed to be a way of life in this place. It started with the deaths of twenty-six police officers as they cycled down the main highway, cut down in carnage of death by ambushing Communists. Then grenade attacks on local buses and burning them out, the innocent beaten and murdered and livestock stolen.

A Communist camp was clearly nearby. This was verified by our presence, along with two platoons from 'D' Company and two from 'C' Company – a total of one hundred and fifty men. Among the group was a handful from HQ including the rare sight of the RSM, and his bristling moustache which he constantly curled with his fingers. This patrol was the big one.

The convoy, heading up north, finally came to a halt beside an open field of lalang, a desolate place in the middle of nowhere.

Moving with cramped limbs the men set themselves down from the trucks and once the tailboards were dropped we grabbed our kit and weapons and set them down at our feet. Me with my old EY waited on the melting tarmac. With stamping and stretching the stiffness gradually faded.

Walking up and down in front of us the Sergeant kept his eye on the moving patrol as they were strung out across the waist high lalang. It was like watching men wade through waves with the strong breeze making the waves on the sea of grass and creating different shades of green in the sunlight. We were reminded of the cornfields back home, high and golden and ready for harvesting.

I buckled the stewpot safely onto my pack while still on the ground before slipping my shoulders through the straps. It was time to move. With a wave of his arm our tracker, Luang, moved into the lalang followed by the red-headed Hank. The rest of the platoon spread out in their wake. We saw the trucks turn and head for base as the head of the patrol began to disappear in the distance into the jungle, edging the perimeter with 10 Platoon in the rear.

Scouts were sent ahead to forage seeking a track to follow or sign left by someone passing that way. A twig broken here, a fag-end there. A footprint maybe in the soft earth. It could be anything.

Our movements had disturbed the flies as we crossed the grass. They were swarming about us, causing us to swat and rub, and show our discomfort by swearing angrily. The men only stopped once they had entered the cooler shade of the trees. For the first time we were going deep into the jungle. We later referred to it as the Green Hell as we got to know it better.

At first, on coming directly out of the sun, it was cool. Then as we strode along we began to change our minds. Our first thoughts were a far misconception from the truth. The trees, rising like giant umbrellas, also held in the heat and moisture creating high humidity. This resulted in a greenhouse effect with the temperature rocketing to well over one hundred and twenty degrees. The sweat stained our clothes like a dishcloth ready to be wrung out. Our clothes stuck to our bodies, causing raw skin and sweat rashes that smarted and itched. Commonly known as Tinear, it was curable but very unpleasant.

Underfoot the ground was alive with ants and centipedes as were the surrounding bushes sucking the sweet sap from them before falling onto the salted clothes. The next minute you were bitten. Feeling a sharp stinging sensation your actions were automatic: use your fingers as tweezers to pull the biting ant clear. But often it left the head still biting into the flesh. We occasionally had to step over a colony of ants on the march where the ground was made smooth by literally millions of tiny feet passing over. A colony could take anything from a few hours to several days to pass by ranging in size from mites to the larger soldier ants. The king of them all, a red and black ant, was over one inch in length.

Stopping for a midday meal, Heapy broke out the Tommy cooker while I sorted out a tin of cheese and the hard tack biscuits. Sitting back on our backpacks we crunched on biscuits and sipped tea at the same time taking in the sounds. From above 'oo-oo-oo-oo' echoed as the threshing of branches loosened leaves and showered the watchers below.

Above us in the trees we caught fleeting glances of monkeys. It was their cries we were hearing, starting at a low pitch and gradually getting louder to finish on a higher note. At night, their amorous cooing irritated the tired-out sleepers. Having said that though, they did make up for it in other ways. They provided the platoon with a secondary guard. Any unusual happenings or strange movements on the ground instantly brought forth a chorus of 'oo-oo-oo's, warning the men that someone or something was near. There were areas devoid of fruit and the treetops were silent and rather strangely we missed their company.

Heapy buried the cheese tin and patted down the soil.

'I would leave some flowers if I were you,' I said.

We both laughed at the stupid joke.

I shouldered my pack, along with the cumbersome stewpot, as the patrol was already underway. As mentioned 10 Platoon was at the rear. Being at the back had its own merits. The tension wasn't as great, and if there was going to be any trouble, the odds were the front was the place it would happen.

The man I was following suddenly crossed his arms above his head, meaning we had come across some tracks. It was in fact a crossroads. Moving on we were to see these tracks ourselves. One veered right, through a man-made tunnel of undergrowth forming an arch over the track. Were we on a Communist route? Only time would tell us. The patrol stayed on this course until mid-afternoon before being brought to a halt and surprisingly told, 'You can make camp here, while a few chosen from among you will make up some short patrol groups.'

Heapy was one of those to go. There were four patrols in all in different directions. It was a precaution against enemy presence in our vicinity. Anyway, Heapy went which left me to sort out the gear and pitch the basher. Before leaving he had slipped off his pack making it quicker and easier to move. I slipped off my own pack and belt and placed them in a pile before drawing my machete and clearing the brush and shoots from the place we were going to sleep. I kept three straight pieces of the longer cut branches back to form the basher frame.

I pushed the first two strong sticks into the leafy ground roughly six feet apart with a fork at the top to hold a longer stripped branch across the centre. This would hold the poncho. I took the poncho out of our packs and rolled them out. I took hold of one and threw it over the centre pole. Pulling out the hanging sides of the poncho I staked them into the ground with cut pegs. This formed the roof. I rolled out the other poncho beneath the ridged canvas roof. This was the groundsheet.

All around the others were doing the same. Kit and rations were stowed away at the far end and used as pillows. I stood back to admire my handiwork, and turned just as the Sergeant came up behind me and told me, 'There's a stream just below the slope over there.' He pointed as he told me, then continued, 'Go over and fill the stewpot with water. While you're away I'll get someone to start a fire. Bring the pot over when you get back.'

I looked in the direction he pointed and nodded back saying, 'Okay, Sarge.'

Picking up the pot by the wire handle I went in search of the stream. On reaching the edge of the camp I heard the sound of bubbling water, which led me to a clear, fast-flowing stream. Crouching down I held the pot partly submerged in the water. When it was a little over half full I turned and walked back up the slope back through the camp lines and over to the glowing fire to hang the pot from the tripod above.

Around the fire lay tins of meat, vegetables and salt, one tin from each member of the platoon. I would add Heapy's and mine later. A tall thin column of smoke drifted skywards barely visible above the trees.

Twenty minutes later and the pot began to boil. We opened the tins and emptied the contents into the bubbling pot and stirred as the stew got thicker. Then someone made a suggestion. The next time could someone bring a bottle of Indian curry to add more flavour? Everyone was feeling quite hungry by now as the savoury smells of the cooking stew had drifted around the ring of bashers.

I sat cross-legged, smoking outside the basher. The next minute I was lying flat on my stomach, my rifle loaded and pointed towards where the sound of breaking twigs was heard. Then into view came the returning patrols. My heart had skipped a beat. On seeing the patrol I applied the safety catch and climbed to my knees. Everyone seemed excited.

Heapy had one of those 'Have I got something to tell you!' smiles on his face. Striding over to the basher and lying his rifle beside where I still knelt, he spat it out.

'On our way back here we found a large Commie camp. And you'll never guess what. It's only a few hundred yards down the track from here.'

I got to my feet as Heapy told the story, and grabbed my mess tin as the stew was now ready for dishing out. I grabbed Heapy's along with mine and strode over to the fire where only a handful were served at a time. This made for a smaller target if caught off guard, instead of a dozen standing around waiting for grub.

Once it was served I carried the steaming mess tins carefully making sure I didn't stumble or spill a drop. Heapy had lit a Tommy cooker for the tea. Setting the mess tins down gently on the uneven ground I rummaged through the packs for a packet of biscuits. Finding them I crumbled two or three into the stew, and left the packet for Heapy who occasionally liked to dunk biscuits into the stew.

We ate the thickened stew, while between mouthfuls Heapy went on and on about the camp. From time to time I thought I heard a baby cry and glanced around the camp only to find those around us eating and drinking. We were in a camp several times larger than those we'd been in before.

We scraped out the bottom of the mess tins and let out a belch. Not from over eating but from eating the hot stew too fast. I continued to listen to Heapy's story as he got to the part where they entered the Commie camp. He then opened a tin of cake taken from his haversack, before he continued with the story,

'Leaving that camp of theirs in such a hurry meant they had either seen the patrol coming or had heard us. The fires still had boiling rice and fish hanging over the embers. There were cups of half-drunk black tea where they had sat. Then Luang heard a whimper.'

Heapy stopped for a drink blowing the flies off the surface of the mess tin.

I sat impatiently wanting him to continue. 'Well, what happened then? You can drink that after.'

Fiddling with the now empty mess tin in his hand, he continued on how they searched the enemy camp.

'We were looking under the blankets that lay beneath the sloping roof made from the surrounding lalang and wood. When lo and behold on pulling up one blanket we saw this crying Chinese baby that had been hastily left behind.'

Heapy was still full of the story and he held me in his grip. The story getting more interesting.

'Guess who carried the baby girl back here? Only old

Knocker.'

That was the nickname given to the RSM. His proper name was Knox. He was the one I had had the slight run in with on Christmas day when I was drunk.

Talking so much meant Heapy was still eating his cake. He sat there munching and crunching away. The embers of the fire began to glow as the light began to fade. Every now and again a wisp of smoke gave way to a splutter as a burst of flame erupted out of the white ashes.

We washed out the mess tins and threw the slops some way from the basher so as not to encourage ants, then stowed them away into the side pockets of the packs. Then we had a fag before it got too dark. Crackling twigs announced the approach of the Corporal with the times worked out for the night's guard. The time given to me was the deadman's watch – twelve till one. Bang in the middle of the night.

Ashes were scattered and lay dormant. From somewhere in the dark the cry of the infant could be heard. I wondered what the child's mother was doing right now. Weeping and inconsolable no doubt, wanting to know what was to become of her child. The baby meanwhile, missing her mother's scent and warmth, whimpered throughout the night but even this didn't keep the tired men awake.

Getting my head down on a pack full of tins may have felt hard but that night I could have slept on a bed of nails. A shaking aroused me from my sleep. Batey from the next basher handed me the illuminated watch. It belonged to Lieutenant Bury and was the only one in the platoon. Yawning I gave him a tap to say I was awake. He whispered, 'Everything's fine, the night's quiet.'

With that Batey slunk back into his basher to finish his sleep. I felt in the dark for my rifle till my hand felt the stock. Holding it I moved to the entrance and went no further. Moving away from the basher would certainly mean getting lost in the dense darkness, although unable to see we could still hear and sounds were all around us of the rustling and splashing of animals as they went down to the stream for a drink. Among them were elephants and the occasional snarling tiger. The tiger was the national emblem shown on most products, the most common one being

Tiger beer. By far the loudest animals were the monkeys though tonight they were strangely quiet. Perhaps the presence of so many humans put them off.

Staring at the ground I noticed a sort of illuminous moving picture. Pieces of decaying matter, such as wood and leaves as well as insects, glowed as they moved under and over the rotting compost. Some sort of chemical reaction from the moisture and matter created a fluorescence and a ghostly movement in the darkness.

Looking into the night sky was like looking into an abyss. I shook my head as my eyes began to close. The biting mosquitoes did their bit to keep me awake. Glancing at the watch the fingers told me it was time to wake the next man on guard.

With outstretched hands I felt for the next basher along. It was only a step away, but felt like crawling on a narrow ledge ten storeys up. Gratefully I could feel the poncho in the darkness. I shook the leg inside, hoping it would be Townsend's. Feeling with my hand I found his and pressed the watch into his palm. I then crept out. I was unable to see him but could imagine him sitting there, rifle between his knees, half-asleep.

Back in my basher I yawned. Heapy had hardly moved. A herd of wild elephants wouldn't wake him, I thought. With my head on the pack, hardly feeling the tins inside, I soon drifted off to sleep.

Morning came and we were soon having breakfast – a mug of hot tea and rather salty bacon before breaking camp. We dug holes and buried the tins from the previous night's meal, along with those from breakfast. We then scattered the ashes from the fire.

Over breakfast a decision had been made to take the baby out. A section, led by the Heban, was to leave at once for the highway the same way we had come. If it was any consolation for the child's mother, the poor mite would be much better off out of this wilderness and be placed in much kinder hands. I wonder if Knocker would be a godfather if asked?

March 1951 – Blind Panic

Looking more like a trekker than a soldier, with my pack and stewpot securely strapped to my back, we crossed the stream. We emerged on the opposite side with clothes dripping and boots squelching.

The heat quickly dried out our clothes but unknown to us the stream swung in a large loop some way ahead. We crossed again only this time the crossing was much drier courtesy of a small log bridge and an embankment of steps, cut into the bank and lined with short strips of wood. This route was used constantly for going down to the stream.

High on the clearing stood the Communists' camp. Everybody was told to disperse as the Sergeant said, 'Don't touch or move anything. Places like these are likely to be booby-trapped. Remember the booby trap in the tree, and the grenade?'

Knowing how adept and cunning they were we searched very carefully.

By counting the shelters we estimated their numbers to be around sixty to seventy. We walked slowly round the lean-to shelters. The floor was raised off the ground and a sweeping roof covered the whole shelter from high at the front to floor level at the back. There were no sides, only two posts holding up the roof at the front. Although dry overhead the front was open to the elements.

Strewn about the floor were clothes and blankets which were used for a bed. Here and there the odd white shoes often called baseball boots were left as well as women's underclothes and some bags of rice. These had spilled over and ants were carrying away the food bonanza. Hanging from a length of string we heard the frantic buzzing of flies. On closer inspection we could make out a brown dried out fish. Brown like leather, it had been cured but uncovered it looked unappetising. I grimaced at the thought of having to eat it but I suppose to a starving man it would be a feast of sorts. Tins of unopened food, some oriental fresh vegetables and white chipped mugs stained with tea and some half full, had all been left in haste. However not one gun was to be found.

Down at the stream Bill Weaver knelt to fill his water bottle. He looked up and there standing in front of him was a Commie soldier, also filling his water bottle. He was unaware the camp had been found. The two saw each other at the same time, and stared for one brief second, before turning and running. They had both been taken by surprise.

Weaver came puffing and blowing hard, shouting as he came. On hearing the commotion everyone swung their guns towards him. At the thought of being shot Weaver threw himself on the ground. Calming down he got to his feet and told them about the Commie down at the stream. We all had a good laugh. I often wondered if the Commie saw the funny side too.

The Lieutenant gave the order to torch the camp. With most of the patrol already moving ahead this left 10 Platoon with the task. We torched every shack and lean-to. Black ash and smoke rose into the air amid crackling flames fanned by a slight breeze. We quickly crossed the log bridge. Behind us we could hear muffled explosions as hidden ammunition blew the camp apart. The ammunition had been hidden in the ground and would have left only a few charred stumps standing. In a few weeks time it would be hard to find any trace of a camp in this area. The jungle is quick to take back its own. Overgrowing creepers and bush would see to that.

The patrol had now broken into smaller groups so that a larger area could be covered. 10 Platoon continued down the track while the rest of the company pushed deeper and deeper into the dense jungle. With eyes and ears open and mouths shut we were fully alert for the slightest of movement or sound. Pushing through the overgrown track was becoming painful as the track narrowed.

Below the underside the giant ferns grew sharp thorns. Like fishhooks they tore at your skin and clothes. The stewpot became entangled in the branches and creepers, and I had to pull and wrestle to liberate it snapping branches in temper.

Without warning the fall of an axe was heard. The sound echoed all around, chop, chop, chop. The man I was following held his fingers to his lips. The patrol came to a halt and we listened. The chopping sounded so near and we tried to pinpoint the direction it came from. We knew that sound travels far in such enclosed conditions, rebounding from tree to tree like echoes in a mountain valley. The Communists must have been extremely confident to start building while we were still in the area.

Further down the track we stopped once again. This time the signal was given by hand. Touching hands above the head meant that those ahead had sighted something. They had spotted some thatched roofed shacks. Suddenly uproar, as there was an explosion from up in front, mixed with crashes, screams and shouts. Then up in front the bushes parted and running straight towards me was the lead section in blind panic.

Their eyes were wild and faces crazed. There was only one thought in my head – that of self-preservation at all costs and I started to run like I'd never run before. Stumbling I scrambled to regain my feet. My legs felt as if they belonged to someone else. The thorns were no longer a worry or even an obstacle. Those behind me also turned and ran. We rushed blindly along but even in panic the body has to slow down. Those in front dropped to their knees bringing those behind to a stop. Each one turned, with rifles raised to make a stand and fight the oncoming menace.

With guns at the ready we waited. Winded by the run we gulped the air into our lungs. The last of the runners came into view. They screamed in agony, the last few falling blindly into the undergrowth holding their heads and covering their faces in a bid to minimise the excruciating pain they were feeling. Those that led them in carried the weapons of those in pain. They slipped the packs off the injured before lying by the side of the track.

The story of what happened was slowly pieced together. It had happened as they stood watching the unoccupied shacks. Unwittingly someone had disturbed a hornet's nest, a clay ball hanging on the lower branches of a tree. Disturbed, the hornets swarmed to defend their nest against the intruder, the unfortunate intruder being the lead section.

In their thousands they had swarmed into a cloud buzzing and stinging. The more the men moved the angrier the hornets had become. The only way out was to outrun these flying killers, as they easily evaded flailing arms. The men chose to run the gauntlet. Mad hornets clung to faces and skin trying to inflict as much pain as possible.

Hutch rushed over to the men as they rolled on the ground in agony. He released their packs and pouches then undid his own satchel strap. He knelt beside Corporal Cole and tried to prise his hands away from his face. Around him the other victims' faces were swelling at an alarming rate.

Through their fingers you could see their eyes were almost closed. Their noses and lips along with their hands were now swollen out of proportion. They screamed for help.

Asking two of the nearest men to assist in holding the men still, Hutch gave each one a shot of morphine.

Luang, with his expert knowledge of jungle remedies for bites and stings, went to help the men. He took the cap off his water bottle and poured the cool soothing water over the first man's head, who was now partly unconscious and shivering from shock. The cooling effect of the water seemed to ease the pain somewhat. On seeing this several of the lads went over and emptied their bottles in the same way Luang had done. Close by, a stagnant pool was found behind some reeds. Going over I parted the reeds and grass and knelt beside the murky pool. I suddenly recoiled away when I saw this huge bull leech swimming away in jerky movements. The two-foot long bull leech, sometimes known as the elephant leech, swam down into the murky depths and out of sight. With eyes scanning the surface of the water I plunged the water bottle in. The 'glug glug' stopped as the bottle filled and I had a quick look for the bull leech before hurrying back to where the men lay.

The men's condition grew worse by the minute. Drifting between consciousness and delirium, the water was the only method we had of keeping them cool. The morphine was for pain only and could not improve their features which by now were grotesque from the large number of stings.

Lieutenant Bury was now facing a dilemma, as the time factor was crucial. With only a few daylight hours left it was too late to push for the road and the injured could not be moved in the dark. He went over to Drak and told him to get in touch with HQ.

Drak quickly set up his system and gave the call sign. Getting a reply after a few moments Drak handed over the mike and earphones to the Lieutenant. He pushed back his bush hat and, holding the one earphone to his ear, said into the microphone, 'This is Lieutenant Bury of 10 Platoon, 'D' Company. We urgently require medical knowledge. Is there a doctor available? We will wait for your call. Over.'

A few minutes elapsed before a reply came; 'Hello. Are you receiving me 10 Platoon?'

The medical officer then asked how he could somehow be of assistance. He was quickly told what had taken place. Then the Lieutenant listened as the doctor told him what to do. All in all he was to continue with the water to keep the temperature down, and give morphine when necessary. Tomorrow we were to get them to the nearest pick-up point as soon as possible where transport would be waiting to transfer the men to hospital for urgent treatment in Kluang.

That night was one of the longest of my life. Delirious with pain the men were prevented from hurting themselves by being strapped to litters we had made from cut branches and ponchos. We all slept fitfully as the unconscious men shouted and groaned throughout the night. All we could do was pray for an early dawn.

The dawn finally came with a heavy mist. Dew had formed on the ponchos, which was quickly shaken off. We found the men's condition had not improved and blisters, where the stings remained, showed signs of infection. These needed to be removed as soon as possible.

Skipping breakfast to save time we were soon carrying the injured parties along the jungle track. With four to each stretcher we were a little vulnerable should we be ambushed and so we did a forced march. The sweat and strain brought the platoon to near exhaustion.

We came out of the tree canopy and into the open lalang in late afternoon, and saw the ambulance had not yet arrived. We struggled through the shimmering heatwave before finally reaching the roadside. Here the bedraggled bunch of men sank to their knees. This was British grit showing its true colours once more, always shining through when up against adversity and sheer bad luck.

A lookout posted on the road shouted and waved his arms to attract the Dingo-led ambulances that were speeding up the highway.

'Here they come.'

The ambulances came to a halt. Still in the waist high grass, barely visible from the road, we carried the injured to the rear of the ambulances. Two orderlies and a medical officer alighted. Each man was given a quick check. The officer then asked Hutch what time the last injection was given. Once the information was given the men were then transferred from the litters to the more comfortable ambulances and their packs and weapons placed beside them.

With a wave from the Dingo driver they were away and the red crosses on the sides and rear of the vehicles were gone before we hit the jungle. Now minus four men, Hank included, Luang had a new partner. Townsend was to lead from the front as the new scout and trail breaker.

We now followed the same track we had covered two days earlier. The undergrowth had quickly swallowed up our tracks as if we had never been there at all. We pressed forward in the wake of the main party who were out there somewhere, even with a twenty-four hour start. Our heavy packs were hanging on slumped shoulders and we were drained of energy.

We desperately pushed forwards for two days and nights. The third day found us on a well worn path when a challenge was thrown out by one of the outlying patrol guards, unseen in the thick undergrowth. On identifying us he showed himself and led the way to the main patrol.

We reported our arrival to the commanding officer of the whole operation. Lieutenant Bury and the Sergeant left the platoon stretched along the track. I took out my fag tin to find only three fags left. I hesitated for several seconds before taking one out. Saying to myself, 'Oh, to hell with it!' I closed the lid and lit the fag hanging from the corner of my mouth. Tomorrow there maybe an airdrop. With only three days' rations left and perhaps five days to the road, there had to be a drop in the next day or so. I drew in another much needed drag.

We found that the main patrol was moving much slower and was not so tiring. The patrol wound like a snake along the green terrain. The green uniforms blended in with the background. Rays of sunlight broke through the canopy and circling in the downward shafts of sunlight were moths and gnats chasing the sun.

Stopping for a rest, I sat down without taking off my pack, and lit my last cigarette. I had just removed my hat to wipe the sweat from my face when rat-tat-atat! Rat-tat-atat! I flung myself forward and in the same moment loaded my rifle. All around the ground spurted up as if alive, as the hidden machine gun hammered out its death sentence. The splintering bamboo canes came showering down around me. There was no cover except for a small mound and I scrambled, praying for protection, managing to crawl to the safer side of the mound. My heart was pounding like a tight drum in my chest. The burst of machine gun fire lifted and moved up the line of sprawling men.

Everywhere was chaos. Men screamed, 'Oh God I'm hit! Oh no somebody help, my arm.'

For some it was arms and for others it was legs. Another burst raked across the patrol, as the men looked for ways of escape. The firing continued to bring down branches and young trees. Bullets smashed through them leaving broken branches swinging perilously.

By now we were returning fire and the machine gun suddenly fell silent. We continued to fire until someone in authority shouted, 'Cease fire! Cease fire everybody. Stop firing.'

The heavy smell of cordite and sulphur hung in the air making some cough and splutter as it entered the nostrils. Shaking from the sudden shock I began to search for the half-smoked cigarette stub with trembling hands. I desperately needed it right now but I only found a ground-in stub. Damn it! I thought as I ground the stub even deeper with my heel.

Feeling relieved at coming out of the skirmish without a scratch, I began wondering why the firing had stopped so abruptly. Shouting continued from up and down the line from men still lying prone. The earthy smell of fungus was apparent. Ants quickly seized the opportunity to suck or bite crazily as the salty sweat oozed from the pores of the now disorientated men.

Suddenly movement from the direction of the firing brought every gun to bear. Snapping twigs sent the adrenaline racing. Fingers tightened on triggers. We were near to breaking point as bushes were pushed aside. The tension broke as an English speaking voice was heard, 'Hold your fire. We are coming in. Hold your fire for God's sake, we are bringing in wounded.'

That sentence sounded like a prayer from heaven. At the same moment, pushing through the thickets and bushes came 11 Platoon. They were carrying two badly wounded men. Oh no, not them! Not our own men. They had opened fire on us by mistake from the flank.

Some terrible mistake had occurred. 11 Platoon were sent to flank the patrol as a cover against ambush. Thinking they were further ahead than they were they had heard voices and not being able to make out what was said thought they had stumbled on a Commie ambush. So unable to see through the undergrowth they had attacked without warning.

The horror and disbelief at what they had done was apparent on their faces. The surroundings were more to blame than they were. Or was it our bad luck continuing? Counting the wounded from both groups it added up to the number four once again.

Each man carried a field dressing in case of emergency. If wounded you could treat yourself in an awkward situation. They were kept in a button pocket on the thigh for easy access. Medics from all platoons were now using these. They worked frantically to stem the flow of blood from the ripped flesh and open wounds.

I grimaced at the sight I was witnessing as the medics went about their work, ripping open dressings to reveal thick wads of cotton wool and lint, which smelt of antiseptic and sulphur. They talked to the wounded trying to calm and soothe their fears.

Placing the cotton wads on the wound and applying pressure, then breaking the tops of the morphine phials and injecting the quick acting painkiller, the sweating medics began to win the battle and brought the wounded to a more stable state. They had won an important victory. Injuries such as these ran the risk, in such a disease-infested hell, of causing gangrene among a list of other ailments. As I moved around the wounded I could see torn flesh as shirts were ripped from their backs to gain access to the wound. One of the victims was Faulkner. He had caught one in the shoulder. Fortunately for him the bullet went clean through leaving a small hole on entry, and a much larger hole where it left. He had lost a lot of blood and his face was white and pinched.

Walking along the line I came to Hughes, a proud Welshman also from 11 Platoon. He was the one with the Bren gun that had had me jumping all around the bamboo mound. His left arm was covered in blood where he had been hit. A bullet had hit the metal casing of his Bren and burst on impact into tiny lead splinters. The splinters had spread way up his arm, almost tearing his thumb off. Thankfully none had hit his eyes or face.

There were two other wounded also from 11 Platoon, whose names I can't recall, suffering from leg and groin wounds. The one with the groin wound had been especially lucky. Two bullets had just missed his manhood and there was a possibility that one of them might still be there. He was though in a bad way still. The fourth man had taken one in the lower leg, just above the ankle. Again the bullet had passed straight through, narrowly missing the bone. There hadn't been any fatalities thank God.

Although partially sedated by morphine the men would ask, 'Is it bad? Does it look bad? Shall I walk again? Are you telling me the truth? I don't want to die. I don't want to be a cripple.'

What could you tell them? What could you say, except, 'It'll be all right, it's only a scratch.'

By coincidence all the victims had been non-smokers. But now, as they talked, they smoked. What a time to start. Holding the cigarette between trembling fingers they looked awkward. As the morphine took hold and they slipped into semi-consciousness, the cigarette would slip from their limp fingers.

I returned to where I had left my pack and saw men scratching and scrambling about their own packs. Some of them had been riddled with bullets. And milk and red Ketchup were seeping through the holes where the tins had been hit. One particular pack had a machete pushed down the inside. A round had hit the blade sending the bullet travelling up the blade and into the Bakelite handle where it had lodged. One bullet had ricocheted and finished up miraculously in a water bottle. I say miraculously because the water bottle was still being worn on the man's behind at the time. With the spent bullet inside he could afford to smile.

At this point we had no sense of time. We only knew it was late. The officers were the only ones with watches, and they told us we were to stay here for the night. Going neither forwards nor back we were in a bad situation.

Finding a reasonable place to pitch our basher I left Heapy to erect it while I went round the men, and asked for water for the evening meal, seeing as there was none at hand. Townsend followed in my footsteps collecting tins of meat and veg. We soon got a fire going and it was in the light of the flames that I noticed how grimy my hands were. It had been four days since I had last had a wash and the same amount of time since I'd taken my boots off.

The smoke and sparks rose as the fire was stoked. Some green twigs amongst the burning wood made my eyes run, and I wiped them with my sleeve leaving dirty streak marks all over my face. I felt dirty and smelt of sweat.

The pot was now boiling and ash floated in the air. Reaching above my head I broke a piece of wood before dropping it into the pot. Any floating ash or dust would cling to the wood, which we could throw out before ladling out the stew.

Kneeling beside the blackened pot, holding one of the opened tins and using it as a ladle, the Corporal poured out an equal amount to each man. We shuffled past careful not to spill the stew then crossed back to our bashers. Sitting at the basher entrance we greedily spooned the hot food into our mouths. This was the first food since early morning.

After the meal I sat there picking my teeth with a match and feeling like a smoke. The smell of cigarette smoke made me turn to see Heapy sat there smoking, a big grin all over his face. Knowing I didn't have any fags he offered me his cigarette. I took a few puffs and rolled the smoke around inside my mouth. This eased the craving that cigarettes have on you. I then handed it back to Heapy. We did this several times until the fag was nothing but a glow on the ground and we were left without a smoke in the world.

Beneath the cover of the bashers the wounded, still being

tended by the medics, were in a delirious state. One was continually calling for his mother to help him as he sank into a feverish sleep. The others would constantly ask for water. The morphine, although good, seemed to last only for a short period. They were in desperate need of hospitalisation if they were to stand any chance of survival.

Looking at our options things looked pretty bad. On the food front we only had enough supplies for two days. We were five days' march from the nearest road – and that was without the added weight of carrying the wounded. The situation had never looked bleaker.

After a restless night morning came none too soon. We were aroused by the sound of cutting down bamboo poles. I crawled out of the basher to face an uncertain day. Two feet of mist covered the ground, and it was strange to see the men walking through it, as you could only see down to their knees.

Over breakfast we found what the day had in store for the platoon. Sipping tea we saw the Sergeant visit each basher and watched as a few of the men threw their bush hats to the ground in disgust as he left. He then headed towards this end of the patrol.

He got to Heapy and me, where a few more of the platoon had gathered, and told us in a grim voice, 'Straight after breakfast we shall be moving out so pack everything as we are the ones taking out the wounded.'

I could not believe what I had heard. My heart sank and was filled with bitterness. Lieutenant Bury had done it again. Using us as his stepping stone for climbing the promotional ladder. He knew we were under strength. Those four good men we had lost were irreplaceable and what with the hornets episode we were shagged out.

The cutting and making of litters continued as 10 Platoon cooked breakfast. The mist began to rise as the sun came up. Even in this stinking place we had variable changes in climatic conditions, waking up in damp clothes and walking through the blazing heat of the day while the natives took siestas during the afternoon. The old saying, that mad dogs and Englishmen go out in the midday sun was certainly true of us.

We shouldered our packs but we carried very little now. With the litters at our feet we waited for the Lieutenant to show. Those of us not carrying litters were responsible for carrying the guns. No one was spared, as each man had to do his share of the workload. With the platoon down to just twenty-two men there was no room for slackers.

Down the line strode the Lieutenant from his meeting with the other officers and told the Heban Luang to scout ahead. I lifted the litter in unison with the other three, saying, 'One two three – up.'

A gasp came from the wounded man as the stretcher closed inwards like a hammock, squeezing and causing pain over which we had no control. The wounded grimaced with pain as they lay there in blood-soaked bandages. The jerking of the litters offered no respite to their suffering. As we started the long trek back the men rolled their heads from side to side, licking their lips as the fever swept through their wrecked bodies. Hutch, the medic, seemed to continually walk alongside the litters dabbing the men's lips with a damp cloth. With shirts open to the waist our thin arms showed every sinew of our puny frames. We would curse at each other if someone slipped. Tempers flared as our mental attitude broke down.

We were making slow progress. Gripping the bamboo poles for such a long period was causing us to lose our grip more and more through cramp. At hourly intervals we changed over with the gun bearers. Not that it made things easier, but at least you could stand upright for a while.

After doing this for several hours the world, in the mind's eye, began to shrink inwards. You felt as though you were in a shell. Your brain went numb and your legs felt as if they had no feet, and you were walking on stumps of bone. We were making our way forward in a dream world, probably caused by a lack of salt. God let this end before we go mad!

That night while eating the last of the stew the Lieutenant told us of the plan to airlift the wounded out and showed us the map of a clearing by a bend in a river where a helicopter could land. This river was another day's march away and the wounded were getting no better. Still delirious they were not eating, only taking in fluids. Their unshaven faces gave them the appearance of gaunt old men.

Lying in the darkness that night full of aches and pains and almost too tired to sleep, we wondered about the clearing. No one mentioned that we could miss it, which would prove fatal to those on the stretchers and perhaps a few of us besides. Talking in whispers and half to myself I said, 'Do you know what I fancy right now, Heapy?'

Heapy, reading my thoughts, answered, 'What's that – a fag. Anyway they're bad for your health.'

I chuckled to myself as I thought of the situation we were in. If a smoke was bad for your health then what the bloody hell are we doing here?

Sometime during the night we heard the pouring rain. The heavens had opened up and the bouncing rain was coming through the sides of the basher splashing my face and soaking through the almost threadbare uniform. The water ran between our bodies and I turned my back to shield my face before falling to sleep once more.

Next morning we woke amidst a quagmire. Soaking wet, my feet felt cold and clammy and it was a good thing I still had one pair of dry socks left. We had a cuppa and a hard tack biscuit with runny cheese, which during the day may turn to dysentery and no doubt give me the shits. I took my socks out of the pack and finally undid my boots. I then pulled off the wet socks. My feet were white and looked dead so I began to rub the toes and feet vigorously. Slowly but surely the blood began to flow and the feeling afterwards was hard to believe. I rubbed in the foot powder and put the dry socks on and then the boots. At least my feet were dry.

I was now packed and ready to go. Standing in the ankle deep slippery mud, I said to Heapy, 'The gods must be against us, even the weather's turned for the worst.'

Heapy nodded in agreement as he shook the rain off the wet ponchos and rolled them up. He then strapped them below the almost empty shoulder pack containing just a little tea and sugar. The milk had all been used.

We stood by the litters, our limbs stiff and aching from yesterday's efforts. Hutch had tended the wounded all night, and looked more dead than alive. His eyes were deep and sunken from lack of sleep. Out of the twenty-two there wasn't a fit one amongst us and we were facing a superhuman effort in order to reach the river.

'Move on out!' The words came from up in front. Slipping and sliding, the wounded were mostly unaware of what was going on around them. They didn't shout if they were dropped and we just struggled on.

Hollowed eyes and raggedy faces covered with five days growth – even our own mothers wouldn't recognise us. Their own sons in this condition!

The ground was now churning to a sticky grey mess. The platoon had only one thought, which drove them forward. Only a few more hours slipping and sliding until we reach the river. The mind deadened by shear exhaustion, the platoon moved painfully on.

The steam rose from the sodden ground and the wet bushes as we brushed against them. The sun was rising, causing the temperature to soar. The humidity was increasing by the minute. We must get there soon. No one, man or beast, could keep this up for much longer.

'Aaah, aah get them off me!'

Cries of anguish and distaste, coming from ahead, told me something was happening. We tried to reach the leading group as fast as we could but we were wading in sucking mud and it was difficult enough to free our feet at every step yet alone move any faster.

We finally saw what had made the leading group cry out a few moments earlier. The night's rain had brought out another of the jungle horrors and another blood sucker at that. Not the mosquito but something far worse that made you cringe and your flesh creep – leeches. The wriggling bloodsucking aquatic worm, its head waving, waited for a passing meal. Whether it be animal or man-made little difference to them. Anything that carried blood. The leeches were anything up to two inches in length. Their thin matchstick bodies were adept at getting through clothes and canvas boots with ease. Just thinking about them made the blood creep and there was no way out but to walk and pray and get clear of this area quickly.

Floundering in the mud the leeches clung to our clothes before burrowing into our skin. The sweat had drained from our bodies with our recent efforts and now the blood was being sucked away too.

Hutch was kept busy handing out salt tablets but there was precious little that he could do about leeches. At intervals those who still had cigarettes burnt the leeches off their bodies. Those that didn't used the blades of their machetes. The blade was used to lift the head from the skin. You made sure that the head of the leech wasn't left embedded in the skin since heads left in the skin quickly turned infectious. The leeches bloated bodies, full of blood, looked like a black peapod. Squelching we trudged through the deep sludge, keeping the ponchos over the wounded to keep them leech free.

Ahead we heard good news. Luang had returned from his forage and reported that the river was within daylight range. We gave a cheer as we pushed, shoved and dragged the litters over a fallen tree which blocked the way. The track had been lost some way down the line.

The sound of the roaring waters of the river drove us blindly on. My feet now felt as though I was walking on sponges. Breaking the cover of the jungle we could see the twisting flow of the river and followed the river bank searching for the clearing shown on the map. Suddenly there it was in front of us covered by at least three feet of lalang.

We were hemmed in on three sides by the jungle and the river on the fourth. We lined the litters side by side beneath the trees on the edge of the jungle, then literally dropped down on the ground ourselves.

Meanwhile Drak began stringing out the aerial high between the trees for a better reception. Once rigged up he began to send out the call sign. Within minutes he was calling the Lieutenant over to him. Squatting down beside him the Lieutenant donned the earphones and pulled them tightly over his bush hat. He spoke into the mike giving out our co-ordinates to HQ from a map he laid out on the ground. The receiver read the map references back to him and we heard the Lieutenant answer, 'That's correct, and you say you will be over here in around thirty minutes?' Still listening and answering the Lieutenant went on to say, 'When I hear you approaching I'll fire a green flare to say it's safe to land. If it's a red flare you see veer away and await further instructions. Out.'

Laying the earphones and mike beside Drak the Lieutenant turned to the Sergeant and explained the tactics of the airlift. Meanwhile, Drak remained by the side of the eighty-eight set, listening for further messages.

As soon as he had finished explaining the situation to the Sergeant, Lieutenant Bury walked towards us rubbing his hands and looking well pleased with himself. 'Anything left to eat in the way of food?' he asked.

Some of the men were scattered under the trees for shade, but we undid our packs and tipped out the contents. There was some cheese and a couple of tins of peas. Eyes were scouting along the now empty packs. A tin of beans, some mixed veg and, lo and behold, a tin of bully beef. Luang came up trumps with what little rice he had left and the Lieutenant threw in a tin of salty bacon.

As someone collected the tins I went down to the river to fetch the water and had to hold on tightly to the pot as the raging water threatened to tear it from my grasp.

The water was already boiling by the time we heard the helicopter and everything that was edible was opened and thrown into the pot. Someone produced a tin of jam and said it was full of calories, so in went that. The steam soon began to rise above us and on into the lower branches.

In the distance was the unmistakable throb of aero engines, and the swish of overhead rotor blades. The sound brought our eyes skywards searching above the surrounding trees. With the pistol pointing towards the blue heavens, Sergeant Cushion pulled the trigger. And bang. A fizzing green flare was sent upwards leaving a green trail in its wake.

The whirling blades were getting ever nearer. With a deafening roar one of the helicopters appeared overhead and the down wash threw us off our legs. Hats and loose clothing, along with grass and dust, were lifted into the vortex before being thrown clear just below the aircraft.

Drak, holding on to his hat, was waving frantically to the Lieutenant. The Lieutenant saw him and trying to avoid the down wash bent down and sprinted as best he could over to Drak. He took the mike and began speaking to the chopper pilot as the craft veered away over the treetops and from sight. The Lieutenant was now able to hear the pilot who was concerned about the over-hanging branches around the jungle's edge. He wanted more room for the descending helicopters so as to control the swaying descent.

The platoon was ordered to climb and cut down the branches while the officers monitored and reported to the pilot. Climbing the trees the men quickly cut and chopped away at the branches. As they fell they were quickly dragged carefully away by those on the ground. We could not afford any more getting hurt.

When the extra space had been cut the Sergeant waved for the men to come down. Like monkeys we dropped down. Drak was then signalled and he in turn signalled the pilot. As the helicopter appeared it hovered momentarily and inspected the clearing before descending.

This time we held on to our hats more tightly as the crafts down wash flattened the lalang and the surrounding trees were bent to near breaking point. Just then a second helicopter appeared.

We waited as the rotors on the first chopper slowed to a mere whisper before lifting the groaning wounded. We bent low under the rotating blades as we carried the first of the litters. The pilot, who judging from the stripes on his arms, was a flight sergeant, was just climbing out of his perspex bubble of a cockpit. He began supervising the way the wounded were loaded. Bolted to the landing gear were two stretchers, one either side of the cockpit, with a hood that fitted over the head and shoulders of the wounded.

Transferring the men from the litters to the aircraft was proving tricky. We removed the ponchos with a one, two, three, then lifted in unison. Strapping him in and pulling the hood cover down. Having done one the pilot moved to the other side where they proceeded to strap in the other wounded man. The litters were finally dragged from beneath the blades as the pilot climbed back into his bubble.

We stood clear and held on to our hats once more as the blades went faster and faster and the chopper slowly lifted, then once clear of the trees, banked and flew out of sight. The way was now clear for the second chopper to land. Over it came, hovering to get into the right position then began descending. Once down we carried the last two men to be strapped onto the perilous-looking landing gear. The thought of flying home that way didn't appeal to me at all.

This time the pilot looked on. He knew we had loaded the others safely. From his breast pocket he withdrew a full packet of twenty Senior Service cigarettes. Lighting one up he looked around to see our eyes staring at him. He opened up the packet and offered them around. Our hands went out and in seconds the pack was empty. He screwed the pack up and tossed it away.

We said thanks for the cigarettes. Seeing the men looking hungrily on and the blackened pot, he declined the offer of a cup of tea. He climbed back into the bubble as we looked on. Those on the stretchers rolled their heads from side to side. Soon they would be in clean beds and receiving the treatment they needed.

As the blades turned faster and faster the helicopter trembled and began to lift above the trees. It hesitated for a moment then like the previous one banked and flew out of sight.

The helicopter's engines soon faded into the distance to be replaced by the quieter sounds of the river as lapping waves and currents broke on the bend of the riverbank. In other times this would have been an ideal spot for fishing.

Below the trees we sat spooning out the thin stew, slurping and wiping our mouths on our sleeves. Manners mean nothing when you're hungry. Never was a meal harder earned.

I finished the stew with a belch and felt behind my ear to see if the cigarette was still there. It was, and I lit it with a burning stick from the dying embers of the fire. I enjoyed the fag, rolling the smoke in my mouth before releasing it in a slow breath. Besides releasing pent-up tension it helped to fill the empty spaces between the ribs. I had a few more puffs before snipping the fag and placing it in the breast pocket of my shirt patting it with a kind of reverence at having such a rich prize.

Soon afterwards the Sergeant came over and told us to bury the cans that were lying about and to scatter the ashes from the fire. Then with empty backpacks and full water bottles the platoon, having done its job, left the clearing and headed towards the semi-darkness of the jungle. We now had less than an hour's daylight left.

We walked all night without making camp, just brief rests. We were without food, which meant we had to find the main patrol before we could eat. Just before dawn broke the patrol stopped once more. Weary from exhaustion we sank to the ground with a sigh escaping from our lips in relief. We slipped off the empty packs and rubbed our aching shoulders. I didn't care where I was as I scratched my stubby chin. I closed my aching eyes, oblivious to the clicking insects and howls from the monkeys above as they welcomed the coming dawn.

I was awakened by a kick to the sole of my foot. I rubbed my red eyes and felt stiff. I sat up and glanced around to see the others being woken in the same fashion by the Corporal going down the line bringing each sleeper back to reality.

Those that had snipped their fags now fumbled for them. I pulled out my own crumpled half and lit it as my stomach growled at me. The match spluttered and threatened to go out as it ignited then burned back to life. My first lungful of the day made me cough and wake Heapy who was lying close by. He opened his eyes and asked, 'You've been holding out on me. How many fags have you got there?'

'Come on Heapy. You know I had this one off the pilot,' I replied and offered him the fag so he could have a drag. We passed it between us until it almost burnt our fingers then I let it drop on the ground and saw the ash leave a dark smudge.

Comradeship such as this carried us through the hard times. We knew we could count on each other, even to death. Struggling to our feet we carried on.

It was early afternoon before we caught the main patrol. They were occupying a clearing high above a slope and beneath the fringe of the jungle. They had been busy cutting a clearing for an airdrop.

Everybody was anxious to hear how their buddies were and if they were all right when they were airlifted. Any contact with the Commies? No, was the answer to that last question. During the three-day interval the two parties had managed to clear an area large enough to be seen by low flying aircraft and our supplies were now non-existent.

The platoon was designated an area to the left of the camp on an embankment some thirty feet above a stream. Here we made our bashers on a more permanent basis, rather than a one-night stand.

The men were spaced out at regular intervals around the perimeter of the camp. All were looking skywards for the slightest sight or sound of a plane. Amongst them stood an officer from 'C' Company. In his fist he held a Very pistol ready to fire as soon as a plane was heard. A white cloth had marked the centre of the drop zone. This was to be the aim point for the aircraft. Far away the drone of engines could be heard. Not a whirring this time but a hum from overloaded engines.

Beneath the trees the wireless operator, who had been sitting patiently, received a signal. Contact had been made with the plane which produced a cheer from the men. The officer answered a message from the pilots asking for a recognition signal and shielding his eyes he raised his hand above his head and fired. The green flare streaked into the blue sky arcing at its peak and trailing smoke. The officer fired once more only this time with a red flare, signalling the dropping zone was clear.

Between the trees two Dakotas came into view at treetop level making a dummy run. In the planes' fuselages we could see large doors opening and men waving from them. The planes banked in a tight circle and began their dropping run. All eyes were now turned skywards.

A large container filled the doorway. As the plane banked the container was pushed out fixed firmly to a raft. It fell for several seconds before a small canopy appeared above the raft, releasing several parachutes which slowed the container's descent. More containers were pushed out and the sky was filled with chutes as the first container reached earth with a resounding bump. One of the chutes roman candled as it failed to open. The package plummeted earthwards in the 1500 foot drop. It smashed on impact scattering smashed tins and broken pieces of wood. Another container swung into the high treetops at the foot of the clearing. It would be retrieved later.

The men waited for the last container to leave the aircraft before venturing out to gather the rations. On the last run the aircrews stood in the doorways and waved and shouted but their voices were lost in the roar of the Dakota's engines. The wireless crackled as the plane's wireless operator spoke to the operator on the ground, 'Enjoy your rations and happy hunting. Out.'

The planes faded. Their work was done.

We were the nearest to the raft that had overshot and was swinging from the trees. Six of us grabbed our machetes and trudged on down the slope before clambering over and through the tangled branches.

Thorns tore at our trousers and being stripped to the waist didn't help either. From a distance recovering the container had seemed easy enough. Close up however was a completely different story.

Standing below a one hundred foot giant wielding our puny machetes, we were faced with an impossible task. We looked up at the swinging container trapped by its parachute cords. We never heard the Sergeant approach us, until he stood behind us, asking in his usual sarcastic way, 'Well, why are you waiting? It's not doing any good up there.'

Seeing there was no way of climbing or cutting the tree down the Sergeant told us to stand clear and producing a Very pistol he told us, 'Stand clear. This is how you do it.'

Taking aim he pulled the trigger. Almost immediately the silk chutes burst into flames. The Sergeant and the six of us scrambled clear. The cords burned and snapped as they were engulfed in a ball of flame. The raft tilted and jerked then, suddenly ripping clear, a burning mass fell thundering to the ground. We moved quickly to smother the burning raft before any more damage was done to the rations.

Some of the boxes had burst open on impact. We salvaged the unopened boxes first and started to pass them back in a human chain that had now been formed. The air was thick with burnt ash and our sweaty bodies were soon covered in black soot. We collected the last of the undamaged tins before picking our way through the pile of bracken.

Once in the open we could make out scattered groups all around the drop zone carrying boxes on their shoulders over to the far corner designated for the stacking of supplies. Breathing hard with my bag of tins over my shoulder, I took my time to reach the area. I was certainly glad to slip the bag onto the ground and leave it to someone else to sort out.

Glancing back down the slope I could see men folding the parachutes and burying them in quickly dug holes. A few branches were then dragged over to cover the freshly dug earth. This effort was to prevent the Communists from using the materials other than empty tin cans.

Shuffling their feet the men moved forward receiving rations that were handed to them. Special rafts carried bread. This came as a total surprise but was very welcome – a small luxury the men would enjoy. Moving up to the front of the queue I was given rations for Heapy and myself. Feeling highly chuffed with myself I carried the box on my shoulder to where Heapy by now would have pitched the basher just inside the jungle.

I placed the box inside the basher and we both opened the rations. We kept the box back in order to keep the ants away from the bread. I cut thick slices of bread with the cleanest of the machetes then liberally spread some marge on them. Finally I put some cheese on. My stomach was rumbling with anticipation of the first bite in nearly twenty-four hours.

Heapy had gone over to the ration area for some fags and fresh clothes from a separate container leaving me to make a brew. Finding the tea and sugar I used my bayonet to pierce the milk tin and waited for the water to boil on the Tommy cooker.

I began wondering where the unflappable Heapy was when up he came with a pile of green clothes. Two shirts and two pairs of trousers. Two pairs of socks and boots. In his mouth was a lit cigarette. He threw me a tin of fifty which was to last me a week.

I unscrewed the lid of the Triple Five brand knowing they would all be gone inside three days. And that was stretching it. With the tea made, a full stomach and a fag, who needed heaven?

Slipping and sliding on my backside down the bank, the stew-pot bounced through the trees as I skidded into the stream. I climbed out and knelt in the water. With the pot washed out and half-full I used the trees to pull myself back up the steep bank. I felt completely knackered by the time I reached the top. I carried the pot over to a dead hollow tree stump where the fire for the evening meal had been lit.

Finding a piece of soap amongst the rations I stripped off the ripped and smelling clothes. Then in groups of four and naked, except for hat and unlaced boots, we went sliding back down the bank splashing in the cold clear stream. I lay there letting the cool water flow and bubble over me. Then soaping myself down I rubbed the thick lather into my skin, freeing myself of the sweat and smells of the jungle if only for a short time. The soapy foam washed downstream.

Next I took the razor blade from my hatband where it had been for several months and replaced the blunted blade within the safety razor with it. I lathered my face and, without a mirror, began carefully to have a shave. With only a few nicks I climbed out of the stream feeling refreshed. I left the others in the stream jumping and larking about like two-year-olds.

I dried myself down unashamed as the boys cooeed and whistled, trying to raise a comment from me. Back on the ridge Heapy had stripped down for his turn at the stream. The camp looked half-deserted. I felt peckish as I pulled on my clean socks and trousers and could see the steam rising from the pot surrounded by empty tins.

Shaking and shivering and wringing wet, Heapy came gasping back as the evening meal was about to be dished out. Carrying both tins I went over and knelt beside the Corporal who was stirring the stew. He could see I was carrying two mess tins and looked inquiringly at me, so I said, 'For two, Corporal. Mine and Heapy's.'

Without further question he ladled out the meal for two and I got back to Heapy as he finished dressing. We sat and ate discussing the events of the last two days.

'Do you think we got the wounded out in time, Heap? You know, without getting gangrene.'

'Sure. I bet right now they're sitting up in bed and cuddling a pretty nurse. Have you got another biscuit there, Ebee?'

I leant back on my elbow muttering, trying to convince myself we had got them out in time.

'We certainly tried, Heapy. We certainly did.'

Patrols for the next few days went out in all directions. As far as we knew the airdrop had gone unnoticed but the patrols were fruitless. The area seemed clear.

Then on the third day 10 Platoon went just a little too far. It was about noon when we found a stretch of water. Luang's sharp eyes picked out stones below the surface used as stepping stones. Carefully we crossed. The stones led to a small raised island which concealed well made lean-to shelters. Unused for months, we made use of the space and settled down for a bite to eat.

We had covered several miles since leaving the camp before Hank realised he had left his pouch containing magazines for the Owen gun behind. Everyone was rather angry at having to return to collect them.

Doubling back the front of the patrol passed us by, led by the red head of Hank, who looked neither left or right as he passed, knowing his mistake was to cost us daylight hours in getting back to base, even having to spend a night on the side of the track without food and only a little water.

Keeping within touching distance we were barely visible in the dark. We splashed and stumbled along. The water had now penetrated our boots and numbed our feet. We didn't even know if this was the right stream that went below the camp. If it was, then we had probably gone past the camp and were now going away from it. Then from out of the darkness came a voice challenging the leading scout. For the next few moments we stood perfectly still and tense as passwords were exchanged. We climbed out of the pool and struggled up the slippery mud bank, hanging on to the person in front and exchanging four letter words. Eventually though we made it to the top.

Exhausted we made our way to where we believed our bashers were. In the darkness I unlaced my wet boots. Then a voice belonging to a dark silhouette blocked the entrance whispering, 'Is that you, Ebee? Only I'm lost.'

'Over here. Come straight on towards my voice.'

He felt with his hands and nearly poked my eyes out.

'Quiet down you lot,' came the Sergeant's low voice. He came crawling into the basher and undid his boots. I could hear the water pouring out of his upturned boots as he used an old cowboy trick from films, where boots are hung upside down on two sticks pushed into the ground. This served to keep out snakes and scorpions and anything else that crawled in the night. It also helped to dry the boots. In the last few months we had learned a lot. We had especially learned how to survive.

I woke early. My ear was feeling dead from sleeping on something hard in the pack. Holding my mess tin I got myself out of the basher and felt my boots. They were dry. I then gave them a tap on the ground and seeing nothing fall out I pulled them on.

Over breakfast we were told the rest of the supplies issued to the company patrol were being split into groups. So over I went to the supply dump and came back carrying a further day's ration box.

Throughout the day at two hourly intervals the platoons moved out burying their cans and burning the old tattered uniforms. I couldn't even visualise the Commies wearing them.

That night 10 Platoon slept alone and slipped away early next morning into the mist. Our packs carried a lot more than normal and it was a good feeling to know we had food.

By midday the platoon stood on a river bank. The swirling currents raced away beneath the overhanging branches and the waters looked dark and forbidding as they lapped the banks. Broken branches from upstream swept by partially submerged in the choppy waves. We looked across the twenty yards of fast-flowing water to the bank opposite where a muddy trail led from the water's edge to a sparse area before disappearing into the jungle beyond.

Gathering toggle ropes from the men we proceeded to loop them together by pushing the pegs on each rope through the loops on each toggle. We did this until we were able to reach the other side of the river. The Lieutenant then asked, 'Who is the strongest swimmer among you?'

Everybody agreed it was Townsend and he came forward

looking puzzled as the Lieutenant explained what he wanted him for.

'Do you think you can make it across?'

'I'll try, sir,' replied Townsend. 'It looks like a strong current. What do I have to do if I get across, sir?'

'Tie the rope end which will be around your waist to a good strong tree.'

The way the officer spoke it was as if Townsend couldn't fail.

Having stripped down to just his socks and trousers the swimmer picked his way down to the water's edge. The Sergeant let the rope out behind him with two or three steadying the rope.

Townsend slipped into the river and instantly struck out against the current. Moving slowly he swam with strong strokes but the current was pulling him downstream towards the centre where the water seemed a lot calmer. As the flow took him downriver Townsend quickly grabbed the nearest and lowest branch. He hung there for several minutes gathering his strength. Then slowly, hand over hand, he dragged himself up the bank on the other side. We gave him a silent cheer by waving our hands. Getting to his feet Townsend undid the rope around his waist then walked up the bank until he stood opposite the platoon.

Picking out a sturdy tree from several on the bank, he tied the rope around it. Then we did the same thing on our side. The rope swung just a few feet above the river. This wasn't a time for faint hearts.

Townsend waved for us to come across. The first one to go was a small man. He slid down the bank with his rifle slung across his shoulders. He then entered the river, where he just hung. The Sergeant gave him a verbal to get a move on. The man was frightened, but more frightened of the Sergeant than the river. His knuckles were going white with holding on to the rope. The water threatened to snatch it from his grip. At times the man went under and gasped as he surfaced. Those who were waiting shouted at the struggling man, 'Hang on you're nearly there. Just a few more feet.'

It was painfully slow but eventually he managed it. With his arms outstretched Townsend leaned forward over the river ready to grasp the exhausted man. Using both hands he pulled the man out. The water poured from his trousers and pack as the man fell to the ground to recover. It was time for the next one to cross.

With half the men across then came my turn. I secured my hat inside my shirt and the EY rifle across my shoulders, then spat into my hands more in defiance than to grip the rope. Holding the rope I steadied myself down the bank and into the water. The water felt colder than it looked and the swift currents tugged at my feet. Hand over hand I moved forwards going deeper the further I crossed. The riverbed, made up of loose stones, made me slip. With my footing and one handhold gone I hung on with the other against the fast-flowing water. While underwater I somehow managed to turn and flung out my free hand blindly while my head was still below the surface. My hand closed over the rope and I came up spewing out water and gasping for breath.

For a moment I thought I was lost. Without the rope I would have washed away downriver. The heavy rations and rifle were helping to drag me under. The thought that my body might never be found gave me added strength. Suddenly the water began to get shallow and the bank was almost within grabbing distance. I saw an outstretched hand and gratefully accepted the offer. Dripping wet and cold I scrambled up the bank and slipped off my pack and rifle and drained the water out of the stewpot.

It was to take another two hours before everyone got across and had recovered sufficiently. While the remainder crossed we brewed tea. The last one across was told to untie the rope and tie it around his waist. He was to wade out and we would pull him across. As he fought his way across a submerged tree narrowly missed him.

We had crossed a barrier. Perhaps this was the first time this river had been crossed. It was said that tribes in these hundreds of square miles had never seen a white man, known as Sakies. We had seen their traps made from twigs and creepers. We had come across small fires of ash and bones of birds and rodents, but the sight of any tribesman had evaded us.

April 1951 – Gardens of Fire

When everyone was just about recovered and everything was packed, we shouldered our burdens as Luang was given the signal to move on. Luang had his First World War Lee Enfield rifle, which was given to him more as a gesture than anything since he would rather fight with his parang than a gun. This fact was emphasised whenever he grinned, and showed his top two teeth were missing.

A few miles had passed and the walking became a little easier. The undergrowth had almost disappeared to just a few sparse areas. Soon we stopped for the night and made camp. This time however there was no running water at hand.

Bashers were erected and the stewpot was swinging over the fire. Generally everything seemed to be going well. Too well for my liking. As we sat there with our meal the insatiable flies covered the food. By now some of us were badly suffering from dysentery. Those that had it could be seen hurrying to the cover of the bushes to do their business, armed with paper and machete. This happened every few minutes leaving the sufferer weak, sore and miserable.

Shovelling in my rice and apricots I felt the urge to scratch my chest. I unbuttoned my shirt and there across my chest was a red rash, the start of a sweat rash commonly known as tinier. It usually started under the arms and groin. Some ointment called Winfields from Hutch's satchel would do the trick. So I asked him, 'Have you got any of that ointment for tinier, Hutch? Only it's driving me crazy.'

'Help yourself Ebee. It's in one of the tins, all right?' he said as he finished his meal.

I started rubbing in the ointment, which burnt the skin. The stuff had a multitude of purposes including curing crabs, sores and other ailments. As long as I didn't catch typhoid or scrub typhus or an even more hideous disease, elephantiasis, I was all right. The latter was when your limbs swell up to an enormous size. There was this one man whose balls swelled up to a huge size. Anyway, that's enough of that.

I stubbed out the last fag of the day as the night closed in on the tiny camp. I wriggled my toes. My boots were upside down on sticks. I had a full stomach. The itching tinier was dying down and I only had nine months of my service to do. Back home right now they were about to have spring. The daffodils would be in flower and buds would fill the trees bursting into leaf or bloom. The thought of home was always near.

With a breakfast of skinless sausage under our belts and the tins buried, the day started like most other days out here. It was cool and easy to live with before the temperature rose. Just the right conditions for drinking and spending some leisure time. All the wrong conditions for humping heavy weights around the country all day.

We shouldered our packs once more and had a hasty look around to see if anything was left. Then the patrol pushed ahead. As we went striding along we could easily see the leading scout – a novelty in these parts.

High overhead, in the crown of the towering trees, we heard the flapping of wings as a huge bird was disturbed from its hunting of the monkeys. They leapt from branch to branch in an effort to escape the talons of the bird. There was one high shriek and one less monkey before everything settled down once more. Then the only sound were our footsteps as we went along in our hypnotic state.

Way out in front Luang had melted away as the undergrowth thickened. A signal to fan out sideways was given. Waving his arms to move up level we sprinted forward. The jungle was now denser. Pushing ahead and bending low we crept forward. Not a word was spoken as we pushed through the vines and creepers entangling our packs and making it difficult to bring our rifles down on any target.

Dropping our packs for better manoeuvrability we crawled the last few yards on hands and knees. We stopped when we came to the edge of the jungle and saw a large cultivated area stretching out before us. There were men and women there. Unaware they were being overlooked, they tended to their crops of corn and various vegetables laughing, talking and feeling perfectly safe beneath their Chinese coolie hats in the hot sun.

We kept quiet and still, gazing as their life went on. To the right of the platoon, beneath the tree-lined edge of the jungle, was a line a shacks. And to the side of these were pigpens. The animals squealed as they rummaged around the earth and roots. Chickens strutted around continually pecking as they followed the pigs around. A mongrel dog bounded out of one of the shacks and scattered the chickens, sending their feathers flying in the dust as they raced squawking for safety.

We turned back to the workers and looked on as they laughed and talked. There was no doubt they were Commies, knowing danger was so close at hand. We lay there waiting for the order to open fire. Our hearts were pounding. It was the calm before the storm as like thieves in the night we waited.

The dog suddenly stopped chasing the animals and looked in our direction. Growling, the dog bounded forward towards the concealed platoon. Then he started barking and snapping which brought the other dogs out of the shacks. The workers stopped what they were doing and looked up, staring at the dogs. A tall Chinese was quick to grasp the situation and came towards us firing his automatic. The dogs had unknowingly made up our minds for us.

We heard the sound of the Lieutenant's carbine first as it returned fire. Then all hell broke loose. Within moments there was pandemonium among the field workers as they ran to escape the hail of death. They ran from the shacks, firing in panic. Their bullets raked the trees and tore the soil in a line of spurts like fountains of water spewing upwards. But the burst was hastily aimed and did little damage if any at all.

The people in the field had to be stopped. I screwed the cup onto the EY rifle and undid my pouch. From inside I quickly withdrew three grenades, which I placed in front of me. In the cup went the first grenade and with the rifle butt well dug into the soft soil I withdrew the pin. With a quick aim I pulled the trigger. Like a mortar the grenade left the cup and exploded above the heads of the Commies. I took another grenade and fired again.

This time a running figure faltered and fell. The explosion echoed around the clearing. Screaming workers fled into the jungle. They didn't have any food or weapons with them and they faced an uncertain end, unless of course they could reach another camp.

Several bodies could be seen in crumpled heaps. The returning fire was growing weaker by the minute as the platoon Bren gunners systematically went from shack to shack. The exploding grenades caused fires to break out amongst the dry wood and thatch and sparks spiralled upwards helping to cover the retreating enemy.

The shooting was now almost over. There was only the 'wuff wuff' as ammunition and fuel exploded sending showers of debris and soot way up into the air and destroying the shacks. We could feel the intense heat from where we lay.

On a given command the platoon advanced, firing a shot here and there at the slightest movement or sound. We kept clear of the searing flames and moved into the jungle on the far side foraging for the enemy. The search ended though without finding a single wounded man. Somehow they had managed to carry them away.

We returned and joined the others searching the gardens, prodding with sticks and turning over burnt wood and charred building materials. Now and then someone found something interesting. 'Over here, Sarge!' as the caller would unearth a document or weapon. There were other finds too such as photos that could be used to identify those lying dead in the fields. This method of identification was far better than carrying their heads back in a waterproof bag.

Three bodies were found in and around the crops. Apart from a few problems we buried the dead with the shovels they had been using only moments earlier. That seemed ironic to me. We covered their graves without chant or verse, just a quick north, south, east and west across our chests. Perhaps those beneath the sod deserved little else. Our next job was to destroy the crops. The dog that barked and started the commotion, along with some pigs, had also been killed.

The Lieutenant went over to Drak. The talk ended with Drak rigging up the aerial, then putting on the earphones Drak turned the wavelength knob, trying to find the strongest signal this far out. We were under the cover of the trees, which made it hard for the battery operated set. Drak however gave a thumbs up to the Lieutenant indicating he had made contact.

The officer gave the call sign Sunray and the conversation went back and forth. The Lieutenant turned to the Sergeant from time to time, who nodded in agreement with the Lieutenant's proposals. We were feeling high from the adrenaline, brought about by the skirmish, as we waited for an answer which came between the crackles and whistles of interference.

A bomber would be sent and we should move to a safe distance several hundred yards away. The map reference was given to the operator and a possible sighting five miles north of the river. The transmission ended with, 'This is Sunray saying out.'

While the platoon waited we cooked a meal and in a buoyant mood we sat and talked while eating the jungle stew. Sometime later the drone of a heavily laden bomber could be heard approaching from the south. It grew louder as we ate the last of the stew.

Drak immediately leaned towards the set and switched it on. Static echoed from the set as he searched for the bomber's wavelength. Through the screeching and crackling we heard the voice of the bomber's operator. He spoke as if through a pinched nose, 'Dog Company. Calling Dog Company, answer me. This is Charlie Fox. This is Charlie Fox. Over.'

On hearing this Drak put down his mess tin and answered, 'This is Dog Company. This is Dog Company. Receiving you loud and clear. Over.'

'This is Charlie Fox. This is Charlie Fox. We shall be over the target area in approximately five minutes. So keep this channel open and keep clear of the bombing area.'

The engines could be clearly heard over the radio as the operator asked for confirmation of the map reference. Laid out in front of him the Lieutenant reeled off the map co-ordinates. Speaking for the first time with the bomber operator, the pilot asked for a red flare to pinpoint our position. The order was confirmed and the wireless left open during the operation so we could all hear.

The bomber, a Shackleton, could be seen sweeping through

the trees. A four-engine heavy bomber, the Shackleton was capable of carrying a twenty thousand pound bomb load. The officer raised his hand and fired the Very pistol and the red trail streaked through the treetops. The bomber now came in on a low run. The scene was almost reminiscent of the war pictures seen down at the local cinema. I never imagined that one day I would see it for real. The bomb aimer lay below the pilot with eyes fixed on the target. The bomb bay doors were already open revealing the bomb racks.

'Steady. Steady there. They're gone!'

The bomb aimer pressed the release button and a stick of bombs fell to earth. They were oil bombs, which caused a devastating fire.

The Shackleton swung round in a wide circle before straightening up and coming in for a second run. The pilot's voice could be heard again, 'Steady. Steady.' Then suddenly, 'Bombs gone skipper.'

The target burst into flames as the black objects fell to earth before being lost from view among the trees. From the direction of the gardens a huge fireball was seen to erupt and spew out across the centre of the area. Black smoke billowed as further explosions shook the ground beneath our feet. All around the smell of burning oil made us cough and splutter, and our eyes smart. The bodies we'd buried earlier were now either burnt to a crisp or blown into tiny pieces.

As the Shackleton made its last run the men vomited from the smell. As the bay doors closed the last words came from the operator, 'They won't be growing anything there for several months. Out.'

Twenty minutes was all it took. It would have taken the platoon hours or even days to destroy the camp. Not only had the crops been destroyed but the ground had been rendered useless as well being contaminated with oil. No one could imagine the terror and panic of those lying beneath such an attack. With the exploding running oil, even foxholes proved useless. The blazing liquid flew everywhere. Those that had escaped death would have been badly scarred for life and possibly sent crazy.

Particles of oil drifting on the breeze left our faces looking and feeling greasy. Without a nearby stream we wiped our faces with anything we had. Some used toilet paper while others used sleeves or whatever. Our luck had held once again as we had come through another skirmish without a single casualty.

Leaving the once blooming gardens in a barren blackened wilderness the patrol went further and deeper into the interior as our packs still contained enough rations for six days.

While on a rest stop Drak reported our position and received orders which altered the platoon's plans. The Lieutenant listened to the new directives as the rest of us waited wondering.

'Your old orders have been cancelled. Your new orders are to move northwards and meet up with a Ghurka patrol. For some unknown reason it has ground to a halt. It is now up to you to meet up with them. Your map references are…'

The voice proceeded to give the new co-ordinates and the rest of the message. With the transmission over the officer called for an NCO briefing.

Since we had left the camp at Labis the patrol had moved in a wide circle, tramping mile after mile, forward and back. Twice we had doubled back with the wounded.

The new orders were given to each section by the section Corporal. The new route took us to Gemas, a town on the main highway. The officer then gave Luang his new orders. Holding the compass and pointing northwards he directed him with an outstretched hand.

We then started to make our way over unbroken ground stopping every few minutes to confer with the compass as we headed northwards. We lost old tracks and picked up new ones. Some belonged to animals while others belonged to those living a Stone Age existence. We came to fallen trees too big to traverse. Trees worn smooth by heavy bodies, such as elephants as they dragged their huge bulk over the trunks. These were the times for helping each other. With the trees larger than normal and the unbearable heat we pushed and pulled and often lifted each other.

The further the patrol penetrated the bigger the trees became, rising like giants with their bases shaped like V rocket fins. The roots steadied these giants throughout the monsoon season while their crowns forever reached for the sun. From their lower branches hung vast water vines. These were in fact aerial roots taking water from below ground and feeding the huge amount of foliage the trees grew. The vines provided us with water by cutting a length away and holding the vine above the head. The water trickled into the mouth and was just enough to keep the body and soul together. There was no undergrowth here, only fallen trees.

It was home to millions of termites. Their internal organs could be seen working as hearts and digestive systems clearly showed through a transparent body. Over the years their skin had lost its pigmentation through lack of sunlight.

As we trudged along the surroundings gradually changed from huge trees to long flowing moss. Replacing leaves the moss flowed like old men's beards hanging from the branches. Underfoot the ground grew softer. A faint gassy smell clung to the nostrils and the jungle became strangely silent.

Cigarettes had run out several days earlier. The rations were getting lower too and there was still no sign of those Ghurkas. As we walked on through the spongy green mud, with the smell becoming ever more pungent, we wondered what lay ahead.

Before long we were wading through knee-deep water. The trees were raised above the water by their roots. Thick green algae covered the surface of the cesspool and the smell became far worse as the surface was disturbed. Was this one of those mangrove swamps that we had read about in school. *Escape from Devil's Island* was the book that came to mind. It was a classic tale of wrongful imprisonment and injustices. If it was, then this wasn't a place for humans or beasts alike.

We jumped from root to root. Our shins became sore and skinned as we missed our footing and slipped and it was a miracle no one broke their ankle or leg.

Rest periods were now more frequent as we waited for those who fell behind exhausted. Morale was now slowly sinking. The blame was put on the officer although the map showed no sign of a swamp. The compass said the nearest route to the road was west. However, this was not necessarily the quickest as we were to find out.

On one particular rest period I sat astride the thick roots of a tree, when some small fish darted below me. The gases of the water were making me feel nauseous so I decided to have a biscuit to help settle my stomach. The biscuit crumbled on each bite and the fish darted for every morsel. Time to move on so I dropped the remainder of the biscuit into the water. The fish would probably enjoy it more than I did.

My pack was now almost empty and the stewpot banged against it as I jumped and scrambled over the roots. The Sergeant had long since given up telling me to keep it quiet. I kept a watchful eye on the water below for anything resembling a snake. I was then reminded of a previous encounter which had happened as I watched a communist prisoner being beaten by the police.

We had sat in a Malayan police compound below some date palms. I didn't know at the time but somewhere close lay a cobra. A king of snakes, it was known to have killed more people than any other. I got to my feet and wandered over to where two policemen were beating a screaming prisoner. For his crime he had promised to lead us to the Communist's regiment, known as the Flying Dutchman's Gang. A prize like this couldn't be missed though he led us a merry dance all day.

From where I had just been sitting came a commotion and I turned to look. Standing with his machete in his hand was Heapy. He was prodding something on the ground. I crossed over to where he stood. There, staring up at me from the grass, was this six-foot long cobra. Its head had been severed from its body. I shuddered. I have a fear of snakes.

The screaming Commie seemed less important to me now. He was dragged back to his cell blooded, half-conscious and minus a few teeth. Within a few days of the beating the man was found dead from a broken neck. He'd fallen out of bed, and the beds were only six inches off the floor.

A lizard, darting about in the cloudy water, brought me back to reality and we leap-frogged our way forwards. Our boots were torn and feet wet and sore. Hours later a few muddy banks broke the surface and the water level began to drop. Mudskippers (similar to catfish) scrambled over the mud flats on flippers that had developed from fins, as they searched for flies and bugs that crawled and scuttled back and forth among the silt. Beneath our feet the ground began to firm up as we left the flowing moss and its eerie feeling.

We emerged from the swamp on the edge of a clearing and saw valuable wood, which had been cut. The workers would have left for the mills carrying a load. A few fires still smouldered as we could see their embers glowing in the dusk.

A road had been made from cut logs. Placed side by side it was designed to take heavy trucks carrying the logs out of the clearing. We kept to the track and made steady progress as the night crept in. Then the smell of cooked chicken and curry began to fill our nostrils. It had been twenty-two days or thereabouts since we had had anything of that nature, having eaten so much stew and other concoctions.

The delicious smells came wafting from a village which lay ahead. The lights from the village oil lamps guided the platoon like ships in the night. As we clumped along the wooden road the sound of twenty or so men brought the scared, inquisitive villagers peering round their slatted doors or lifting one piece curtains. Dogs barked with their hackles high while other more adventurous ones ventured towards us making tentative moves to snap and then pulling back as the tired soldier kicked out uttering threats as to where they would be kicked if they came too close. From somewhere we heard a scuffle and a squawk. Probably a chicken disturbed as it roosted.

The Sergeant went off in search of the village elder to gain permission to stay at the village school overnight. Permission was granted and we trooped into the building. The first man struck a match and found a paraffin lamp hanging from the school wall. He lifted the glass globe and lit the wick. Soon flickering shadows began to form on the walls as the men settled around the school walls amongst their packs.

We made ourselves as comfortable as we could and the floor was hard but at least it was dry. It was then that Heapy produced the dead chicken. The squawk we heard earlier was when he pulled the bloody thing's neck.

'You crafty bastard you. It was you I heard pulling that bloody bird's neck,' I said keeping my voice low so as not to cause any suspicion.

'It's chuck chuck tonight, Ebee. Get the mess tins out while I gut and feather it.'

The smell of the cooking chicken, as we entered the village, had whetted my appetite and although it was a small woeful looking bird, Heapy busied himself pulling out the feathers and cleaning it out before cutting it into small pieces along with the bones. Still having a tin or two left we sorted out some beans to go with the chicken. One mess tin with beans and the other with chicken were topped with water and placed on two Tommy cooker frets.

I looked around the room as Heapy stuffed the feathers and remains into the empty bean tin. We had more paraffin lamps now and could see the school had neat rows of desks, and a blackboard at the front. On the blackboard was written the day's work of some simple equations. A few posters adorned the lalang woven walls. Behind the teacher's desk hung a coloured print of the present King George in his naval uniform and to the side of this was a map of the world. There was the occasional rustle overhead in the roof rafters. Probably from a bat or some other rodent which was nesting there. Little bits of straw and dust floated down in the half-light as they ran across the roof though it created little interest amongst us. The only thing that interested us at that moment was cooking and brewing tea.

Tonight Heapy was our head chef. The chicken bubbled as he stirred in a pinch of salt with the steam rising from the mess tins. He was really enjoying himself and sat there smiling. As soon as it was cooked and ready, those around us were each given a small piece. They may have been small pieces but to a hungry man it was a meal fit for a king. So I raised my bit of chicken towards the King's portrait. All this time a guard stood outside in the shadows constantly probing the darkness.

I picked my teeth with a matchstick and looked down at the bones in the mess tin. My stomach rumbled. Oliver Twist was asking for more. Moths and mosquitoes buzzed around the lit lamps. Occasionally one got a little too near and singed its wings before falling to the ground, where it wriggled and died.

For the first time in days I felt at ease with myself. We had all been through harrowing times these last few weeks and it had taken a simple schoolhouse and the taste of chicken, plus your own free will to do whatever you wanted, to bring this about. This is what we fought, and in some cases died for.

Corporal Gwilt, known as Nodder because of his habit of rolling his head, came round and picked out those who were to go on guard. He pointed to me.

'Two till three then Gowey follows you.'

With a nod from me he stepped over the outstretched legs and picked out two more. This completed the guard until morning. The lamps were turned out soon afterwards and the school was filled with paraffin fumes. We settled down on the hard floor which to us was like a feather bed.

It felt as though only a moment had gone by when I found myself outside the schoolhouse door, leaning against the wooden structure. From inside came a cough that brought a low growl from a dog. The night was cool as the sky twinkled with stars. It was the simple things in life that you missed though you never realised it at the time.

Time dragged on. Only the hum and bite of a mosquito, followed by a slap as it met an abrupt end, kept me from dropping to sleep. I looked at the luminous dial of the watch but in my tired state the fingers and numbers merged into one. I slowly closed my eyes and opened them again. The figures had now steadied and the time was just a little after three. Quietly I went inside and found Gowey. I shook him and gave him the watch. On his way outside he tripped over someone's legs, which brought out a nasty remark, 'You clumsy big oaf.'

There were only a few hours till daylight and I tried to make the most of what was left of the night.

A crowing cock awoke us. Well, some of us anyway. Heapy was still asleep. Was there anything that would wake him? It would be just like him to fall asleep on his wedding night. A dig in the ribs from my elbow finally brought him around.

'What's up Ebee? Made the tea yet?'

This I couldn't believe and I answered, 'God help the poor cow you marry, Heapy.'

Heapy stretched and yawned, like some old shaggy dog. I half-expected him to roll over for me to tickle his stomach.

Picking up the unwashed tins from last night's meal I made for the door. In the daylight the village looked different. Women were gathered around a well washing and pulling up buckets of water. Some filled white chipped enamel jugs, while others poured water over their heads, threw their hair back and wiped the water from their eyes. We waited for them to finish before going over and we didn't have long to wait. Carrying their buckets and jugs on their heads they hurried back to their primitive living conditions. Their homes held precious little in the way of value. With just enough food to carry them from day to day, their needs were much simpler than our own. The men were working as wood cutters and clearing the jungle during the day and their world was lit by a paraffin lamp at night.

The well was now deserted and the platoon was able to wash for the first time in days. Even a pig would hold its nose if one of us came too close. We pulled the bucket up from the well and filled old used buckets on the well head. Bending over one such bucket I cupped my hands. The water felt good as I bathed my face and let the water trickle down through my beard and onto my chest.

After washing both mess tins and filling the empty water bottle I stood gazing. The village had sprung to life. From where I stood I noticed that the village boasted one shop. Like so many shops in Malaya it was owned by a Chinese, the shopkeepers of the east.

I went through my pockets and found a red five dollar note. Enough for what I wanted. The note, having crossed rivers and swampland, was grubby and wrinkled but it was still a coin of the realm and spendable. I straightened out the corners and walked over to the shop.

The elderly gentleman greeted me with one of those oriental smiles. Like the spider saying to the fly, 'Come into my parlour.'

I glanced around the well stocked shelves of canned goods before finding what I was looking for. On the dark shelf behind the shopkeeper, neatly placed in rows, were the cigarettes. The brands were all Chinese. There were no English. Anyway one cigarette looked much like any other and one brand in particular looked familiar. It was a packet with the motif of a motorbike on the front. I pointed to the shelf and Chinaman turned and moved his hand over the cigarettes until I said, '*Brinti*', one of the few words I knew in Malay, meaning stop.

He handed me the packet of twenty and I gave him the five dollar dog-eared note. He changed it under the counter. 'Okay Johnny, okay.'

His wrinkled face broke into a grin as he spoke the only English he probably knew.

Feeling pleased with myself I left the shop and hurried back to the schoolhouse. The smokers gathered round as I handed out the cigarettes over a cup of tea which was the only rations we had left. We lit the cigarettes after a smell and look at the tobacco leaf. They were maybe a little greener than we were used to but a fag was a fag. Soon though we began to cough and splutter. They tasted and smelt like a compost heap and everybody shouted at once, 'Ebee, what are you trying to do? Kill us all with these bloody things!'

We all threw them on the floor. Well, I did try. Later as we passed through the village I gave those that were left to a Chinaman. I began wondering if this was the reason that the Chinese had yellow skin.

With the village behind us we clumped our way down the wooden road passing some of the villagers on their way to market. They carried poles on which were balanced baskets of fruit and vegetables. Some balanced stalks of bananas on their turbaned heads as they walked at an easy gait. Some were without shoes and others were wearing a kind of flip-flop shoe.

The early start soon brought the platoon to the main road. Here we scattered and lay down to wait. Cyclists and bus passengers stared at the poor condition we presented. Ripped uniforms, unkempt hair and beards. We were a sorry hollow-eyed bunch. Did they realise it was all for them? Did they care one way or the other?

Further down the road, trucks were spotted approaching fast. We got to our feet, gathered our gear and awaited their arrival. Reversing up the track they turned around. They stopped just long enough for us to throw the gear onboard and climb aboard ourselves. The last one on closed the tailboard then the cab was given a thump to let the driver know we were all aboard.

The road back to Niyor lay some way to the south. A road sign said 'Kluang 96 miles', while the one pointing north read 'Gemas 7 miles.' The platoon had travelled over a hundred miles north. Just how far we had penetrated we couldn't hazard a guess.

We were now facing a journey of over two hours and tried to take advantage of the rest. Dozing between bumps and jerks, we sprawled out half-lying across someone's legs.

The sound of a klaxon horn brought the small convoy, a Dingo and two trucks, to a crawl. The horns continued to blow as the heavy logging lorries passed by. The dilapidated vehicles had long seen better days. The cabs didn't have any doors and the huge tyres showed bare canvas treads ready to blow at any time as they carried overweight loads of timber. The Indian driver could be seen in bare feet.

The giants passed and as we looked on in the dust cloud we could make out a man sitting high up on the rear of the logs.

May 1951 – On Leave in Singapore

The convoy bustled through towns and small villages alike. On one occasion we slowed for a flock of geese crossing the road in single file. A bus chugged up a hill in front of us. Its roof was laden with crates of chickens and a goat lay on its side, barely able to move. Passengers waved as the bus stopped with steam hissing from its overheated engine. Gowey sat opposite me with legs crossed in front of him. He was dreaming aloud.

'Right this very minute I could just down a pint. And a smoke would do nicely.'

Each and every one of us felt his sentiments at that moment. Then someone shouted, 'Shut up Gowey, you're making me ill just thinking about it.'

Then an empty pack was thrown. Gowey caught it, preventing it from going over the side.

We passed a road sign that read 'Segamat 3 miles', and 'Kluang 10'. The men were stiff. Their backsides hot and sore. Midday was upon us and we reckoned we had close on another hour before we reached Niyor camp. We soon passed over the wooden river bridge at Segamat, towards Labis the home of 'C' Company – the place where this epic story began.

As we approached the village we could see a vehicle on fire and smoke billowing across the road. The convoy slowed again and we could see the vehicle was a bus. On the driver's side was a covered body, that had been dragged from the burning shell. Shot no doubt for his defiance by some irritated Communist thug. The platoon had gone in search of these butchers and marched hundreds of miles to find them so near. A voice in my head said, 'Why don't they come straight out and fight? Let's get it over with once and for all.'

Passengers waved their arms in protest as their crates of live-stock crackled and burned. A red flag hung limply from a nearby tree. One bare-footed man stepped from the crowd and ripped the flag from the tree, before hurling it onto the burning skeleton of the bus. We left. There wasn't anything we could do.

We reached the base at Niyor sometime in the afternoon. The platoon handed in what was left of the ammunition including the grenades. Weary and feeling filthy we then made our way to the line of tents, where cigarettes and a clean bed lay. The first cigarette tasted sweet. A wash and a shave came next though there was no rush to be first. Sharing mirrors and razors we eventually shaved away the three weeks' growth instantly looking ten years younger. Under the showers we soaked our sore and bruised flesh. The red scratches and leech marks felt sore as the water opened the festering sores. Our ribs were almost bursting through our ribcage from the loss of weight. Our poor feet were white and wrinkled. Some had the beginnings of foot rot and some of the men left the shower block limping.

In freshly laundered and starched clothes we looked and felt clean and more human. The clang of steel upon iron signalled us to our meal. I hoped they had cooked some horses since I could have eaten one right then. I hardly cared what the food tasted like as long as it filled the hole in my stomach.

Around the table I couldn't help but notice a paper being passed around. It was *The Daily Singapore Times*. The daily out here meant three weeks. This one was near that age as it reached Heapy. He read the front page and immediately pointed to one headline beneath which were the smiling faces of the helicopter pilots who had lifted out our wounded. The headline read 'A Gallant Air Rescue'. The story went on to describe the event of snatching the wounded from the jaws of death in a jungle skirmish. This was the story of what *we* had done. It was us who had struggled carrying out the wounded to that river clearing yet nothing had been said of this. Nothing at all.

We felt as though we had been screwed for a fifty cent packet of cigarettes given to us by one of the pilots. And we all vowed not to buy this rag of a newspaper again, which was then screwed up and tossed in the bin.

Eating with us were the victims of the hornet encounter. They were now looking more like themselves, laughing and joking. Those wounded on the patrol later were still in hospital. Only one of these had ended up serious. His leg had turned gangrenous and had lost a lot of sinew and muscle. He would be a cripple for life.

Before going out on the last patrol I, along with another member of the platoon, had put my name forward requesting a week's leave. The request was granted and I had two hundred dollars back pay from money which had built up over the months due to us on patrol and therefore we could not withdraw. This was to be our spending money while on leave.

Pouney, who was the other member of the platoon going on leave with me, carried the suitcases that he had borrowed. We waved to the men who had come down to see us both go, from aboard the ration trucks. We were bound for Kluang where a train would take us on down to Singapore. Wishing the men were joining us, we moved off in a cloud of red dust.

Carrying our cases we presented the big Sikh ticket collector with our documents. With a grunt he rubber-stamped the commencement date and return date on the travel warrant. We moved onto the platform where hawkers pestered us as they sold drinks from metal containers carried on their backs. Some were filled with sweet tea and others had soft drinks. We had been warned beforehand not to buy loose drinks made from unknown sources of water as they could cause all sorts of problems, which we didn't need right now.

The hawkers moved and shoved through the waiting crowd of passengers filling glasses of tea from the canteens for a few cents at a time. In the distance, through the heat haze, which made the rails dance, a loud whistle blew, signalling the approaching train. On seeing this, the crowd began to jostle to be first on. The ones on first got a seat while the rest had to make do with whatever room there was.

The passenger train was proceeded by an armoured car on a flat wagon, coupled to an engine, some forty yards ahead. This stopped some way up the track beyond the platform. The passenger train then slowed to a halt alongside the platform. The pushing and shoving then started in earnest. With suitcases above our heads we managed to get aboard. Once on we managed to find a window seat.

As we waited an Indian ticket collector asked for our travel warrants. He was searching for non-paying customers. The train shuddered trying to gain traction as it began to move. The steam hissed as the pressure was released. Two blows on the whistle signalled the train ahead that we were ready to leave. We placed our suitcases between our legs for safekeeping as the train gathered speed.

Through the glassless window we could see those in the fields working looking up from their labours as we thundered passed. The old carriages still showed unplugged bullet holes in the walls and roof from previous journeys. They were also badly in need of a coat of paint. The carriages were like ovens inside. We bought bottles of luke warm beer from the various stations we stopped at which was warm and tasteless and hardly quenched our thirst at all, but made us sweat even more.

We ate the sandwiches the cook had made us for our journey and this turned out to be a good thing. The hawkers and vendors had sold food and fancy cakes from trays hung by a strap around their necks. But they were covered in flies and wasps which was both unhygienic and criminal. Other vendors sold fruit from baskets – dates, bananas, oranges and pineapples – shouting, 'Ten cents. Twenty cents.'

The smell from the station toilets was overpowering as passengers hurried back to the train, the hissing steam warning them we were leaving. Onlookers scattered on the platform lest they were scalded by the rising steam.

Johore Baru, the capital of the state and the gateway to Singapore, was the last of the mainland towns. The crossing from here was by the Causeway Bridge. The clatter of the train's wheels echoed on the steel and concrete structure spanning the two miles of waterway that separated the mainland from Singapore Island. The breeze from the sea blew through the carriages. Those clinging precariously to the roof on the outside held on tighter. Armed with goods and crates to sell on the open market for a handsome profit, they dared the perils of falling from this weekly journey.

Running parallel with the railway was a road with rickety trucks overloaded with fruit and vegetables which were also on their way to the island.

Once over the bridge we could see, near the railway embankment, kampongs built on wooden stilts amongst the coconut and fig palms. Their curved roofs blended with the background. We were now near the equator.

The scenery then changed. The kampongs gave way to rigid looking concrete structures. Their whitewashed colour dazzled the eyes as the sunlight reflected off them. The buildings became higher as we neared the centre of Singapore and the end of the line.

Everyone was hanging from the windows as we entered the station. The train slowed and then stopped. People pushed onto the platform, eager to join the crowds. The pair of us collected our meagre luggage and stepped off the train before joining the crowd heading for the entrance. We gave another ticket collector our travel pass. He glanced at it for a second then waved us through.

Once outside the station I felt as though our holiday had truly begun. Around the taxi ranks the usual pimps and hawkers asked, 'You want girl, Johnny? You want clean girl. For jigger-jig, Johnny. Only ten dollar, Johnny.'

They kept asking and asking until I turned round and gave them my answer, 'Piss off will you!'

We made our way to the three-wheeled trike taxi rank. The Chinese cyclist was told the address we wanted taking to. The Saunders Home Hotel was one of only two hotels which was allocated and catered for British troops while on leave. We sat in front of the cyclist, our suitcases under our seat. The Chinese, in his pith helmet, confidently pedalled in and out of the traffic.

Blaring horns and gesticulating drivers vented their anger on the unperturbed cyclist. We zigzagged our way along, passing Chinese coolies pulling heavily loaded carts, from the docks to the local shops and warehouses. Their labour was cheaper than motor transport. They were the oxen being used as the beast of burden.

We finally reached the hotel and the cyclist pulled in front of the foyer. We paid the taxi fare and climbed the white scrubbed steps. Inside we took in the tasteful décor before giving the young Malayan receptionist our booking forms. 'D' Company's pay clerk had made a reservation for a double room with single beds earlier.

We followed the porter who carried our light cases past the outdoor swimming pool. The cool water looked very inviting. The porter stopped beside a door and, producing a bunch of keys, he unlocked the door and opened it. He led us into a twin bedded room with en suite facilities. He handed me the keys and left after I handed him a tip.

We threw the cases on the bed and inspected the bathroom, which had a shower. Then we opened the French windows to allow a breath of fresh air into the stuffy room. The French doors opened onto a balcony. With a room like this for a week and money in our pockets to burn, we had everything we wanted.

That evening in the dining room we ordered steak and chips. Then fruit and real ice cream for afters. Smoking and drinking coffee for the first time in months was a real treat for us.

Earlier we had made plans for the night, starting with a walk. The night glittered with lights as we window-shopped. One place we wanted to find was a clothes shop. We didn't have any civvies, only our army uniforms, and in these we looked a bit conspicuous. It wasn't long before we found one to our liking.

The tailors here boasted they could measure you up one day and have the suit ready to wear the next. But tonight all we required were some shirts and slacks, made from a material we had only heard about – sharkskin. We came out of the shop with the trousers and shirts costing us eight dollars each, the equivalent of around seventeen shillings each back home.

With parcels under our arms we turned our attentions to the jewellers and inspected watches of all shapes and sizes. We were especially interested in the ones with luminous dials. We eventually came to a price, after much haggling with the shopkeeper.

Tired from the journey we returned to the hotel for a last minute drink. Later, whilst lying in bed, I had a feeling there was something missing. Then I had it. There weren't any biting mosquitoes, only the wall lizards which darted for the flies.

Next morning a knocking on the door awakened us. We groaned at the early caller. 'Who is it? Come on in. The door's not locked.'

The door catch turned and in walked one of the dining room waiters carrying a tray. He placed it on the bedside table between the beds. He then left without saying a single word. On the tray was a pot of tea, two cups, milk and sugar on a side plate along with a few assorted biscuits. It was nice to lie there with a lighted cigarette, without the fear of the Sergeant shouting in my ears, 'Wakey wakey, let's be having you.' Even here his haunting voice could reach me.

We stood under the canopy of the hotel in our new civvies and hailed a tri-taxi. Within minutes one stopped right beside us. Pouney asked, 'Where to Ebee? The town centre or the bar?'

'No, to the nearest church you dope. Of course to the town centre, then the bar. Let's get our priorities right,' I said sitting on the tricycle's bench seat with a wave and a word to the cyclist, 'Take us to the town centre.'

By now the barefooted cyclist was standing up on the pedals to start us moving forward. His bare feet and legs pumped up and down. Horns honked and we gave the motorists some suggestions on what they could do.

Reaching the busy centre we paid the fare and began browsing round the shops. One shop in particular created more interest than the others. It was an apothecary and herbalist where several preserved poisonous snakes and jars of reptiles were on view. Powdered rhino horns and tiger bones and other forms of aphrodisiacs used for love potions. Some were sold to the public for relief and some for added pleasure.

All the shops were open from the streets and there were no glass-fronted ones. The only shops like this back home were the fishmongers and the greengrocers but here only the jewellers used glass display counters. The milliners and the food stores were all open shops.

Every other shop was either a dentist or barber's and one of the Chinese barbers beckoned us in. While Pouney sat reading the funny pages, the barber gave me the full treatment including a neck massage. Through the mirror I peered and wiped the loose hair from my face. I could see he had given me a crew cut. With both of us sporting new hairstyles we paid up and stepped out into the bright sunlight.

We passed bars where the Malayan and Chinese, having nothing better to do, played their game of mah-jong and sipped tea from glasses. They would get excited whenever they held the winning piece and bang the table with it. We stopped outside one bar and sat in the open beside the pavement. The barman quickly came over to take our order which was two bottles of Tiger beer and a cigar.

'Make sure the beer's ice cold, and bring some salted nuts.'

The barman soon returned with the beer. Condensation ran down the outside of the glass. He had also left the salted nuts, which I was partial to.

Idling the time away we watched the passing traffic. We were fascinated with the way of life of the expressionless porters pulling their carts with eyes that seemed transfixed on the roads as they leaned forward for more pushing power. They were oblivious to the surrounding traffic, labouring like animals for a poor pittance of a few cents an hour. The world of Malayan, Chinese and Indians was rushing to nowhere in the blistering heat of the day.

Under their parasols the young ladies paraded past, some in cotton slacks and others in decorative frocks. We chewed the peanuts as we drank. The tensions of the last few months began to feel like a bad dream.

Just before twelve we drank up and hailed a tri-taxi to take us back to the hotel for lunch. After a wash and brush up we made our way to the dining room. The cool breeze from the overhead fan felt quite pleasant. There were white table napkins beside the place settings and fresh iced water in glass jug tumblers lay on each table. A menu lay half-open in the centre.

Reading the menu it showed a good selection of cooked meals and cold salads. Choosing roast chicken and sauté potatoes with green beans we tucked in. We were making the most of everything before going back.

Going to Singapore without visiting the world famous Raffles Club was like going to Paris and leaving before having the pleasure of seeing the Folies-Bergère. Paying the taxi we gazed at the rather unimpressive building. So this was the place where the famous gin-sling was supposedly to have originated. The Raffles Club. A place of high society. Let's give it a go.

No one gave us a second glance as we went through the main foyer. The arrow on the wall pointed towards a smoked-filled bar and who should be in there but two from 'B' Company. One was a right tearaway named Palin. A troublemaker and right now the worse for drink, in the company of some American rubber planters down for the weekend for a quiet break.

One woman with a rather strong American accent was also the worse for drink. She wanted to get to the bar right where the rowdy Palin stood. Shoving past him she snapped saying, 'Out the way you cock sucker. Let a lady through.'

'What did you call me?' he asked, wanting to know what she said.

'Out the way. You're only fit to be shot at,' she retorted.

'Why you...' Palin started to say something then raised his glass. The woman paled. She realised she had spoken to the wrong type of guy.

'I could do that to you.' As he spoke he squeezed the whisky glass only inches from her face. The glass broke into pieces between his fingers and the blood slowly trickled down his hand.

She screamed as if the glass had caught her. The whole bar was now in uproar. It was only a few weeks ago, when I was on the police, that Palin had been released. He'd done six months for breaking up a bar in Segamat causing several thousand dollars worth of damage. Quickly some waiters closed in and descended on the two and escorted them into the car park.

Keeping to ourselves Pouney and I drank up and left. We never did taste the gin-sling. Outside the swearing Palin was shouting from the car park. We left him to it and hurried away to find another quiet bar.

Later that night we were lounging on the poolside chairs, swimming and generally mucking about. The time was somewhere around midnight. The moon provided the light as we dived off the springboards and raced against each other. We did this well into the early hours before calling it a day and going to bed.

Over breakfast we read the morning papers which were provided free. With the paper opened on the advertisement page I read aloud the amusement column for that night. I also read out the films. Some of which were the very latest on release.

'There's a cinema here showing an Esther Williams film. It's her latest, called *One-piece Bathing Suit*. How about that one for this evening?'

'Sounds interesting. What time does it start?' he asked as he pushed his breakfast to the side.

'Err,' I said trying to find the time, 'Nine o'clock the last showing. Just time for a drink before we go in,' I said scanning the section once more. That night just before nine both of us stood looking up at the figure of Esther Williams in a diving pose, above the entrance to the foyer, outside the reputed world's largest theatre, The Cathay Cinema. Under one roof you had two 1000-plus seat cinemas, a hotel with swimming pool, a restaurant, a bar and a shopping arcade thrown in. Tonight was the first showing of the film we had come to see.

Inside the theatre was air-conditioned as we watched the coloured musical from the balcony. The show was so-so. Not too good and not too bad. After the show we joined the crowds trickling out of the cinema, took a stroll around the arcade shops then went out on the street. Across from the theatre was the notorious Lavender Street. We had come to see the sights so down we strode being accosted by the street girls every few yards. 'You look lonely, Johnny. You like pretty girl? You buy me drink, I make you feel better.'

Their painted faces hid their ages. Some were as young as twelve and worn out before their teens. We turned away saying, 'Not tonight, love. Go home to your mother.'

Seeing we had no intention of taking up their offers they turned their attentions and charms on the next potential customer following on behind us. In shop doorways they stood. Some were showing their naked breasts, flirting and giving us the come on. It was a sight to be seen as they shouted, 'Over here, Johnny. Only seven dollars. Twenty dollars all night.'

Coming to the end of the street the lighting got better. Taking advantage of the short leave we stayed up late and walked freely around listening to the eastern music coming from the open shops. Walking from one shop to the next we browsed and on occasions bartered for a lower price on articles we didn't want. Doing it just for the kick and laughing and arguing with the seller, saying, 'Too much, Johnny, too much.'

If no agreement was reached on a price we would walk away

pausing and hesitant. More often than not the proprietor would call us back with the words, 'Okay, Johnny. You have. You have at that price.'

Around the town the lights began to go out so we hailed a tri-taxi. They were always on call. With the cycle lamp barely shining he pedalled us to the hotel and left us at the foyer to walk to our room and bed.

After such a late night we stayed in bed the next morning until twelve. The tea by the side of the bed was stone cold so the tea boy must have been early. Swinging my legs out of bed my head started to bang from the hangover. The same pained expression was on Pouney's face as he said, 'What the hell did we drink last night – surgical spirit?'

Seeing the tea was cold he got out of bed and went for a cold shower to wash away the cobwebs. Under the shower I was singing a song I'd heard being sung last night. I tried to remember the words.

'Rose. Rose I love you with an aching heart.' Then suddenly I remembered it was called 'Rose of Malaya'. It was such a catchy number.

Feeling better after the shower I slipped on my trousers and shirt and joined Pouney down at the bar for a black coffee and a late lunch.

The four days left we spent much the same way. One night we came out of the Empire Cinema, after seeing a western, to mingle with the jostling crowd on the cinema steps. From nowhere a police wagon swung to a stop in front of the crowd. Jumping from the rear came a dozen armed Malayan police. Some had Sten guns. A white inspector took charge and encircled the leaving crowd.

I shouted to the onlooking Pouney, 'Let's get out of here. They must be looking for somebody and don't look too bothered how they do it.'

Pouney needed no encouragement. Breaking through the mass of bodies, then being allowed through the police cordon, we hid behind an old Victorian cast iron post box at the roadside for protection. Any provocation from the crowd could end with the armed police opening fire and a bloodbath. Or perhaps an escaping terrorist would produce the same result. At that moment two of the biggest police officers went charging through the militant crowd. Scuffles were breaking out. Fists were flying, boots were going in and truncheons were being used. The skirmish finally ended when the two police dragged a struggling man covered in blood and frogmarched him to the back of the wagon. There he was spread-eagled on the floor between the seated police.

Sheltering behind the red colonial pillar box we watched the saga end and the police wagon speed away.

After last night's police raid keeping in the open air seemed a safer bet. Paying two dollars each we made our way through the turnstiles and into the pleasure gardens. This particular one was known as 'Old World'. Around the island were scattered other parks going by similar names. There was 'Happy World' and 'New World'. All were tuned for enjoyment. Dance halls, theatres, bars, sideshows, shadow theatres, wrestling, kick-boxing and the usual call girls. Strung along the paths from tree to tree were lit Chinese lanterns swinging in the breeze. Coloured bulbs flickered on and off spelling out various entertainments. At one of the many bars we sat drinking and smoking in the open air, occasionally being propositioned by call girls. They would come over asking for a cigarette or a drink, and saying for ten dollars they would show us a good time. We gave them their answer, 'For that much I can get drunk and still have change.'

Besides we could catch something by going with such women so the pair of us declined their offers and this often caused a reaction from them.

'You frightened, Johnny? Me clean girl!'

They eventually left us to continue our drinks as they looked elsewhere.

As we came through the entrance we saw that the posters were advertising wrestling tonight. So we decided to go and see the show. Pouney looked at his new luminous wristwatch saying, 'Drink your beer up, Ebee. The wrestling match starts in twenty minutes from now.'

I lifted my glass and emptied the contents then stood up and pushed the cane chair under the table.

We walked past the shows. Some had open fronts so all could see. One of these was the Chinese Shadow Theatre, which dated back to the time of Sod. Lit by lanterns, the cardboard and papier mâché figures were moved below the stage on sticks in unison with the storyteller's voice. The audience was held spellbound like children.

The sign beside the big pay box read 'Queue here'. A light in the pay box flickered on and we saw a young Chinese girl, sitting cross-legged on a high stool, selling tickets. Once we had paid we climbed the stairs which led to the wrestling hall.

The ring was raised some three feet above the floor and was surrounded by wooden benches. We sat two rows back from the front as the hall rapidly filled. Around us were a mixture of men and women of all races come to support their local hero – the Far East heavyweight champion who weighed in at around thirty stone. Ducking through the ropes the night's MC introduced the first contest of the night – the light heavyweight bout between a Somian and a Chinaman.

The two in the ring gave their all as the onlookers bayed for blood. In the fifth round the Somian knocked out the local hero with a tremendous drop kick. The Chinaman lay still and was counted out. The boys booed and cried down the winner for beating their local lad. The next two contests went the whole distance. Then came the main bout. A championship title match for the heavyweight belt of the Far East. Through the curtained doorway lumbered this giant overweight monstrous white man, a Dutchman with the ring name of King Kong. His opponent was a mere nineteen stone Chinaman by the name of Chang. The programme stated though that he was a master of the drop kick.

From the first bell Kong showed his strength by lifting the challenger with ease before throwing him across the ring. Chang replied with a drop kick. The champion barely rocked. The only thing that Chang had now was speed. The fans were now shouting and in a frenzy. The women screamed out abuse. The match went first this way and then that with both men sweating profusely and breathing heavily. The end eventually came with King Kong lifting his opponent again in one massive show of strength above his head. He then flung him backwards in a flying superflex showing incredible mobility for a man of his size.

With his opponent knocked out the huge man stood, draped in a towel, in the centre of the ring. The referee raised the huge arm of Kong amid boos from the hostile crowd. The ring cleared and the MC said goodnight to the fans as they left leaving wrappers and bottles under the seats.

It was now midnight and still an hour before closing time. We left the wrestling hall and strode over to the open-sided dance hall. Glittering with lights and blaring out loud eastern music it drowned out most of the other amusements. There were painted hostesses who charged punters twenty cents a dance. One particular dance was called the 'Jogget' where two couples moved forward and back, never touching the opposite sex.

We were at a loose end for what to do so we stopped a tri-taxi and got the cyclist to give me a try at riding it. Pouney sat in the passenger seat, laughing at my attempts. I gave up when I nearly broke my neck.

Back at the hotel the pool looked very inviting so we went to the room to change into our swimming trunks. The moonlight was shimmering on the water's surface. Diving into the warm water we knew now how a millionaire lived.

The last night of our leave came all too quickly. After these last few days in Singapore, with its nightlife and hotel, we would find it difficult and extremely hard to leave. After all these home comforts we would be leaving to go back to God knows what. Spending all those nights under ponchos with the leeches and ants, hungry, wet and frightened. Yes, we were frightened to die in all that blood and shit.

We agreed to end the night by going to the flicks for the last time, after spending the day lounging around the pool. From the foyer we caught a taxi. We chatted and smoked, pointing here and there. A broken down cart and a girl arguing with her pimp – and so early in the day. This was a place of many extremes.

We stood outside the cinema. Running around the canopy edge, like ticker tape, were moving lights that told us the programme that evening. Besides the main feature there was the latest Pathé News from Korea and the French Indo-China wars. Climbing the stairs to the balcony we found two seats. By the light of the film we could see the overhead fans swishing round and giving a cool, more bearable atmosphere. The lights came on at the interval. First house had finished and people got up. Some went to the foyer shop while others left. We could smell the heavy scent the eastern women wore.

From the rear a bell sounded warning those who were away from their seats the second house was beginning. With the interval over the lights dimmed and the curtains swished silently open and a white cockerel introduced the Pathé newsreel.

First on was the Korean War. The Americans and United Nations were being pushed back to the sea. Near Seoul, American artillery and air strikes were bringing the Communist forces to a halt. A troopship had landed British troops into Korea from their nearest base, Hong Kong, to strengthen the UN forces.

There followed news from Indo-China, another hot spot. Again it was bad news. Like the British in Malaya the French forces, as colonial powers, fought the Communist enemy at a place called Bien-Dien-Phu and they were taking a terrible beating as the Communists closed in for the kill. Only the British in Malaya seemed to be holding their own. The future looked bleak. If the tide didn't turn we could find ourselves out here for years fighting. The government had already raised conscription to two years. I turned to Pouney and read his thoughts. They were exactly the same as mine. My thoughts turned to home and the following film was meaningless to me now.

I lay in bed that night wondering what the future held. We knew what to expect when we got back to Niyor but for how long? My mind went back to the Second World War. I was thinking of the famous Chindits, our forerunners, who fought the Japanese in the jungles of Burma. To me they were the best fighting force and our training was based on the same principles. Could we, their sons, beat these bastards on their own turf? We would die trying.

Before leaving we gave the room waiter a tip of five dollars apiece. Then after breakfast we booked out of the hotel. We were going back with a few more things than when we came. We even had a bag of sandwiches we had made up by the hotel's cook. Then paying the tri-taxi his fare outside the station we went to join the bustling crowds.

A crowd already filled the station for the early morning train. We stopped to buy a paper from the kiosk to read on the journey back and kept it for the lads back at camp. Information about what was going on in the world was as rare as chicken's teeth.

The station resembled a market day back home. People old and young shouldered pigs in slings. Live chickens, their legs tied, fluttered about with bloodshot eyes upside down. Home woven baskets were filled with groceries. Others carried rolls of decorative cloth used for sarongs and saris. Among the crowd a few police mingled, looking for pickpockets. Vendors weaved through the waiting passengers, shuffling impatiently as they waited for the arrival of trains.

The departure time came but no train. Then an announcement over the tannoy system said the train would be late. The heat, sweat and smell of the animals were strong as the crowds closed in all round.

A feeling that something had happened further up the line began to heighten when another train was seen getting steamed up in a nearby siding. Shh, shh, shh, as steam jetted out from beneath the train's boiler. The steam hissed as the engine clanked over the points to where it was coupled to a line of empty coaches. From there it was shunted alongside the platform and everyone made a mad scramble for the seats. Pushing, shoving, elbowing and at times swearing Pouney and me struggled aboard but managed to find window seats. The smell of human and animal sweat was ripe and we were glad of every bit of fresh air we could get.

Again led by an armoured car train, our train slowly moved and rumbled over the points as we left the waving relatives on the platform in the distance.

We crossed the causeway from Singapore to Johore Baru to the first stop. Passengers alighted with struggling pigs while those boarding pushed their way on. The old people would give us a toothless grin, making us laugh at their comical expressions.

The train gathered speed once more. The journey was taking longer than we expected – timetables out here could be as much as a day behind. Way past noon the train came to a stop and I stood up wondering what the hell the trouble was now. Alongside the track and towards the front of the train, leaning on shovels and holding crowbars, were gangs of immigrant labourers – mostly Chinese and Indian – who were replacing bent and buckled rails. Along the bottom of the embankment, for close on two hundred yards, lay the twisted and broken passenger train that we had waited so patiently for in Singapore. We could see the decoy train had caught the full force of the explosion on the bend of the track. The track had been ripped from the sleepers and as the following train failed to stop the coaches had jack-knifed into the air. Then they had rolled down the embankment gouging out great lumps of earth and exposing tree roots. From what we could see, most of the passengers must have been killed on impact.

Both engines lay there with their shining wheels pointing skywards, giving out the occasional pssst of steam as though they were monsters drawing their last breath and dying. The coaches were crushed and splintered into nothing more than matchwood. Bogies were ripped from the undercarriages and partly buried in the flattened undergrowth. Broken crates were everywhere. Ducks and chickens pecked around the inert bodies and a pot-bellied pig, enjoying the plentiful roots, chewed contentedly away.

Moving about the edge of the jungle armed guards, survivors of the crash, protected the passengers and immigrant platelayers from further attacks by the Commies. Not having any guns Pouney and I felt rather vulnerable.

Beside the track lay the dead and injured covered in blankets and clothes. One coach on our train was cleared to take the injured and dead aboard and the passengers dispersed between the remaining coaches. The passengers understandably showed some resentment, being overcrowded already.

I turned to speak to Pouney who was staring out through the window. Looking down his eyes filled with tears, I turned to see where he looked and could see tiny feet protruding from a blanket, the small brown feet of a child. What I wanted to say was of little importance, as no words could define how we felt at that moment. A child dying from illness was unfortunate. But to die like this unnecessarily was unthinkable and such a waste of a life.

The platelayers finished laying the track and the train steamed on leaving behind the area of carnage and devastation. The rest of the journey continued in a sombre atmosphere.

Reaching Kluang during the night the train stopped just long enough to drop the passengers. The beam from the armoured car swept the area before continuing its journey northwards.

There we were, left alone on a closed station in the dead of night. Only a single light shone on the station's name high above the platform. It brought a comment from Pouney, 'Well, Ebee, it looks like we will have to spend the rest of the night on the station. There are some benches over there. We can get our heads down.'

We picked up our luggage and started walking when we heard a motor engine coming from the station entrance. We carried our cases and hurried out to see a jeep. Behind the wheel, beside a Sergeant, was a Ghurka driver. Seeing us the Sergeant waved us over. We threw in the cases and jumped in the back seats.

The jeep sped through the town which was also still alive with bars and some shops still open.

We headed towards the Ghurka barracks. Once there we passed the guardroom and jumped out. The Ghurkas ushered us to the canteen. For the next few hours they feted us like heroes, once they knew we were part of their brigade.

Morning found us only a few hundred yards from our own HQ. We thanked our hosts and left to report our delay to the officer of the day. From there we left to wait at the supply depot. We managed to scrounge a breakfast from the dining room while waiting for the trucks from 'D' Company to arrive. The guard this very day came from our own 10 Platoon.

'How was it in Singapore, Ebee? Did he lead you astray Pouney?'

The questions came thick and fast. Helping to load we quickly had the rations onboard. The Corporal signed the supply sheet saying everything was in order. Then we drove off still being bombarded with questions.

June 1951 – The Bugle Gang

Four men boarded the trucks whose shoulder flashes said they came from the REME. Their neatly pressed uniforms were creased and starched like new toys straight from the box. They sat amongst the fruit and vegetables, their kitbags at their sides, while Pouney and I sat with our suitcases.

Going back to Niyor was a bit like going home. Big Gowey, one of the men on guard duty, was yelling as we bounced up the track about the changes that had taken place while we had been on leave.

'There's a new Sergeant for 10 Platoon. Named Charmers, a right so and so, Ebee. No time for conscripts like us, he calls us part-time soldiers. Have you seen the new men on the trucks?' He waffled on and on. God we are back, I thought.

Before long the trucks passed Niyor village. The children, with wide eyes and running noses, waved. Next we passed the open factory where clanking rollers turned the latex into more manageable mats. Then we were through the camp gates and stopped at the cookhouse.

Those on fatigues peeled spuds while others swabbed down the tabletops or washed the greasy pans. We jumped down and walked over to the office to report back. We knocked on the door and were told to enter. Looking up from his workload was our platoon commander, Lieutenant Bury. He returned our salute.

'And how was leave in the big city?' he asked us.

'Very nice, sir.'

After a few casual questions we gave him another salute before making our way to 10 Platoon's lines. There a chorus greeted us, 'The prodigal sons have returned.'

Seeing that we had the daily papers they snapped them out of our hands. Others more curious at what went on in Singapore. The main question was did we have any women while we were there. Pouney winked at me and said, 'Sure plenty. They were like leeches all over us, right, Ebee?' Pouney gave them a load of bullshit as they asked for details, only to be told, 'You're too young to know.'

I suddenly realised I hadn't seen or heard Heapy. I looked around to where his bed was. The mattress and blankets were neatly folded whereas the other beds were made. Worried, I asked the others where he was.

'Where's Heapy then. What's happened to him?'

Apparently he had been sent on a three-day course while we were away to learn about water purifying. On what to drink and what to leave well alone. Plus the possible places to find it. Well, we all knew Heapy. While on the course he picked up the bug typhoid. It was the bug he was supposed to be learning to prevent. I couldn't help but laugh. Trust Heapy to do something like this.

Pushing back the tent flaps the new Sergeant of 10 Platoon led in two of the new men. Knowing Heapy was my partner, and he being away, I was short of a partner. The Sergeant spoke to the taller of the two.

'There are two bunks over there. Sort yourselves out a new partner each, and Swindles,' that was the shorter guy, 'you will be the Lieutenant's new batman. Report to him later.'

The batman at present was Weaver who wanted to be released from the post.

From the moment I met Jones, my new partner, we hit it off. Jones instantly became Jonah. Like myself he was from the Black Country, a place called Tipton. Or as we say in the Black Country 'Tipun on cut'.

With the Sergeant came his pedigree. Seasoned as a fighter in the theatre of jungle warfare he was not known for spit and polish. He was firm but not frightened to lead from the front. The only thing against him was that he didn't like conscripts but time would tell.

The first time we crossed swords was while filling sandbags to place around the slit trenches. The Sergeant came walking over and his first words to the party were, 'Can't you lazy beggars work any faster. You're just like those sandbags. Only fit for stopping bullets. Any trouble and I'll leave you to it.'

We now knew how we stood with him as National

Servicemen. My new partner was quick to answer him with, 'If that's the way you want to play it then I personally will be keeping an eye on you. Any trouble, as you said, you will leave all right. When we all leave or not at all.'

The Sergeant looked surprised at the remark. He left us all in silence. He knew he couldn't charge Jonah because his remark to us was a discrimination against the men. Still filling the sandbags I said, 'Good for you Jonah.'

It was now in the Sergeant's corner whether he accepted us or not in a platoon already established by our own hard work.

We were sitting in the sun peeling spuds at the rear of the cookhouse around a galvanised bath. Talking and smoking the cook came periodically to empty the peeled spuds into the black cooking pots for boiling leaving us to fill the baths all over again. I stuck the knife into a large spud so as not to lose it and lit a fag. Like so often in life, when you decide to do something the opposite happens. Around the corner came the Sergeant with a look of urgency on his face.

We dropped everything as we heard him say, 'You three drop what you are doing and get over to your tent and change. We are going out. All you'll need is your gun, ammunition and water bottles, get moving.'

We answered by sprinting over to the tents. Those already there were changing from shorts to battle dress. Lacing up our boots we tried to pull on our shirts and grab the bandoleer from the locker with the other hand. I grabbed the EY from the rack as I rushed over to join the others who were waiting. We all listened as the Lieutenant told us, 'A few moments ago we received a message from one of the platoons asking for help. They've been badly hit. When we go out be on your toes, let's go.'

Needing no further encouragement we raced over to the revving trucks and jumped aboard as they lurched down the rough track. We moved away from the village and headed towards where the previous morning they had dropped 12 Platoon.

Twisting and turning and often skidding over the dusty bends, we were thrown from side to side. Then braking hard the lorries stopped in a cloud of red dust. Coughing and spluttering we jumped from the tailboards then scattered around expecting the worst. With Luang in front we followed in the steps of fairly new tracks. With no added weight to carry we literally smashed our way forward through the undergrowth of the unkempt rubber plantation with the adrenaline rising the further we went.

We stopped as the leading scout was challenged. We had made contact with 12 Platoon, or what was left of it. We followed the sentry through the undergrowth. One of the men who had recently joined the platoon, named Todd, was still shaking from the events. He led us to the base camp where our Lieutenant had a quick exchange with 12 Platoon's Lieutenant Morris, before setting off once more. But not before noticing Sergeant Cooper. Only by the grace of God was he still alive. His head was swathed in khaki bandages where the red scorch mark of a bullet had crossed his cheek taking the lobe of his left ear clean off. A fraction more to his right and he would have had scrambled brains.

We went off in the direction Lieutenant Morris had pointed out towards a missing section and a missing man, out on his own. 'Let's hope we can find them alive.' Again we leaned on Luang's tracking skills. If anyone could find them he could. At the same time he kept us from being ambushed by clearing the traps left by the Commie gangs. By now we were ourselves also adept at clearing booby traps.

Slowly and cautiously and fully alert to the dangers, we hardly made a sound as we came across one of the bodies of the missing men. Without thinking, Townsend bent down and turned the body over. It was the missing Leadam. This foolhardy action brought an angry response from the Sergeant. 'You bloody fool! What do you think you are doing? If that body had been booby-trapped there would be dead and wounded all around here by now. In future, all of you remember leave the bloody thing to me, all right?'

Townsend went to say something but knew the Sergeant was right. A bit of swearing at times emphasised the situation just right. Only last night I had sat with Leadam in the mess hall, a quiet and most inoffensive chap as you could ever wish to meet. A man of few words, he was now lying stripped of his webbing, packs and boots. He was left in just his blood-splattered uniform.

All around the body lay spent cartridges from the missing Bren gun. He had clearly given a brave account of himself. His eyes were still open staring in death but looking alive. He had faced the enemy front to the very end. Later we learned he was shot through both legs. Unable to move, he covered the retreating section of two men, forfeiting his life to save the others, knowing that the Commies never took prisoners.

We wrapped the body in his poncho cape and carried him with us as we searched for the second section. The soft ground became hilly as we moved more and more cautiously in case the missing section opened up, mistaking us for the Communists.

Hank was up in front with Luang just for this purpose if and when contact was made. An occasional rustle from the undergrowth, maybe a lizard or a wild pig making off into the bush, brought nerves close to the edge.

The little track brought us round the base of one hill. A shout from up the hill caused the platoon to freeze. Then the shout was heard again. It was the missing section. The four men had stayed put as they had hit the second laid ambush. This was probably what had saved their lives. Only one of the four was slightly wounded. They had come under heavy fire but had returned fire as the Chinese charged. They had even blown a bugle trying to demoralise the defenders and had screamed several times, but each charge had failed as they were driven back by grenades and automatic fire. Lying in a depression in the ground the four had stayed put knowing a search party would be sent to find them. With the element of surprise now gone the bugler had sounded the recall and from their position the defenders had seen the Commies come out of their hideaway carrying the wounded as they melted away into the greenery.

We made a brief search of the Commie positions but found no bodies or anything else. The theory of nothing left behind made them look even more invincible and far superior at jungle fighting than us. But we knew this was only propaganda and that they had learned this theory from the Germans, who were past masters of the game.

On more than one occasion we had stumbled upon graves. One of the men from our own platoon was having a run out.

Standing astride as he took a piss he looked down as the streaming jet slowly uncovered a piece of cloth. He had bent down to unearth it with his machete and discovered a shallow grave of decomposing bodies. The uniforms confirmed they were the flesh and bones of dead Communists. We left them as we found them, in unmarked graves.

Joining the platoon the four retraced their steps back to where we waited. Back at base there was a lot of backslapping when both parties met but we were also saddened at the loss of Leadam. With all formalities over, and the camp cleared of bashers, the two platoons pushed back to the pick-up point. The trucks found us waiting and we loaded the body still wrapped in the poncho. Hutch our medic and Beddows, 12 Platoon's medic, were looking after the Sergeant and the other wounded man telling them that within the hour they would be in clean beds in Niyor. Then early tomorrow they would be moved to Kluang's military hospital, along with Leadam's body.

Hutch had had no previous medical knowledge or experience but had been chosen from the platoon to carry the medical bag. Again he had done a good job tending and dispensing medicines to the sick and wounded.

Dusk was upon us as we entered Niyor. The wounded were more settled now they were in a clean bed. Without having a wash we sat down for the meal we had peeled the spuds for earlier. The sausage was hard from standing too long and only the tea was hot.

Over breakfast I sat with Jonah and Jim Swindles. They had asked me what it was like to be under fire. Well, they had seen yesterday's combat. The great adventure and the gung-ho 'I was there' attitude was gone. Though only a day older they had grown in stature, soon to become veterans in killing and dying. Out here life could be very short.

New orders came down from the hierarchy. Outlying farms and small communities were to be resettled in larger camps therefore making it easier to protect them. This also helped to cut the supply routes for the Communists.

From their homes they carried their belongings: pots, kettles, old oil lamps, and large bundles of clothes and blankets. The kids chased chickens, laughing and tumbling. They treated it as one huge game. They loaded their possessions onboard lorries that we had provided. They resented us for uprooting them from their homes. They had lived there since they could remember, being born and buried in the same soil as their ancestors. This to them was a new beginning.

We lifted goats and pigs as the old men and women held on to their rope leads. They looked bewildered as the animals bleated and grunted. Chucks were caught and crates stacked on a forward lorry. Next we helped the old people onto the trucks before climbing on ourselves.

Sitting in bundles of clothes the old women cried. They were very disorientated leaving their homes. The younger ones laughed and giggled as they held on to the sides of the trucks as we rumbled down the tree-lined road. The older ones were now resigned to the fact they were being taken to a much larger settlement, a plantation village surrounded by barbed wire and armed guards. The guards had been hand-picked by the villagers themselves and they were trusted.

We arrived at the gate and the guards opened them and directed us to where newly erected huts stood. We drove to the end of the huts and helped to unload everything. They now had a new home and a shop and, well, a new village. The new village was called Bukit-Siput and had a population of between 150 and 200.

With no word of thanks, just a wave from the children, we left them to it. After driving through the gates the guards closed them and we bumped on down the road.

After lunch the army cinema truck, followed by the ration trucks, drove through the camp gates, a sight seldom seen but nevertheless very welcome at any time. The old tennis court, now used as a parade ground, would tonight become the open-air film show ground and tonight of all nights I was on guard. Hank had been talking to the projectionist who told him the name of the film was *The Egg and I*, a comedy about chickens. From our tent we could see the erected white screen on a stand. Tonight, benches from the mess hall would be filled with smoking and drinking film buffs from 10 and 12 Platoons.

'Pity you're on guard, Ebee.'

I'd forgotten about that and Jonah reminded me. I wasn't even ready. I muttered to myself, 'Fancy forgetting about guard.' Speaking louder I asked Jonah, 'What time is it, Jonah?'

Before he could answer I heard the Sergeant's voice shout out, 'Guard mounting in five minutes.'

I'd already missed early tea, which the guard always had. Now if I didn't hurry I would miss the guard mounting.

'Can I borrow your rifle as mine isn't too clean,' I asked.

His answer was nothing less than I expected. 'Sure you can, Ebee. Is there anything else you want?'

Quickly thinking I answered him, 'You can get me an ice cream at half time. And keep your hands off the usherettes.'

I felt my chin to see if I needed a shave. Well it was much too late to worry if I did. Tonight it was our Sergeant who was guard commander. Pulling on my bush hat I grabbed Jonah's rifle and said, 'Be home early from the pictures, lads!'

Carrying my rifle I joined the others, seven in all, outside the guard tent standing to attention as Sergeant Charmers walked behind the inspecting officer. Tonight that was 12 Platoon's Lieutenant Morris. He walked between the ranks inspecting our rifles and general appearance. He stopped in front of me.

'You haven't shaved have you soldier?'

'No, sir,' I replied. It wasn't worth lying to him. I knew myself I needed one.

'Take his name, Sergeant, and put him on report for tomorrow.'

Saying that, the officer moved on to the next man. Once he had finished the inspection he read out the duties and the times of the guard.

Dusk, and I was feeling hungry. I slowly walked around the perimeter going in the opposite direction was Todd from 12 Platoon. From the mess hall we could see the men having the evening meal. Those who had finished carried the benches over to the parade ground ready for the show. When the mess hall was just about emptied and everybody seated the projectionist was ready to roll. The lights went out and the screen lit up.

First up was the news. From where I stood I had a perfect view and could hear the commentary although from behind the screen the characters were the other way round. Standing quietly behind the screen I didn't hear or see the approaching Todd until he was beside me. He nearly gave me heart failure as he spoke.

'What are you doing Ebee? You're supposed to be on guard.'

Somehow I had to convince him I wanted to see this film.

'Nobody will come tonight, it's too light. Anyway, this is a good film, stop worrying,' I whispered back hoping he wasn't going to be a smart-arse and say come on we can't stay here. It was a moonlit night and we stood in the shadows where nobody could see us. We looked up at the screen and stayed there till the end. It was also the end of our stag. We only moved when the watching audience carried the benches back to the mess hall. We didn't think of the consequences if we'd been attacked suddenly. Todd gave me a nudge and a whisper.

'See you round the other end.'

Next morning I shaved with Jonah at my elbow, brushing his teeth. Between brushes he spoke of last night's film.

'You missed a good show last night, Ebee. A really good comedy show.'

I smiled as I answered him, 'That was a good part when the chickens got loose.'

'Yes, that was a good laugh,' he answered laughing. Then suddenly realising what I had said he asked me, 'How did you know about that?'

He frowned as he spoke and I tapped my nose as I answered him, 'Ah, that would be telling.'

With my towel over my shoulder I left the shower block whistling and Jonah looking puzzled.

After morning parade I stood outside the office waiting to go before the Major. The charge – being of improper appearance while on guard parade. The Sergeant stepped out of the office, brought me to attention and marched me in on the double.

'Right left right, pick those feet up there. Come on, pick them up there.'

After saluting I was ordered to remove my hat. Standing to attention like a submissive fool I stared unflinching, over the head of the presiding officer who was my judge and jury. The Sergeant gave the officer the charge sheet. After a glance he read the charge out to me. Looking me in the face he said, 'Have you anything to say?'

Replying to his question I said, 'No sir. I'm sorry, sir.'

He looked down at the paper then said, 'Then seven days extra duties, and I don't want to see you before me again. That understood?'

'Yes, sir.'

I knew when he read out my punishment that it was all cut and dried before I went in. Anyway, at least he didn't dock my pay.

I was working in the cookhouse paying off my jankers, a term used for punishment, when the ration trucks from Kluang rolled in. Another part of my punishment was unloading the supplies. I dropped the tailboard and whom did I see? The grinning Heapy was looking healthy after his illness. He jumped down and we stood shaking hands. He asked me to walk over to the tent lines with him but I told him I was on jankers. Later that night we enjoyed a drink together and a chat at the old Char Wallah's.

July 1951 – Bukit-Siput

The trucks were loaded and we sat perilously on the open back, watching a Malayan regiment take over the Niyor base. Rumour had it we were going to Segamat for a rest period and this soon had the men's morale sky high. The platoon from the Malayan regiment was there to take charge of the vacated camp. Waving and wishing them luck we left with no regrets.

We left the area for the last time and drove past the village we were leaving to be protected by their own kind from the Communists. We journeyed through the rubber, passing 'B' Company, giving them the news that we were leaving the area. Talking and smoking we were soon entering Segamat.

This was the town where I had done my police patrols and I told the lads where the best places to go were. The trucks eventually pulled into the old lines of 'A' Coy. Then followed hours of unloading and unpacking.

All spent out we lay on our beds, planning the strategy for the night down in Segamat. I had a few dollars and a postal order from my old boss from back home to change. That night after tea Jonah and I walked down to the station and cashed the postal order. The feeling of freedom as we wandered downtown was great. Finding a bar we sat drinking until it was time to go.

We lay in bed the next morning and failed to hear the reveille until we were shaken by the Sergeant making his rounds while the others were at breakfast,

'Hello, what do we have here? The two sleeping beauties. Let's be having you, you're both on a charge. Sleeping while you should be on parade.'

He left quickly and we got out of bed, dressed and joined the others on parade. The following morning we received seven days' jankers. Instead of Segamat that evening we were scrubbing out the offices and each night we attended the guardroom for extra duties. One night we stood out there, waiting to see what piece of equipment the guard Sergeant wanted to see.

'I would like to see your machete shining like chrome.'

Back in the tent, from under the bed, I pulled out my old machete. Taking it out of the scabbard I could see the blade was red with rust. I looked at Jonah who had much the same in his hands. We both burst out laughing. There was no way we could clean them in time. We went round the tents trying to find two clean machetes. We at last found two in HQ, and with a bribe of twenty fags each we had our machetes. Standing on jankers parade we pulled out the machetes and the Sergeant inspected the blades before looking at us. We breathed a sigh of relief as he fell for it. This was the last night of jankers and it was well worth the twenty fags.

With a few more patrols and no mishaps during our week's rest, we found ourselves on the move yet again, this time by train. Again wagons were loaded and unloaded at the station's sidings. This time the journey was north and the crowded train was filled with soldiers and supplies.

We stopped at Kuala-Lumpur, having only stopped once for fuel. Trucks were loaded once again and 'D' Company left for a place which was unknown to us. Tired and exhausted we didn't care where we went and just before dark we reached a place near a town on a hill.

We woke the next morning on an already erected base overlooking the town of Klang, the old capital of Malaya. It was perched on a hill beyond the jungle. From the treetops rose a shining dome, the home of the Sultan of Perak. We were now in the State of Perak, a hilly and dangerous place.

Time was spent on short patrols and camp duties until the familiar call came one day. 'Everybody get fell in. There's an emergency on.'

Standing there in three ranks we were told the Governor of Malaya had been killed in an ambush on a road east of Klang. The convoy had broken down and was left unarmed, except for two men and the driver of the car. Alone they stood little chance of survival. We mounted the wagons dressed in our battle dress and carrying weapons. This was the most serious and largest kill yet by the Communists.

We went through Klang with horns blaring. With a twenty-four hour ration pack and a poncho to cover our heads for the night, it looked odds on we were going in search of the killers. The few cars, carts and cyclists pulled onto the side of the road as we sped past.

Some miles down the road we came to the bullet-riddled government car. A police wagon had already arrived. On the back seat, slumped in blood, lay the Governor. Every window in the vehicle had been smashed, even the headlamps. The leather upholstery had been ripped and tufts of the material were sticking out. The two bodyguards, one in front with the driver and the other in the back, had died instantly.

The trap had been laid as an opportunist ambush hoping for a planter to ride by in his jeep, or perhaps a softer target, a bus full of passengers to rob, or drag the women and screaming children into the nearby jungle to molest and murder them. But they had the supreme target in a thousand to one chance.

This was a real eye-catching news item for the world to read. To leave an armoured car, as he had done, to keep a golf date seemed highly irresponsible for a man in his position.

From the bank where the hidden Commies had opened fire we could see the positions clearly trodden down. They may have hidden here for ages. This position led us into the jungle where the newly broken twigs and track were easy to follow. Again we moved with caution so as not to fall into the same ambush. The track ended on a hillside, inside a rubber plantation. We stopped as the platoon officers mulled over the situation. We then noticed a new officer in the group. This was our first glance of the company's new Commanding Officer, Major Mitchell. Known as Mad Mitch he had a habit of chewing peanuts.

The signs of the Commies' tracks had now dried up so we made our way back to where the incident happened. The vehicle had been moved and only an oil stain on the road marked the spot.

The camp overlooked the railway station. A long flight of steps led the way down a shorter route than the road. Klang's station had inherited the same features as the larger stations – a large beer bar. It was clean and used by the local planters. Jonah and I soon became regular customers while stationed there getting to know the planters and police officers who were mostly European retired army personnel.

In civvy street Jonah was a bricklayer. I was a plumber myself. Every night we were asked, 'Why don't you come and work for us when you've finished your service in the army. Stay out here and get rich.'

They also knew we were seasoned fighters, which was a real asset along with our trades.

Those inquiring were gold dredgers. They used large mechanical dredgers on lakes of water to sift the gold from the extracted ore and mud. After thinking carefully we declined their offer, as the call of home was greater than the lure of money.

We had now taken to playing football at the base. Playing on the camp pitch soon brought challenges from the local police sides. Jonah and I played for the company, to the shouts of 'Foul!' and 'Did you see that ref!' The slighter built police were sent sprawling as they tried to jinx their way to goal. Because of the heat the time was reduced from ninety minutes to eighty minutes and the game usually ended with a win for the army.

'D' Company had only been here four short weeks when news came through that the Malayan replacement regiment were losing the upper hand to the Communists. The situation was getting serious, and the Malayan government called for a demand for our return there.

Once again we packed the company's supplies and equipment. At the station we were in a sombre mood. We played cards as we rattled along, sometimes snoozing as the swaying train rocked you to sleep then being disturbed as a winning hand was played and a large kitty was won.

That evening we unloaded the freight wagons and loaded up the trucks. Through the unlit town we drove with little help from the moon. The racing clouds were a sure sign that the dreaded monsoon season was drawing near.

We climbed down from the trucks. The darkness stopped any unloading and erecting till morning so we were told to make the best of what we had and in most cases that meant the ground you stood on. Jonah and me in the meantime had confiscated a little shed left by the Malayans as unwanted baggage and used it for our sleeping quarters for the night. We crawled through the door and lay down exhausted. The journey had taken its toll.

We woke early next morning covered in foul-smelling shit (is there any other?) and scratching at the biting red mites, left by the former occupants. It had been used as a chicken pen! We dashed straight down to the swimming pool and plunged in fully clothed. The water instantly brought relief. The others gazed in amazement. When they knew what had happened they had a field day at our expense. We were reminded every time we had chicken, 'Is this one a member of the family, Ebee?'

The villagers recognised us from our last stay and often waved as we went past their village. Life was now more secure at our return.

One lunchtime I was sitting opposite Jonah, talking and sipping lemonade from the tin mug, when Sergeant Charmers came over telling us, 'When you've had your lunch get your gear ready to go out after dusk.'

'Does this mean I'm off jankers, Sergeant?' I blurted out. He nodded yes. I had been given another seven days jankers on the last day at Klang for talking while on guard mounting. I had claimed I was a victim of mistaken identity but still got the seven days and still had two left to do.

We packed the tinned rations tightly into our packs before going down to the Char Wallah's to buy two hundred Rough Rider cigarettes. This was the name given to the cigarettes bearing a cowboy riding a horse and shooting a rifle. From the box on the table I sorted out a few packets of biscuits, thinking I could put them in between the mess tins as a small added bonus in the jungle.

I got back to the lines as the grenades and ammunition were being distributed. They were packed into the two front pouches and held on the front by the shoulder straps so every bit of weight was balanced out around the body.

Dinner came and went and we waited. Our webbing belts, carrying the machete, water bottle and bayonet, and if your weapon was an Owen gun a magazine pouch besides, lay on the bed ready to be hooked on to the waist. The heavy packs lay alongside.

At around ten o'clock, as some of us were dozing on the bed, the call came. Without shouting the Sergeant poked his head around the tent flaps. 'Outside and do it quietly. There's no need to tell the world where we're going.'

Closing the tent flaps we slipped quickly and quietly into the night. The only sound was that of our jungle boots as they fell on the track. Even that died away as we entered the rubber. Tied down tightly even the stewpot, which I had regained, remained silent.

The darkness had its own way of making the hearing more acute than normal. We could hear the clicking and whirring insects that during the day we would never have given a second thought to. Occasionally we disturbed fire flies as they attracted a mate, blinking, flitting and dancing as they went about their love life in the most extraordinary way.

Somewhere up front came the sound of a muffled cough. The cloak of darkness gave nothing away as to where we were going. It was like walking in a dream. Our senses were all at sea. Under the feet the ground suddenly changed to hard track. A mishap now could put the whole operation in jeopardy.

Through the night the men trudged only stopping for short rest periods and a drink. Then the seemingly endless night was broken by the coming of dawn. The rising sun gave out its rays of heat and the cool of the night gave way to the humidity of the day.

We progressed on amongst the rubber plantation trees. The early rising Tamils, the immigrant labour force imported in great numbers, could be seen moving from tree to tree emptying the cups of latex into a large metal container held on their backs by a strap around their foreheads. They hardly gave the patrol a second glance. I wondered how long it would be before the Commies got the information we were in the area.

We kept an eye on the rubber tappers. Their very presence meant a village was close at hand. News was coming down the line that Hank had reached a village and had turned into it. Since daylight the patrol had strung out and now covered some two hundred yards. This meant that information was late getting to those towards the back, and it was some time before the last man went through the village gate. It then occurred to me that I had seen this place before. This was the resettlement village of Bukit-Siput.

Entering through the barbed wire gates we found the rest of the men beginning to settle some thirty yards inside the perimeter. To the right of the track, on a fairly open grassy area, was a likely place for the camp. I slipped off my pack, groaning as I did, 'Thank God we're here. A cup of tea is all I want right now.'

The rest of the platoon lay on their packs talking, while a few smoked. Two guards were immediately placed on the top gates down the centre of the village. A single track ran to the far end where another set of gates stood open and two more guards were dispatched to guard them. They were given the same instructions – to stop and search any villager entering or leaving the area.

This left the rest of us free to erect the bashers and cook breakfast. Opening the pack I extended the three-legged Tommy cooker while Jonah raised the basher. Opening a tin of sausage and placing a knob of margarine in the mess tin, I placed the tin on a lit tablet and turned the sizzling sausage from time to time.

Elsewhere the smell of bacon being cooked filled our nostrils. Using one of Jonah's mess tins I filled it with water, ready to replace the cooking sausage with the water for the tea. Holding the hot handle with my rolled up hat and using the point of the bayonet I rolled out Jonah's share of the sausage into his other tin. We ate the sausages with our fingers letting the greasy fat trickle down our chins. We made the tea between mouthfuls and sipped it afterwards while having a smoke.

Finishing, we were told to take over the gate at the bottom of the track and relieve those on the gate for their meal. With rifles slung over our shoulders we marched down the slight slope through the village. A few barking dogs ran from the doorways showing their ribs through their sides. A few badly aimed kicks sent them squealing and howling beneath the wooden shacks.

We took over from Gowey and Hutch. By now the returning Tamils were waiting at the gate to be searched. Their latex-stained clothes smelt to high heaven. Some carried a cloth made satchel while others a reed woven shoulder bag. Each one was searched. Holding and carrying nothing of importance they shuffled away in their flip-flop sandals.

Behind them came the Chinese workers in groups of threes and fours in their casual black styled pyjamas, peering through slit eyes as one of us rummaged through their possessions while the other trained his gun. With a wave from the gun they were allowed through.

I glanced at my watch and saw Townsend and Pouney coming down the track. This time of day was a quiet period. With the temperature soaring, the villagers had their siestas till mid-afternoon. Relieved from gate guard duty we ambled up the sleeping village passing a well where the village water supply was taken.

After lunch we were told to gather round and form a half-circle. In the centre stood the officer and a little way to his rear was the Sergeant. The officer began to explain to us the reason why we were here.

'We have strong information there's a force of three hundred Communists moving through this area in the next few days. If they show we hold our positions until help arrives.' Tapping his foot with a stick as he spoke, he eyed up the listeners and then continued. 'We shall guard the perimeter throughout the night, at different points each night we stay. If put under attack, during the day or night, drop back to this position. Understand, this position.'

We answered with a chorus of, 'Yes, sir's.

'There will be slit trenches which, after this talk, you will dig. The Sergeant will show you where to dig them.'

Jonah raised his hand to put a question to the Lieutenant. 'Sir, how long after the call for help would the response take to get backup?'

'Last night we covered a little over eighteen miles. Maybe the roads are bumpy but they are clear to drive on. That gives us thirty minutes. After that it won't matter. If that's all Sergeant, carry on and get the men digging.'

Moving three or four yards from the bashers towards the camp gates the Sergeant pointed out various spots to dig. Using trenching tools we'd brought along we first marked and then cleared away the turf and stubble. We found the red soil easy to dig in the heat. We were soon stripped to the waist cutting the trench in an 'L' shape and throwing the excavated soil in front of the trench. The 'L' shape gave the occupants two firing positions and some defence against a grenade attack. If one unluckily dropped in the trench you quickly moved to the other side and avoided the explosion. We stopped occasionally and tried the height by pretending to fire at an imaginary enemy target over the firing rim. Once we had reached the depth we stamped the bottom of the trench flat. The sweat now oozed from every pore in our bodies.

Waving a piece of paper at us the Sergeant called us all together. Allotted in groups of three we were given the area we were to guard that night. I was with Batey and Corporal Nodder. The Sergeant pointed with his finger and we followed his gaze. On a rise stood an old temple. We were at least on high ground.

'You three will cover that area down to the next group below you. Oh, and before I forget, keep out of the temple. You know how religious they are. Any sign of trouble or movement come running, okay?'

With that he turned to the next group and told them where they were to go.

Just a little before we put the stewpot on and cleaned the dust off the rifle, I became aware of the wireless operator, Drak, talking to the Lieutenant and Sergeant Charmers. In Drak's left hand was a smaller 36 set which we called the walkie-talkie. He was pointing to the larger 88 set. I saw the Lieutenant nodding in agreement to what was said while the Sergeant stood taking sips from his tin cup. Something had gone wrong I could sense it.

Carrying the walkie-talkie with him the Sergeant headed over towards our basher. He called Batey over to join Jonah and me. Then he explained, 'It looks like the walkie-talkie may be defective. It needs testing and the only way to do this is to take the set some distance from the base, to about three miles. It's the only way to test the bloody thing.'

'You must be joking, Sergeant. There's three hundred Commies out there and you're asking three of us to test the bloody thing,' I said half-laughing.

Immediately the Sergeant's mood changed and he thrust the

set into Jonah's hand. 'You will do as I say. Grab your weapons.'

From the way he said it I knew he was deadly serious but Batey by now was insistent it was too dangerous and refused to go. He was immediately placed under open arrest for disobeying orders. On active service this was a very serious offence. In days gone by he could have faced the death penalty. He would now face a court martial at a later date. Batey had taken a foolish but stubborn stand.

Hutch replaced Batey as the Sergeant instructed Jonah on the rudiments and call sign of the walkie-talkie. He walked over to the gate with us saying, 'Walk down the track for forty minutes by the watch. When forty minutes have elapsed you should be close on three miles away, then make your call sign.'

I changed my EY for Batey's Sten gun that had more firepower if we ran into any trouble. The three of us in turn then went through the barbed wire gate.

It was here where no man's land started. We hoped it wasn't the road to paradise. We left the track straight away and moved into the undergrowth for cover. Soon we were on our own. At every sound we stopped and dropped to one knee, only continuing when everything seemed all right.

The fear and tension mounted the further away from base we got. If we ran into trouble now our chances of survival were almost nil. We knew if we did anything stupid it could be our last mistake and so kept low and quiet. We passed the rubber tappers with fingers on triggers. No one spoke. A stare or a nod was sufficient. Jonah stared at his watch and gestured with his hand. We all agreed we had come far enough, as the time was now forty minutes. Dropping on one knee we were below the height of the undergrowth. Keeping a sharp eye open we gave the surrounding area a quick once over to see if it was clear. Jonah then pulled the antennae from the walkie-talkie, mouthing to himself what he had to say. Then with his hand partially over the mouthpiece and keeping his voice to just above a whisper, he pressed the send button and spoke.

'Calling 10 Platoon. Calling 10 Platoon, this is zebra. Over.'

He released the button and waited for a reply. There was no answer just a lot of static and crackling. He turned the antennae in the direction we had come and tried again.

'Calling 10 Platoon. Calling 10 Platoon, this is zebra calling. Come in please, come in. Over.'

The crackling suddenly gave way to a voice.

'This is 10 Platoon. This is 10 Platoon calling zebra. Receiving you loud and clear. Everything all right your end zebra? Over.'

Jonah looked at both of us and raised his thumb, telling us the set was working perfectly then he answered the base's last question. We then waited for the call sign to return to base. A few moments elapsed before the reply came. We were told to return and to keep our heads down.

Hutch led the way, I was next and finally Jonah brought up the rear. Taking our time we began to cover the forty minute distance which seemed to take hours before we reached the guard on the gate who let us through. I was never more pleased to see a place in my life, and I did a quick north, south, east and west on my chest.

Nodder, the Corporal, dipped the empty can he held into the boiling stew. A few pieces of meat floated to the surface of the pot. Then using the lid as a ladle he tipped the stew into my outstretched mess tin. Starving, I hurried over to the basher and rummaged through the pack for the hard tack biscuits. I crumbled two into the stew and sat cross-legged to eat the meal which I enjoyed as though I was sitting in the Ritz.

Darkness fell and we slipped quietly out of camp to the lonely positions the Sergeant had pointed out earlier. With the groups dispersed only a handful were left at base to help any group should they be put under attack. This meant there were wide gaps in the perimeter unguarded.

Through the night Nodder, Batey and I approached the bottom of the hill leading to the temple. When we were near the temple, where the lamps cast shadows, we left the path and kept to the shadows. We knew even amongst the villagers there were Communist sympathisers willing to give our position and strength of numbers away.

To the side of the temple we found a small depression well away from the light thrown by the suspended oil lamps from the temple rafters.

We placed our rifles beside our water bottles and grenades and settled down as best we could. From there we looked down on the village below. The only movement came from the shacks within. We had restricted the villagers' movements by warning them anyone found near the barbed wired fence risked getting shot. The gates had been closed and chained since early evening as the last of the tappers had entered.

Lights below shone through the slats of the shack walls. The sounds of a gramophone squeaked out some old music, along with someone singing to it. The smoke and smells seemed stronger way up here. The aromatic cooking of spices with fish and rice mixed with onions, mingled with the heavily scented joss sticks that smouldered in the temple in sand jars below a golden sitting Buddha.

Dogs barked and howled in the night, their sixth sense, a throwback to the wild, telling them there was something different this night. Strangers such as us were still here. Perhaps we could make use of their ears during the night if anyone or anything tried to get through the barbed wire.

Gradually the lights went out one by one leaving us to talk in whispers. We kept away from the subject of why Batey had refused the order. Although he was on open arrest he could still be called upon to do his duty, such as he was doing right now.

The other two caught up on some sleep while I took the first watch on guard, and I tried hard to focus my mind on something to keep me from falling asleep. The paraffin lamps continued to burn in the temple. I could see red painted woodcarvings below the roof eves, and ornamental wood scrolls picked out the worshippers in gold leaf and taking great care of their temple was the fat Buddha who sat crossed-legged in the centre of the altar. The golden painted statue, with its eyes half-closed and eastern features, was one of the biggest symbols of Buddhism. Along the base of the altar stood jars of joss sticks. They were waiting to be bought for just a few cents each. They would be lit in remembrance of a friend or relative as they knelt on the bare floor. Footwear was forbidden in the temple and worshippers would leave their sandals and flip-flops in one corner before crossing the tiled floor.

Holding my wristwatch towards the temple light I could make

out the luminous fingers. It was time to wake one of the others for guard. I turned to Batey and gave him a nudge. He woke a little startled then settled when he saw it was me. I slipped the watch off my wrist, saying, 'Nodder's on a twelve o'clock.'

I then settled down myself, pulling the brim of my bush hat over my eyes and trying to ignore the constant humming of the mosquitoes.

A shaking woke me. It felt as though I'd just closed my eyes. I pushed back my hat and felt a hand close over my mouth. Staring into the darkness I made out the face of Batey who had one finger up to his lips. Once he realised I was awake he withdrew his hand. Then I heard it – twang! Then again – twang! It was as if someone was trying to free themselves from the barbed wire. Hardly daring to breathe I whispered to Batey and held out my hand.

'Pass me two of the grenades. They sound as if they're just below us. I could sneak down and before they knew it I'd have the grenades amongst them.'

The Corporal whispered back, 'There may be too many to handle. Go and tell the Sergeant. Let him decide what to do.'

Voted two to one against I slipped down the slope in the pitch darkness. Almost blind I felt my way with my feet. I knew I had to cross the dirt track but all I felt at that moment was grass and twigs. I shuffled my feet and suddenly found the smoother ground, which must have been the dirt road running through the village. I fixed a mental picture of the bashers in my mind and made for that direction. Let's see now, the camp's about thirty yards to the right, I counted as I went blindly on. Almost stumbling over a basher in the darkness I regained my senses and called out softly, 'It's me Ebee. Don't shoot. You know, Ebee, it's me.'

I felt the hair on the back of my neck stand up. Although I could not see them I knew there were at least half a dozen guns trained on me at that moment. The Sergeant's voice broke the silence, 'Come like that again and you will get shot. What's the bloody trouble now?'

Excited and slightly breathless I told him about the noise and the twanging barbed wire. On hearing what I had to say the Sergeant and two other men followed me back. Guided by the lights of the temple we crept back as silently as we could.

From the temple we peered into the black hole from where the noise had come from. Now it was as silent as a tomb. There wasn't even the sound of a cricket chirping. The Sergeant made his decision.

'If there was anyone down there they've gone by now. In the morning, at first light, search the area. Now get back to sleep.'

The three left and went back down the slope. I felt more at ease now and settled down once more. But I didn't sleep again that night.

Early in the morning we woke in a sea of mist. The roofs broke through the mist like islands. A crowing cock and a barking dog slowly brought the village to life.

The mist lifted leaving a damp and cold feeling in the air. We got to our feet and stretched out the stiffness in our joints caused by lying on the hard ground. The three of us half-ran down the slope before we came to a stop. Looking at both sides of the barbed wire we were convinced by the trodden down grass that someone or something had been there. The flattened grass led from beyond the fence on to this side of the wire although there wasn't any evidence of clothing or hair to be found hanging from the wire.

Over breakfast the Sergeant questioned the three of us before we relieved the guard on the bottom gate. Most of the workforce had already left. Only the odd one or two were left going to town on their bicycles, some carrying a child on the rear carrier behind the saddle. We again searched their belongings before they left the compound which some resented and felt they were being harassed.

As the cyclists left, the Tamil Indians arrived carrying a pole on their shoulders. Coiled round the pole was a dead black mamba snake. The mamba was one of the world's deadliest snakes. The Tamils jabbered at us as they pointed to the snake. Then putting their fingers to their mouths they conveyed to us that the snake was very good eating. My stomach turned at this and we moved back. Even in death the mamba looked ominous. The Tamils walked in rhythm to the bounce of the pole with their bare brown legs. Chewing betel nuts they would spit out a stream of red juice which stained the ground.

We felt hot and dusty after coming off guard and the suggestion of a wash sounded good. Stripping down to our underpants, Jonah and I along with others went down to the village well. The first one there had the bucket, with rope attached, standing on the concrete slab. The bucket was then thrown into the well and filled. My turn came and hand over hand I lifted the bucket until it cleared the rim. I then emptied the bucket over my face and body. From nearby other buckets were found. Suddenly someone threw a bucket of water and our wash-down turned into mayhem. The horseplay caused the concrete to become slippery and dangerous around the well. We were fooling about and falling about on our makeshift ice rink until the Sergeant noticed the danger, his voice snapping out, 'Stop fooling about down there, or I will stop it and that will spoil it for the rest of the men.'

Jonah said what he felt. 'Moaning sod. If he comes down here I'll drown him.'

We walked back with our underpants hanging from us soaking. We must have looked a humorous sight.

We had a cold midday meal of cheese and biscuits. Crunching on the hard tack we were entertained by the local dark beauties as they bathed at the well, pouring bucket upon bucket over their long black dresses and saris which gripped their slim bodies, showing outlines that we had almost forgotten existed and swishing around their long sleek black hair. The water sparkled as it sprayed in the bright sunlight. Chanting and laughing they knew the men were looking at them and they teased us by giving us side glances. They dried their hair but were still wearing the wet saris. We followed with our eyes their hip-swinging walk, which brought comments for the men.

Rotating the guard to different positions broke the boredom a little. Tonight, instead of the temple, we were guarding the bottom gate. As well as the area the Sergeant also rotated the men. With me tonight were Jonah and Hutch.

With the Sergeant leading the four of us strode through the middle of the village, where the Chinese and Tamils sat. Beneath the shade of the overhanging porch men lay around smoking and scratching at the odd bite from a bug or fly. The older women were washing at the well, beating the clothes with a stick or smooth stone as squawking brats clung to their mothers' sides with fingers in their mouths. Other young ones, without a stitch on, paddled in the water bending down and patting the water with their hands.

Above the embers of a fire a black pot hung. Around this stood a small group of red, betel nut chewing Tamils. The steam rose as the ingredients boiled. It was probably the black mamba snake we saw earlier though we didn't recognise the carriers, as they all looked the same.

Dogs hung around sniffing the air in anticipation. They were brutishly kicked and hit with sticks by the onlookers, as they waited patiently for any morsel thrown their way. A stone, thrown by a young boy, caught one dog and it yelped and limped away. The other dogs scattered only to regroup and slyly return.

Standing outside one gaudy looking shack where Chinese music was constantly being played stood a group of young Chinese girls. They giggled and waved as we strode on by. They were the village brothel girls, and wore heavy make-up, bold red lipstick and powdered faces with dark lined eyes. They also had red ribbons in their hair. This wasn't unusual for a village of this size which often had houses of ill repute.

Next to the brothel was the village shop. Having no glass windows, the shutters were propped against the timbered wall. This provided the shop's security when closed. Inside the shop hung dried brown cured fish from a taut rope stretching across the front entrance. Various dried meats also hung there, maybe months old. Flies buzzed and crawled all over the uncovered meat. There were barrels of rice and flour everywhere. In the flour were ants. Both dead and alive they looked like currants sticking out. Dusty tins and bottles of every description stood on the shelves from curries to medicines and balsams – most guaranteed to cure all known ills.

A small hut with a red cross on the door provided the village with a permanent nurse and visiting doctor once a week. On the bench outside sat a pregnant woman. Beside her sat other women holding babies. They too were pregnant. Runny-nosed kids played with grasshoppers poking and prodding the unfortunate insects.

We reached the gate and moved to a spot where the Sergeant

gave us our orders for the night. He threw in his bit of wisdom before leaving us.

'Keep your virginity for the girls back home. Forget about sowing your wild oats and don't visit the girls.'

We left Jonah with the key to the padlocked gates which were to be opened in the morning. We all looked round the chosen guard position. It was a bit exposed to say the least, with some old tree trunks scattered about. Thinking these would have to do I turned to Jonah, asking for his help.

'Grab hold of the other end and drag it over here. Hutch can you manage that smaller one over there?'

In no time at all we had built a solid wall in front of us, a shield of timber capable of standing a grenade attack or rifle fire from the front. Now we all felt safer.

With the light fading fast we lay with our backs to the wooden barricade and had our last smoke of the day. From here we had a clear view of the rear of the village shacks. The cultivated plots of vegetables and greens were laid in neat rows. Behind the gardens sat a roofless building. From time to time both male and female would enter. It was some kind of prayer hut. Beyond this, in one cultivated patch, was a healthy looking garden full of my favourites – pineapples.

As the night progressed the village settled down. Men and women continued to visit the fenced in buildings, which may have been a problem for what I had in mind. I was still thinking of the pineapples and how nice they would taste on a warm evening like tonight. I got up, not telling the others what I had in mind, just saying, 'Fancy something nice, something juicy?'

'What have you in mind, Ebee? A pint, or has the sun finally got to you?' Hutch answered uninterested, thinking I was pulling their leg, which I often did.

Moving into the dark I crept along in the shadows keeping clear of the light thrown through the wall slats by the paraffin lamps and keeping a wary eye open for sleeping dogs. I stopped as a villager appeared carrying a lamp. The lamp threw out dancing shadows onto the wooden walls and the ground. The light fell onto the lower half of my body which was camouflaged by the green uniform. I stood there motionless as the figure passed. The light momentarily fell on the pineapple patch. I now knew exactly where they were. Drawing my bayonet I crept over to them and stooped. I felt through the leafy top and picked the biggest, these being the juiciest, then moving my hand lower down below the fruit for the stalk. Collecting three in all I checked everything was clear and moved back towards the barricade.

However, on the way I decided to satisfy my curiosity and crept up to the entrance of the banana woven fence. Using great care I moved more like a cat burglar than a soldier. I peered over the edge of the fence and there sitting on a long pole overlooking a trench, which ran the full length of the pole, was a Chinese, grunting and straining. I'd found their bogs. I could hardly contain myself from laughing. Still holding the pineapples I backed away.

I crept over to the other two who looked up in surprise as I dropped the pineapples at their feet.

After their thanks and questions we trimmed away the hard skin with our bayonets and threw the remains over the fence to get rid of the evidence. The ripe centres oozed with juice and dribbled down our stubble chins as we ate the fruit.

We had barely finished when we heard someone coming. It was ten o'clock and the Sergeant was making a surprise visit. To show him we were alert I rattled the bolt of my rifle as if loading it, hoping this would scare him.

'Cut it out, Ebee, you know it's me,' he said quietly. Coming closer he saw the log barricade for the first time. 'That shows some sense. You've got some protection in front of you now.'

He stayed only for a few minutes then disappeared into the night, his footsteps fading in the soft earth.

Before settling down for the night I undid my webbing belt and produced four hand grenades from the pouches. I placed them within easy reach by the water bottle. Peering at my watch the fingers told me it was ten past eleven. The village was now in complete darkness and the dogs were quiet for once. The only sound came from Hutch, who was snoring. He would occasionally smack his lips at the lingering taste of the pineapple. I thought to myself, I hope that the Commies don't pick tonight to show. If they did strike the trenches may be too far away for the three of us to reach. The bottom gate would be some sort of early warning for the rest, which made us expendable.

Morning seemed late in arriving. Being the last on guard I was able to see the village come to life. They came from their homes in groups of two or three. They crossed the track and headed up the slope towards the temple leaving their footwear before entering. Once inside they would approach the jars full of joss sticks and light one from the candle in front of the fat Buddha. The joss sticks gave off highly scented aromas. They would then start to back away from where they had knelt swaying backwards and forwards and chanting in a kind of rhythm with the other believers.

Meanwhile the non-believers threw out the previous day's refuse to the waiting pigs which grunted as they ate cabbage stalks as if they were fish heads. To a pig anything was food. The dogs would also join in if anything looked remotely edible.

The time was approaching 6 a.m. Jonah unlocked the pad-locked gate and swung one half open so as to prevent anyone from sidling out. The ones with cycles carrying latex collecting canisters, formed a queue waiting to be searched. Some tried to push through but were stopped at gunpoint and shouts of anger, '*Brinti. Brinti.*'

We searched each one in turn before telling them once again, '*Pigy, Pigy, manor pigi*,' meaning you can go, hurry along.

As they passed through we counted their numbers. This was to stop any infiltration by the Commies and mingling with the returning villagers.

Down the track behind the waiting queue came our relief. One of the men was Weaver, who had learnt to talk Malay in his spare time. He began talking with a young good-looking Malayan girl named Zarrow. She was aged about seventeen and worked as a nanny to the rubber manager's children. We left him to it. Our stomachs were rumbling for the breakfast we had yet to cook.

As we walked up the track we noticed the only place that remained closed was the brothel. It looked like the girls had had a rather busy night as they were still in bed.

Heavy eyed I sorted through the rations, saying to myself, 'How about some beans? No. Er, how about sausage and beans?

That sounds better.'

'Jonah, fancy some beans with sausage?' I asked.

'Yeah Ebee, that will do me. I'm not fussy, just tired,' he replied.

Throwing the tins out to him I found the Tommy cooker and a dry box of matches. Meanwhile Jonah had opened the tins and placed the contents into different mess tins.

With the cooker lit we soon had the sausages sizzling and we were soon eating them and spooning out the beans. Out here manners was a word seldom heard of. We heard laughing and giggling coming from the nearby well, and turned to see the mothers bathing their children. Their little world was still an innocent place of fun while outside the wire death roamed.

Pulling out my pack from the rear of the basher I searched for some boiled sweets I'd saved from the rations. The children, now washed, played by the well as their mothers washed out a few meagre belongings. They looked at me warily as I approached. Bending down in front of them I opened my hands, beckoning them to come to me. Wide-eyed they turned to their mothers before coming to me. A few words passed between them as they approached sheepishly. First one then another, but once the barrier was broken I knew I had their trust. I left them shouting, 'Johnny, Johnny.'

I crossed back over to the basher and could hear Sergeant Charmers giving Jonah the day's duties and rota.

'You two, I want to see patrolling the perimeter, and no funny business, understand?'

We picked our rifles up by the slings and threw the dregs of tea across the littered ground then turned to start the long walk around the edge of the village, following the barbed wire fence.

It was now eight days since we had first arrived and as each day passed the hollower our eyes looked due to lack of a good night's sleep and the continuous guard duty.

We stumbled up the slope to the temple, which was now empty. The Buddha's smiling face seemed to be laughing at us as he looked down on the village. I stared back at it and said out loud, 'Somebody must have told him a good joke. He's been laughing every time I've seen him.'

At which Jonah let out a tired laugh.

We passed the place where the wire still sagged from where we had heard noises the other night. The grass no longer showed any signs of tracks. We kept an eye on where we trod, going round places where the ground had been broken. There was no point tempting fate.

Women hung their washing out and a few hoed the vegetable plots as we continued along the wire. When we reached the bottom gate we stood and spoke to the two guarding it before moving on. A revolting smell rose from the enclosed lavatories as the heat made the contents ripe, and we quickly hurried past. The pineapple patch brought a smile to our faces as I pointed out the bare patch to Jonah.

To do a complete circuit of the wire took approximately forty minutes and it was another two circuits before we were relieved for a smoke and a mug of tea. During the afternoon, with the odd times of having guard changes, the stewpot was kept boiling from lunchtime so that everyone had a hot meal during the day.

Night-time, and the rota came round for me to take my turn on the temple guard. Lying there dozing, I became aware of a distant drone gradually getting louder and louder. I woke the other two and sat peering into the sky trying to get a fix on the direction it was coming from. A lone plane appeared from the south and we could see it was a British bomber although we could not tell what type. Flying low over the trees it swept over the village. At the same time a Very pistol was fired from below and a burning white flare rocketed upwards from the base camp. The circling bomber now had the exact position of the village. He came round, heading for the spluttering flare only this time he dropped his own, which hung in the sky on miniature parachutes. They seemed to hang for ever. The light they emitted illuminated the whole area, from the barbed wire fence to the rubber beyond. It was like broad daylight. Nothing stirred. Shadows thrown by the trees stood our eerily but nothing was seen and we wondered what was going on. Another flare was fired. This time it was green, signalling to the pilot to reduce speed. Again he swept in low feathering his engines and afterwards we could see his bomb bay doors being closed. We assumed the pilot was doing a spot of night-time bombing practice – with us as the imaginary targets!

Below us the village had come to life, as people ran outdoors, pointing to the plane. The villagers hadn't experienced a low flying plane over their village before.

Dogs howled and ran round in circles as the bomber's engines faded once more into the night. The hanging flares spluttered and died out leaving us again in complete darkness. It was some time before the village settled that night.

With the night over a new day began which found Jonah and me on the top gate. We were well into the morning when a billow of dust signalled the arrival of a ramshackled and overloaded lorry. It swayed and lurched as it turned on the rutted track into the village and came to a stop when we threw out a challenge.

Sergeant Charmers strode over to inspect the vehicle. Jumping onto the canvas covered back he lifted it up and revealed the weekly supplies for the shop – bags of veggies and boxes including some powerful smelling dried fish which they evidently found tasty. They were given the signal to pass through by the Sergeant who was still on the back. The lorry lurched on down the track and stopped outside the shop where the suspicious Sergeant watched the unloading.

Eating the stew that night we had a real treat. The stew was laced with curry and thickened with rice which the Sergeant had brought back from his trip down to the shop.

We were now on our fifteenth day since arriving and the Commie threat seemed over. Apart from losing sleep the operation hadn't been too bad. It was far better than pushing your way through the jungle, or wading through a swamp.

Down from the temple came the guard putting in an appearance for breakfast. Leading the three was Batey. He was walking fast and blurting out a story about a ghost. Interested in what he was saying I wandered across to listen.

'We all saw the ghost, didn't we?' He turned to the other two, who were with him, to confirm this.

Standing there were big Gowey and Corporal Cole. They both answered, 'Yes, he's right. The three of us saw the old Indian.'

Batey continued the story as the Sergeant smiled from the back. 'Well, this old Indian geezer appeared first on the old temple steps. He walked across towards the Buddha then turned to the right of the altar and he walked straight through the door without opening it. Straight through.'

Batey was questioned about the door, but he was adamant.

'We looked at the door this morning and found it locked.'

I couldn't hold it back any longer. I had to ask, 'Did the old Indian take his shoes off?'

There was huge laughter. Some believed him but the rest treated it as a huge joke.

We were told to break camp which we half-expected to happen. We took down the bashers and folded the ponchos, packing everything away, cleaning the area and burying the cans. We left the village to go back to its previous habit and the trenches for another time.

Transport arrived for the journey back which saved us another long walk. In our half-asleep state we didn't feel any bumps. Only the braking and jerking of the trucks brought us back to reality. The vehicles eventually stopped and we slipped from the tailboard and waited to get fell out. Finally the Sergeant waved us away.

Once inside the tent I threw my kit under the bed and sat on the edge. I undid the laces of my boots and let them slip onto the floor. I felt the comfort of the bed with a long drawn sigh. I heard the tent flap being lifted and through half-opened eyes I could make out the Sergeant-Major. He stood there holding a stone gallon jar.

'Get your mugs out and have some of this all of you,' he ordered.

I pulled out my mug from my pack as he came round pouring out a good measure of black rum. It was one hundred per cent proof and as thick as treacle pudding. It was diluted with water but still tasted potent. Before he left the tent the Sergeant-Major warned the men, saying, 'I don't want to see any of you on your feet during the next twenty-four hours. The only time I want to see you is at meal times and for the toilets. If I see anyone anywhere else, they will face a charge.'

We sipped the rum, issued only in cases of severe shock or trauma. Within the hour everyone was fast asleep. It was the only time I can remember being ordered to bed without being ill.

August 1951 – The Tangerine Orchard

We stopped for a rest in the centre of a fruit orchard where the trees were laden down with the fruit. On looking a little closer the green skin looked familiar. We plucked one from a lower branch and peeled the thin skin, which brought forth the smell of a juicy tangerine. My thoughts turned to Christmas back home where the tangerine was a favourite fruit though they would be ripened and coloured a sweet orange by then.

We sat beneath the branches and made use of the shade having covered several miles searching the open countryside for derelict shacks and for signs of recent occupiers using some as half-way houses between attacks. The only things we found though were cobwebs and dust.

From where I was sitting I could see the former fruit owner's home, a thatched roofed shack in the far distant corner, a few hundred yards from the orchard. The owner had had to leave due to the resettlement plan. He would either enjoy the company of others or hate every minute of it after living in isolation for so long. As the time frittered away we began to wonder why we were waiting, as no order had been given to make camp. From the front of the patrol some movement could be seen. Striding down the line men from 10 Platoon came the leading scout from 11 Platoon. Nick, a well built figure of a man with blond hair and sporting a two-week-old beard, came clumping past. There was a big grin on his face as he cradled the three hundred rounds per minute Australian Owen gun in his arms.

'Have you seen anything out there, Nick?' I asked. He was a Black Country man like myself.

'Nobody and nothing, Ebee. All I want right now is that bottle of beer down at the Char Wallah's,' he answered without stopping.

'So long Nick,' I shouted after him.

He waved his hand to show he had heard me.

The rest of the platoon was happy in the knowledge that they would be sleeping in their own beds with mosquito nets to keep the biting little perishers out. They were biting me right now.

With two platoons operating in the same area we knew only too well the dangers involved. We got to our feet as the order to move was eventually given and left the orchard using an old track which ran parallel with the shack. It seemed we had only been going for a few minutes when the peace was shattered by gunfire. The platoon scattered quickly beneath the tree-lined track. A Commie patrol had emerged from the rear of the shack from the edge of the jungle.

Above the noise I could just make out the Sergeant's voice yelling, 'Get that EY firing. Let's have some grenades on that shack. What the hell's keeping you?'

With the grenades laid out in front of me and one already in the cup, I gazed upwards. Because of the canopy of trees one wrong move and the grenade could bounce back on us. I picked a sparse spot between the branches and pulled the trigger, praying that the grenade would find a way through. From the direction of the shack came a bang and a yellow flash, then the sound of the deadly shrapnel whistling downwards. Almost as the grenade exploded I fired again. The exploding hot metal started fires on the thatched roof of the shack and sent black smoke drifting over to our left.

The order to move forwards travelled along the platoon and we fired from the hip, pushing the enemy back into the jungle. They ceased firing as they crept into their jungle lair and disappeared from sight. Shouts of 'Cease fire!' ran up and down the line as the linemen advanced to the shack.

As on so many previous strikes the Commies had carried away any dead or wounded. With the amount of fire we laid down they must have had a few casualties. Later at the ammunition count we learned that over six hundred rounds had been fired along with half a dozen grenades.

Evening came and after tracking the Commies all day we made camp. The ground was hard but the area was thick with ferns. Jonah and I began to cut and lay a good bedding of ferns beneath the poncho. Neither of us was on guard duty that night and, with the soft bedding, we slept deeply all through the night.

Waking next morning we were unaware that we had visitors during the night. A group of Commies had entered the camp perimeter. Heapy was on guard at the time and they took him by surprise. He must have been dozing and they must have been surprised also. The barking of their dogs must have brought Heapy to his senses, but he was unable to fire his Bren gun in fear of hitting any of his own men. The alerted camp stood guard but the Commies had already made good their escape. All this had happened and Jonah and I had slept through the whole episode. We listened to the story all right but kept it to ourselves in case of comebacks.

During the following days we laid ambushes lying for hours on end. The flies and ants found our sweat irresistible to leave alone and the flies buzzed incessantly in and out of the filtering rays of the sun that bore down through the foliage. The ants meanwhile scurried beneath us carrying eggs from one defeated ant's nest to another. They would hatch the eggs and raise them as slaves.

My boredom grew. Just for something to do I lifted up a piece of rotten wood and underneath was what looked like a nest of wriggling black worms the thickness of shoelaces. I used a stick to push them back into a hole. We had now given up on the ambush, and I replaced the rotten wood as we returned to base.

It was while having stew back at camp that night that I found out the worms were actually the most poisonous snake, known simply as the bootlace snake. One bite and it was goodnight Charlie. It wasn't only the Communists that killed out here.

We were now down to one day's rations. Next day we broke camp and started following animal tracks. We found this easier than trying to cut our way through. We would end up disturbing the odd animal though, sending it crashing through the under-growth. Using a compass to guide the way we reached the edge of the jungle late in the afternoon where we made the last camp of the patrol.

Finishing a late meal I sat picking my teeth. A piece of corned beef had wedged in my mouth. I finally released it and chewed it again at the same time rubbing the bristles on my chin that formed a barrier against the mosquitoes in the fading light. We crawled into the bashers talking in whispers until one of us fell asleep. The quietness was then only broken by the sound of a cricket.

Over a breakfast of beans we reminisced about how things had turned out back home. One storyteller was nicknamed Myrtle after the girl he constantly talked about. His story would begin with, 'One night me and my girlfriend stood outside her house, when it began to rain. To get out of the rain we both went into her father's garage. It was rather dark and there were no electric lights. I knew her father tinkered with cars and had a workbench littered with spare parts. Well we started smooching and were getting rather amorous so I edged her over to the workbench. Almost at once a shadow came swinging out of the darkness…'

We were all by now picturing the scene as if we were there. His hands helped to describe what happened next as he went on.

'I was sent sprawling onto the floor partially knocked out. My girlfriend screamed for help that brought her old man running into the garage with a torch. In the light he found me lying under a car wing. It had come over like a boomerang as I'd pushed her backward against the workbench.'

I nearly choked from laughter as I visualised him lying there in the torchlight, looking up cock-eyed and dazed with his love-making cut short.

We were still some distance from Niyor but the early start meant fewer miles to walk under the baking sun. Although empty the backpacks now acted like a body warmer making the sweat trickle down the shoulder blades and our sodden shirts cling uncomfortably to our skin. We were dried out but we refrained from drinking since the more we drank the more we sweated.

I shielded my eyes from the glare as we stood on the perimeter where the jungle met the lalang. Gazing across the sea of grass I saw a plume of black smoke rise from a train's smokestack and heard its clattering wheels echoing through the still air. The labouring train ran on unseen rails on the horizon like an old tramp steamer far out at sea. Some twenty minutes later we crossed those same rails that carried the prairie schooner on down to Singapore.

September 1951 – Beware of Woodcutters

Waking the following day I pulled the mosquito net from beneath the mattress, before pushing it to one side. Like a blind man feeling for a lost coin I felt for my shorts. My eyes were still shut. Next came my socks and then boots. With soap in hand, towel under my arm and eyes still shut I made my way to the showers.

Once showered I felt more human. I had heard the breakfast call while showering and found the others had already gone. I strolled over to the cookhouse and joined the queue. The cook placed two rashers of bacon with a fish turner into the mess tin then scooped up a rubber looking egg and placed that on top of the rashers. In a droll, couldn't care less attitude he asked, 'How many bread?'

'Two,' I replied.

Moving up the table, where the tea bucket sat steaming, I dipped in my mug before moving to a seat by the rolled back tent flaps.

'Morning, Ebee.'

I looked up from my mess tin and there stood Jonah.

'Mornin'.'

Only I wasn't thinking that. Eating rather salty bacon, a slice of ant infested bread and chewing a rubber fried egg. It was rather a good start to the day and grand to be alive to enjoy such comforts, I must say.

Later, sitting on the edge of the bed, I watched Batey packing his kit for this morning he was being taken into Kluang, under escort, for a court martial. He was facing charges of disobeying orders at the wrong time and the wrong place. His attitude at the time was enough and no more what everybody felt at one time or another. But the best policy was to keep mum on such occasions. Silly lad. He would now have to face the consequences. Shouldering his pack he left for the rations truck and slinging his kit onto the back he turned to wave as the lorry left.

The humidity over the last day or so seemed to be getting stronger and it came as no surprise when we heard the splatter of rain on the sagging canvas roof. The dry khaki canvas quickly took on a darker shade as the heavens opened and angrily lashed the ground. The clouds exploded in fury and the sheets of rain made it almost impossible to see beyond a few feet. One minute the ground was a dust covered bowl, and the next it was a muddy lake. Everywhere men hurried to take in the washing from the lines.

Clem the monkey cowered beneath his tree in fear while Poncho the dog ran for shelter below the open floor of the bungalow before peering out of his drier home.

Above the deluge the returning ration trucks could be heard. With them came the news Batey had been given three months. He had been made an example of and others would now think twice before refusing a direct order. Batey had to look forward to some hard work and severe discipline.

For the next few days the deluge went on unabated. The monsoons had started with a vengeance causing floods and disasters over the whole countryside, washing away crops and domestic animals. The rivers burst their banks causing death and destruction as floating debris, homes and uprooted trees were caught up in the raging torrents and became dangerous to both man and beast. Deadly reptiles swam as they too tried to escape the swirling waters.

Day after day we waited for the end, as we could only look and watch. We walked to meals with ponchos over our heads and walked through the mud as we carried the food back to the tents. Everyone was becoming irritable in the humidity that accompanied the monsoons but gradually the rain began to subside to a much more tolerable rate.

We received the weather forecast from the wireless operator. The weather was becoming more settled and the rivers began to subside. With no more rain forecast the ration trucks were made ready – all the fresh vegetables had been eaten and the stores were generally getting low.

I was chosen as one of the guards for the journey and I was quite looking forward to going to town. It broke the monotony of camp life or what little of it there was. I stood overlooking the driver's cab. The truck slithered through the thick mud, wheels spinning as the driver wrestled with the controls battling to keep traction. We had to keep moving forward. Abandoning a vehicle would mean blocking the single lane track and we would have to cut and clear another track around the vehicle.

We found the going no easier when we got to the main road which was under several inches of water. Crossing the river bridge was nerve racking as the roaring water was running just below the arch of the bridge. We climbed into the higher part of the town which had escaped the flood but the streets had been turned into a muddy bath. There were a few street traders who tried to sell salvaged crops. The buyers standing in the mud haggled over the high prices.

Whilst loading the trucks with the supplies from the quarter-master's stores, we heard a Dingo driver was missing. It had been three days since he was last seen. Charlie Marsden, the driver's name, was long overdue. But he was known to be a strong swimmer and if he was stranded and could reach safety at least he stood a chance.

With the water subsiding there was a lot of talk about mounting a search party. We half-expected to find him in some village marooned with his broken-down Dingo.

Well loaded for another week, we started back for Niyor where the conditions were just as treacherous. Floating on the side of the road were bloated oxen and pot-bellied pigs swarming with flies. This was the prime time to spread dysentery, typhoid and scores of other diseases.

Entering the rubber region the lead truck became bogged down. Jumping down from the wagon the guard cut down nearby branches, and laid them beneath the spinning wheels. They eventually found a better grip and the vehicle was lifted onto firmer ground. We were covered in mud from standing knee deep in the brown oozing water, which the heat turned to cake on our uniforms and bodies as we sat there amongst the bags and boxes.

Every day the water level diminished a little more. News came that the body of Charlie Marsden had been found. Apparently he had been found by a group of field labourers out searching for stock caught up in some wire fencing. He was covered in snakebites and had been partly eaten by some animal. It was fortunate the body had been found before it was washed away for ever. The Dingo was found some way from the scene half submerged and on its side. It had been washed away during the heavy storm and remained underwater. The turret had been open and it was likely the driver had attempted to reach the nearby farm, but for some unknown reason he had failed. Wading waist deep through the paddy fields the rescue party had carried the body to the waiting transport on the road.

Charlie's death had brought out an interesting story I could confirm myself, which may be a coincidence or just another stupid superstitious story. But I will let you be the judge of that. This is the way it happened.

Someone remembered Charlie having a pet monkey, while at Nee-Soon barracks on Singapore Island. The monkey was with Charlie night and day perched on his shoulder. However one night after a heavy drinking session, Charlie was the worse for drink. In this state he was best left alone, but for a man who craved attention this was like a red rag to a bull. He began taking out his frustrations on the poor monkey. He held a mock trial, making the monkey the scapegoat, and sentenced the poor animal to death. Before anyone could stop him he brought the bottle he was drinking crashing down on the monkey's skull. The scene was sickening to watch. Picking up the body from the table, Charlie went stumbling out laughing.

Folklore in Malaya had it that anyone held responsible for the death of a monkey would not leave the country alive. I wonder what Charlie's epitaph would be. Here lies Charlie for monkeying around. It makes you wonder, don't you think?

The weather was now much improved and the patrols resumed. Our new OC, Major Mitchell, had a peculiar habit of chewing peanuts as mentioned previously. His peanut chewing featured in one patrol he dreamed up.

Peanuts, which were full of vitamins and lighter than tinned food were to be carried for a trial period, as the diet on the next patrol. The experiment fell on the shoulders of 12 Platoon. The platoon lined up and each man was handed a bag of peanuts, along with milk, tea and sugar. They said they were lighter than the average rations by fifty per cent. On paper it looked full of promise. Five days later the patrol returned looking hungry and angry. Two days into the patrol the men had began to feel uneasy and unwell. The peanuts had played havoc with their digestive system.

I spoke to Todd on the night they came in. He told me, 'After eating so many nuts they felt like a ball in my stomach. And the pain. Well, on the way back we passed a pineapple patch and the men couldn't wait to get their hands on them.'

Needless to say that put paid to the peanut patrols.

Jonah, Heapy and I sat on upturned buckets around the water-filled bath. A fag hanging in the corner of my mouth, I was peeling the ever popular spud. Jonah let the peeled spud fall with a splash and sprayed us with water. Reaching out towards the sack for another we looked up when we heard the revving engines.

'Hi hi, here comes some more trouble,' Jonah announced as the Sergeant appeared. The three of us looked up.

A few moments earlier, unknown to the three of us, the stumbling figure of Fownes from 12 Platoon had come through the gates. He was an athletic type of character and a fanatic for fitness. He had collapsed at the gate with terror written all over his face. He had run through the rubber for miles in blind panic.

'12 Platoon's in trouble. Lots of trouble,' he blurted out between gasps of air, his chest heaving from his exertions and dust caked on his reddened face.

Someone offered him some water and he drank eagerly. Only half the water made it to his mouth, the rest went down his chin and chest. By now he was beginning to calm down.

'They walked straight into them. They didn't realise you see. Oh God what a mess! The woodcutters just threw the axes down. Just threw them down. Next thing we knew they were firing on us. We stood no chance. No chance. They're getting shot to pieces. You have to do something,' he babbled on, mumbling we had to do something.

All this went on as we peeled spuds until the Sergeant came and told us to drop everything and get kitted out for combat. Everyone sprinted from various jobs back to the tents changing as rapidly as we could into jungle greens. We pulled on trousers, laced up boots and filled up water bottles. Within minutes of being told we were ready outside the bungalow.

From the bungalow rushed Lieutenant Bury and close at his heels was the Sergeant joining in the sprint towards the waiting lorries. He jumped on the tailboard as it started to move and pulled the last of the men up in the scramble.

Swerving and bouncing we hung on for dear life. The dust was making it almost impossible to see beyond the gate of Bukit-Siput. We stopped at the dropping point where 12 Platoon were last seen. The tailboard was dropped quickly though some didn't wait as they vaulted over the sides to take up defensive positions.

In the distance gunfire could still be heard echoing through the surrounding area. But this didn't mean we were anywhere close. The high trees amplified the gunfire, making you believe it was closer than it actually was.

We were told to keep close as the platoon moved at a fast pace. Luang was at the front as usual and Hank was a close second. Pushing aside the branches and undergrowth breathing in huge gulps of air as the going got harder. Even without the packs the fifty rounds held in bandoleers together with the rifles and Bren guns made you feel the pace. The rifles got entangled in the creepers from time to time as we ran.

The gunfire had now ceased up front and we slowed down to a steady walk and emerged into a valley clearing where until a few hours ago local lumberjacks had been working before the Commies laid their cunning ambush.

Cleared timber was piled high to one side of the track. The cut and stacked thorn brush formed a gully between the cut and uncut trees which made an impenetrable barrier that stretched far up the other side of the valley. At the centre of the valley floor was a stagnant pool bridged by a fallen tree, now minus its branches.

There was movement coming from the valley floor. Small groups were seen tending the wounded and covering the dead. We moved on down the side of the valley searching for more signs of the ambushers but we saw only deeply scarred trees, empty cartridge cases and smears of blood on the freshly cut stumps. These were all the signs of a fierce skirmish. Cordite and wisps of smoke clung to the air. We waded across the stagnant pool littered by branches and thorns picking our way before emerging on the opposite bank.

We avoided the felled trees and saw axes and saws where the bogus woodcutters had discarded them and grabbed their hidden guns, completely surprising the patrol who had passed woodcutters many times in the past.

Empty brass cartridges lay everywhere. Although the Communists had an early advantage, they could not drive it home by providing the killer punch. 12 Platoon had held their ground after loosing their officer early on in the ambush.

We moved among the men who relived their stories so soon after the short but bloody encounter. We came across Todd who showed signs of being in a state of shock. I knelt beside him for a moment but he didn't recognise me at first and his mind took time to register who I was. I then listened to his story as he stuttered, still in shock. Beside us lay a body stained with blood not even cold.

'That one's beyond help, Ebee. He got caught early on.'

I got to my feet and looked down at the body. Then in a low voice I asked, 'Who is that, Todd?'

'Young Dykes. He never stood a chance. The bastards shot him at point blank range,' he mumbled staring at his trembling hands.

I lit a cigarette and gave it to him. I moved my eyes from group to group stopping when I saw a couple of medics trying to stem the flow of blood as the wounded man threshed about on the litter in agony. A snub-nosed bullet, made to cause maximum damage had blown his smashed knee and calf away. They had been outlawed but were still used by such regimes.

In a trembling voice Todd told me what happened. 'It all began last evening. You know Ebee, we should have known something like this was bound to happen.' He stopped to take a long, long drag from the cigarette he held. His eyes relived the ordeal as they peered into space. 'Last night we made camp up on the hill. Lieutenant Morris placed two men out on stag on the edge of the camp. The two on stag were Hughes with the Bren while at the other end was young Dykes here.'

As he spoke he glanced down at Dykes's body. Before he spoke again he broke down, his eyes filling with tears.

'About this time Beddows, the medic, was putting some Whitfields unction on my backside. I've got this rash and I had my trousers round my knees.'

Hearing this I could picture Todd in this compromising position. A chuckle escaped my lips.

'It's no laughing matter, Ebee,' he snapped back at me.

Trying to keep a straight face I apologised to him as he continued with the night's events.

'Well as I said, Beddows was dabbing on this ointment when Hughes's Bren opened up at something he had seen in the undergrowth. Down at the foot of the hill I heard the returning fire and threw myself onto the ground, leaving my Bren leaning against a tree. I crawled towards the tree, my trousers rolling further down my legs. They were now well below my knees.'

Pausing, his eyes drifted in a dazed state. His head shook in disbelief as he continued.

'After that incident the camp tried to settle down but we knew they were out there somewhere. Then this happened.'

Getting to my feet again I left him to recover. I picked my way through the tiny groups trying to understand how the men had felt as they passed the Commies masquerading as workers. They had looked genuine enough and had gone to great lengths persuading the real workers to leave their work and tools. Their plan had worked out well as they appeared to offer little threat. They had waited patiently while the stretched out platoon moved over the pool and began to climb up the slope opposite.

Throwing their axes and saws to one side, they had picked up their weapons, hidden beneath their feet, and fired from a few yards. The rounds had ripped into the forward section, completely taken by surprise the lead scout had been the first to call, the others had desperately tried to fight back, though they were sorely wounded. Todd had tripped over the branches of a log that spanned a stagnant pond. He struggled to free himself and once free used the log as cover. Cocking the Bren gun he looked for targets, seeing one grey uniformed figure ducking and weaving from tree stump to tree stump, firing then going to cover.

Sighting the Bren, Todd had anticipated the Commies next move. He had waited for the figure to rise and when he did his finger trigger tightened. From the Bren's muzzle had come a string of tracers which had entered the man's left shoulder, literally tearing the flesh away, smoke rising from the burning phosphorous tracers had left the man screaming.

Further up the platoon line the Lieutenant had been directing those around him from a standing position regardless of his own safety. He was hit several times, before going down, only to rise again and rally his men, before going down and staying down.

Rawang the Heban tracker had moved quickly to stand over the body. Fighting ferociously with his drawn parang, he had slashed at the charging Commies and had thrown grenades found on the officers body, scattering the advancing Commies. The howling charging ranks scattered as the grenades landed amongst them, although not exploding. Meanwhile, although hit in the leg and wrist, the young tracker forced them back. Later we were to learn why the grenades failed to explode: no one had taught the Heban how to pull the pin out to explode them.

Still missing from the platoon was Corporal Stanton. The last time anyone had seen him alive was when he was being dragged screaming away by the Commies. Wounded in the thigh he had managed to take out his own field dressing and dress the wound himself to stem the blood flow. Then from the enemy lines had come, 'You bastards, let me go! Let me go. Help me, someone help me! You yellow bastards.'

His voice had made the defenders more determined to hold out.

Searching for him later we found his body lying face downwards half-hidden in the undergrowth. Using the toggle ropes we lifted his one leg carefully and slipped over the noose before moving to a safe distance. Lying down we pulled the rope taught and pulled the body along the ground, again carefully. If there had been a grenade under his body it would have gone off by now. We went over to the body and gently rolled him onto his back then turned away quickly, not expecting to see what they had done. Some sadistic minded animal, not satisfied with just killing the Corporal, had tortured him and bayoneted him in both eyes. This war was turning out more criminals and cold-bloodied murderers than fighting men whose sole interest was in freeing their country. They had now sunk to depths of barbarism.

Before wrapping the body in a poncho, we washed the faint trickle of blood from his bruised eyeless face, distorted with pain. We then gently lifted the corners of the poncho. We didn't wish to degrade him any further by carrying him on a pole.

Carrying him back was no easy task, as we had covered some rather rough ground. Still alert to the dangers, our eyes searched every corner and we found evidence the Commies had withdrawn this way. One more find was a Chinese left in a sitting position next to a tree. He had either crawled to the spot, or had been left by comrades to die from his wounds. The Corporal's face was still fresh in our minds, so instead of burying this Commie, we grabbed both his arms and legs, and swung him back and forth, counting, 'One, two, three, let him go.'

From where we stood we threw him down a steep bank sending the body crashing and rolling, head over heals, through the undergrowth before coming to rest somewhere at the bottom. He would provide some animal with a meal, if it could stomach him. Our feelings for the enemy were that grim.

We reached 12 Platoon with the body but their hopes of finding him alive had already gone. Anger was written on their faces, as they wanted to view the remains. We advised them not to unwrap the body.

'Sunray. Sunray. Calling Sunray. Please answer, Sunray.'

Suddenly, from where he sat, Todd quickly got to his feet. His face full of rage, he picked up the microphone next to the 88 set and yelled down the mouthpiece, 'Sunray's f***ing dead. He's f***ing dead I tell you!'

He dropped the microphone beside the set and turned away as the agitated voice of the receiving officer, resenting being spoken to like that, answered, 'Hello. Hello. Who's that speaking, answer me. Hello.'

The voice petered away as the platoon made ready to leave, taking the dead and wounded back to the place where the pick-up would be waiting. Lifting them onto litters, the flies buzzed all around.

Once back at the pick-up point we laid them side by side on the trucks, then slowly drove back to Niyor. We were in no hurry now. The Char Wallah's that night was the quietest we had seen for some time. There was no laughing or singing, just a quiet drink. Our thoughts were with the dead and the wounded. This game of cat and mouse had become a stalemate going first one way then swinging back the other, with no actual winner in sight. Over the last few months, 12 Platoon had taken a beating and lost half its men in wounded and dead.

October 1951 – Revenge is Sweet

I lay on my bed reading a comic book called the *Wizard*. Well, half-reading and half-listening as Jim Swindles, the Lieutenant's batman, was engrossed in an argument over religion. I could hear him say, 'How could a man, this Jonah geezer, live in a whale's stomach for weeks without food. Tell me how he could live?'

Hutch and Gowey were in on the argument. 'That's what they call faith, if you believe in God,' they both answered. Backwards and forwards went the argument. It ended with the cook clanging the tyre rim, summoning the platoon to dinner. They were still arguing as they collected their mess tins. I pushed the comic book under my pillow before following them out.

We ate the boiled fish and potatoes as if we were robots. Life hardly held any meaning for us. We packed loads like animals, slept like animals – we even died like animals. Our lives were like a roll of the dice, or waiting for your card to turn up. Was it your turn next?

The Orderly Officer interrupted my black thoughts. 'Any complaints with the food?'

I gave my reply without much thought to the matter. 'We could do with more fresh meat, sir. But everything else seems all right.'

'Mmm, leave it with me. I'll see what can be done.'

I thought to myself that was the last I'd hear of that. But I was wrong.

Next morning, at the end of parade, Lieutenant Bury told the men of 10 Platoon, 'Get your gear. This morning we are going pig hunting. Bring along the toggle ropes.'

We changed from shorts to trousers and paraded for the pig hunt. But where the hell were the pigs? Surely we weren't going into the jungle after them.

After a short journey we stopped at an isolated village resettled some months earlier by the platoon. We jumped down from the tailboards into the centre of the village which showed real signs of dilapidation. Thatched roofs were caved in. Doors were hanging lopsided. Once well worn paths were now bursting with new growth. The earth was beginning to take back what it had lost.

We heard a scuffling in one of the dilapidated shacks. Hutch, being the nearest, stepped quietly forwards, clutching his gun to investigate. He peered inside then suddenly ran out shouting. The biggest pot-bellied pig you would ever see was following him. The pig squealed as it chased the unfortunate Hutch. Those watching scattered and the pig charged after them.

The pig halted in the centre of the village as it was surrounded by the platoon. It took up a threatening posture as the men made ready the slipknots in the toggle ropes. We closed in. Then without warning it charged through. The encircling group bowled over Gowey and Townsend but their hurriedly thrown ropes ended hopelessly in thin air. The pig seemed to be enjoying the chase.

After further attempts failed at catching the slippery customer, the Lieutenant drew his revolver. 'Stand back and stay where you are. There's only one way of doing this.'

Which he promptly did. Taking aim, he shot the bloody pig. The pig fell squealing, its nerves twitching in its death throes before quivering and lying still.

While others carried the pig's carcass onto the pick-up, we began chasing the numerous chickens left by the former owners. Even catching chicks wasn't easy. We tried to entice them by calling them like dogs, 'Here chick-chick-chick. Come on nice chick.'

As they got close we dived forward. But all we got was thin air and feathers. The escaping chicken, clucking and flying, usually evaded the frustrated men. Somehow though we caught the majority of the birds. But the pig was the main prize and the conversation piece. Having had so much salty bacon, the thought of a good old-fashioned pork chop and fresh bacon brought the taste buds watering.

I looked at the carcass where it lay. Its eyes were still open and a smear of blood was around the dark puncture wound in its head. Its tongue was protruding between the green stained teeth. Its death meant food for a company of lean men who needed meat for strength and endurance, which it now lacked.

However, this was not to be. Next morning over breakfast the cook told us that during the night the pig had turned bad. The heat and humidity had turned the meat into a putrefied, fly-blown, maggot-infested piece of rotten flesh. The sickly smell hung in the air. With handkerchiefs tied around our faces the group of volunteers unhooked the meat from where it hung and dragged it to a safe distance before burning the carcass. The aroma now was much better than the rotting smell. That night we ended up having chicken instead of pork, our cowboy days finishing on a wrong note.

Like on so many occasions we sat smoking as we were driven to an unknown destination. We only knew the direction the road went, north or south. Today it was north as we passed through Labis where the land was getting back to normal after the heavy flooding and the farmers were already sowing and planting in the fields. Back home, harvesting was done once a year while over here it was continual, apart from the floods.

Ahead a small traffic jam held up the way forwards. The air was full of the smell of burning rubber and black smoke could be seen billowing. Looking over the driver's cab we could make out another bus had been stopped and burnt. As we moved alongside we saw the charred remains. The very presence of the police seemed to add to the chaos as they prevented the passengers from recovering possessions.

As we pushed ahead the air became clear and there was a slight breeze, which was very welcome, as we sat in the full glare of the sun. A slowing of the trucks once more found us looking to the front. Up ahead were several armoured cars known as Diehards from the Hussars' armoured battalion. They were the proud Lancers of yesteryear and had gone from horseflesh to plate armour over the generations of changing warfare.

From the rear of the Diehards they unloaded three-inch mortars and set them up on a nearby bank, overlooking the rubber trees and jungle beyond. Stripped to the waist the Hussars toiled and laboured carrying the barrels and ammunition, setting the base plates and bolting down the barrels before sighting them towards the rubber. Meanwhile Lieutenant Bury and the Hussars' officer debated over a map spread out before them. Their discussion ended with the map being folded. Our officer crossed the road to have a word with the Sergeant. We heard him say, 'Right Sergeant. Get the men strung out and move them in that direction.' As he spoke he pointed towards the rubber at the entrance of the plantation.

Once we were standing on the road, the temperature dropped to a more comfortable level. Drak was to the front of me carrying the wireless. The small green triangular flag on the extended aerial bobbed from side to side as he walked with a rolling action.

After covering something like half a mile the platoon was brought to a halt. The officer looked at his watch as if expecting something to happen. Suddenly there was a 'phut-phut' followed by explosions in quick succession. All about us treetops and branches were brought down. The noise deafened the eardrums and made the senses reel.

Rushing over to Drak, the Lieutenant tried desperately to get in touch with the commander of the mortar section. The bombardment suddenly ceased, leaving us dazed and it took several minutes for us to recover. We had never been more grateful for the trees. Their protection had almost certainly saved the platoon from being wiped out by flying shrapnel. Our officer ranted over the net, tearing pieces out of the mortar officer.

The mortar sights were adjusted and they began to fire again. The 'phut-phut' this time made the platoon instinctively crouch as the bombs passed overhead. Way up front of the platoon came the 'crump-crump' as the bombs began exploding. We knew how the enemy must have felt at this moment as we had experienced it ourselves only moments earlier.

High up in the trees monkeys tried to make for safety. One monkey attempted to jump but miscalculated and ended with a thump on the leafy ground. For several seconds it lay still, as if dead, then got to its feet and scampered up the nearest tree to join the others in their flight.

The barrage ended and we waited for our orders to move. My fingers were nervously fidgeting with the old rifle sling, wondering what to expect. Probably nothing like on previous occasions.

High on our right came the lone hum of a single-engined plane. The sound grew louder and louder, and we searched the skies until we finally sighted it. It was a Hurricane class single seat fighter. We saw it dive from right to left in the black smoke rising from the mortared area. Slung beneath the Hurricane's wing were rockets. Suddenly they streaked earthwards, leaving a white trail of smoke. They became lost to us in the black smoke, until a muffled bang was heard. Circling, the fighter came in low again, firing the remainder of his rockets. Then he circled once more and fired cannon shells from the wings. Tracers hammered home into the objective. Sweeping round the fighter gained height and dipped his wings from side to side. This was an old pilot's way of saying good luck as done during the Battle of Britain. Then the sound faded and he was gone.

This left the platoon to finish the job. Our ears were singing and buzzing from the explosions as we waited for the message. Then Drak received the all clear to move on. The softening up had been completed. With some waving of his arms the Sergeant got the platoon in a line facing the jungle. From the centre he looked up and down and his voice rang out, 'Fix bayonets. We're going in. Don't falter or fall behind.'

All along the line came the clicking as bayonets were locked onto the end of the gun barrels. This came as a shock to most of us. My heart pounded when I realised we were going in like this. My chest began to heave and my knuckles turned white as the grip on my rifle tightened, making my hands ache and tremble. Relax, relax, I kept telling myself driving my body forwards as my legs refused. The jungle in front seemed to be coming towards the men fast. The roof of my mouth was dry and I licked my lips. I was trained for this purpose and for moments like this but I still asked myself, could I kill a man, face to face? This would be answered in the next few strides.

Slowed momentarily by the undergrowth the jungle closed in around us. Ahead there was noise and movement screened by the undergrowth. We charged forwards, smashing through the remaining few yards. We surprised the unsuspecting Commies, who'd thought the attack had come to an end. The aerial bombardment had done little damage as shielded by the massive trees their small halfway camp was still intact.

They overcame their surprise and picked up anything they had at hand for defence. As we fell among them shots rang out in the air. Lunging forwards with bayonets we sank them into soft flesh. The recipient sometimes grabbed hold of the barrel, holding in the embedded bayonet in a vain effort to stem the flow of blood. The blood began to trickle through the fingers. We would then pull the trigger and literally blow the Chinaman several feet away.

Even this didn't stop some bayoneteers as they struck again and again. Whether their victims lay on the ground or not, the screams and blood-curdling rants pierced the eardrums. During these frenzied moments, the scenes seemed to play in slow motion. The adrenaline made the senses reel and turned men into raging animals whose only thought was to kill, kill and kill again.

Like fighting cocks the men had gone crazy. The enemy's sword and parang proved no match for the British bayonet. Those trying to escape barely reached the edge of the clearing before being brought down.

The hand to hand fighting was over in minutes. As the charge carried over into the jungle, we could see that only minor damage had been caused by the rocket attack. The trees had acted like a steel umbrella over the enemy.

Silence brought the carnage to an end. Taking in the full scene we could see what the ferocity of the attack had left. Nine bloodied bodies and some weapons. We were sweating and breathing hard. The adrenaline was still running high. The job of clearing up began, and the dead had to be carried back to the road which meant another hard march. Cutting down branches to make poles we lashed the bodies to them hand and foot. It was a rare but satisfying feeling to be carrying their and not our own dead. Suffering from only slight cuts and bruises the platoon's casualties were light and needed only slight attention from Hutch.

Getting back to the road took three times as long. And by the time we did reach the road, the Hussars had already stowed away the mortars and were waiting for us. They could now see the enemy at close quarters for the very first time as swinging bodies lashed to poles. They had heard the gunshots as we attacked, and were now seeing the results.

Exhausted, we lay the poles on the tarmac and gratefully accepted the cigarettes offered by the Hussars, though they were more interested in the bodies than us. Some were more adventurous than others and pulled the poncho covers back. Their faces paled at what they saw. Some turned away and vomited on the roadside. We had a quick laugh at their expense. We ourselves had been hardened many times in the past.

The bodies occupied the centre of the trucks, and we sat on the steel sides watching the high-wheeled armoured Diehards moving in the opposite direction. Worn out, we hardly noticed the burnt-out shell of the bus, resting on the blackened axles and scorched road. When cold it would be pushed over into the gorge below.

Singing in the Char Wallah's that night the atmosphere was more boisterous then usual. We were celebrating one of the men's birthday and, as the first round of drinks were free, I chose a bottle of Carlsberg from one of the clinking bottles floating in the nearly full galvanised bath. From around his neck the Char Wallah produced a bottle opener. With a click the metal top flew off. I took my first drink and nodded to the birthday boy as the party got into full swing.

The merrier the men got, the ruder the songs became. Then the party began to play jug-a-lug. Everyone took it in turns to sing and anyone refusing had to pay a forfeit. The forfeit was to drop ones trousers and bend down, showing your behind. While doing this, ashtrays and beer dregs were emptied up the rear accompanied by howls and derision from the onlookers. Plucking up courage as my turn came round I sang a song, which I had heard Heapy constantly singing. I completed the song in an atmosphere of smoke and cat calling and finished by taking a swig from the bottle.

From then on the night's recollections faded into a drunken stupor. It was early next morning when I realised my mistake of drinking so much. Standing in the sun, my head was about to explode. I said to myself, never, never again.

November 1951 – Forgotten Days

Between patrols we spent much of the time in two groups. Our chores and pastimes helped to break the boredom. We would play badminton behind the officers' mess or basketball on the parade ground. Spectators, amid shouts and bad language, urged the heavy tackling players on. The games often ended with knackered players on both sides.

Beneath the showers the cool water soothed my bruises and stiffness, aches and pains. I forgot everything as I relished this small pleasure for a moment. With a towel around my middle and unlaced boots on my feet, I strolled over to the tent and as I ducked under the tent flap I caught Hutch asking its occupants, 'Have you read the bulletin board outside the office today any of you?'

There was a chorus of no's from the men. So Hutch obliged them with the news word for word.

'Awarded for bravery in the field. The late Lieutenant Morris has been awarded the Military Cross. Private Leadam gets mentioned in dispatches. But wait for it, the Heban tracker Rawang gets the George Cross.'

It wasn't long before a crowd stood around the notice-board reading the awards. From near the back someone was heard to say, 'Think they've heard back home yet?'

News like this could have a double-barrelled effect on those hearing the awards. While it was good to feel proud of your son or brother, it also meant you were in the midst of trouble which was more worrying.

Late that afternoon 12 Platoon came through the camp gates on foot. They were bearded and bedraggled and rattled by the encounters. Perhaps the news of the awards would help to bring back some kind of purpose. Something they could build on.

Their new officer was Lieutenant May, a baby-faced man whom they instantly nicknamed 'Blossom'. They operated without a Sergeant, since Sergeant Cooper had gone home. They had even lost the services of their Corporal, Corporal Chadwick. He had been the victim of a freak accident when a Bren gunner had placed the loaded weapon sharply on the ground. The faulty safety catch caused it to fire prematurely, hitting the Corporal in both legs. Fortunately for him the bullets had missed the bone.

Although not wishing them any harm, 12 Platoon's return meant 10 Platoon were next out, and would be going within the next twenty-four hours. Rations were issued after the last meal of the day, which meant an early morning start. That night was spent down at the Char Wallah's celebrating the news of the awards in honour of their dead, and the wounded George Cross winner Rawang. We also left with a supply of cigarettes.

Fully kitted out in the early hours we stood waiting outside the office and helped each other make sure everything was secure. Holding the packs high on the shoulders we altered the straps for more comfort. A badly placed pack would cause the carrier to have sore shoulders while a well balanced pack would avoid all this. Patiently we waited. Then the officer came through the door, fiddling with a twisted shoulder strap and holding his crumpled hat in his fist. He asked the Sergeant if everything was ready. The platoon was then brought to attention and the lead scout was ordered to the head of the patrol.

Just at that moment the clerk rushed from the office and called out, 'Sir, sir, this has just come over the wireless.'

He passed over the paper and the officer glanced at me. My first thought was, What have I done? Then I thought it must be someone back home. The words he spoke came as a big surprise.

'Private Parkes. You are to stand down.'

I was still puzzled and mystified.

Then he completed the sentence. 'You are going home.'

His words had only half sunk in. My tour of duty was over. Finished. Ended. Another five minutes and it would have been too late. I would have been walking down the track with the rest of the platoon. In disbelief I unslung my pack. I was still bewildered by the sudden news. I handed over the stewpot into someone's outstretched hands, and said hasty goodbyes to my friends. Over the last two years they had become my family, and seemed to take precedence over my good news. Quick handshakes and a 'Good luck Ebee, and don't forget to have a pint for us!' were the last words, still vivid in my mind.

Jonah, my partner, asked me to go and see his mother. 'Tell her I'm all right, you might want to say, Ebee.'

They were waving as they went through the open gate. I would never see some of them again.

Still bemused by the news, I walked back to the tent which was now empty. Carrying my pack I let it fall on the bed. My eyes roamed around the empty beds.

Other shouts went up from nearby tents as they received news they were going home. Then came orders we were to leave early next morning by ration truck. During the day the others and myself packed out kitbags. That night down at the Char Wallah's I paid off my slate. I regretted the fact my last drink here wasn't with the lads and in the silence of the tent that night my thoughts turned to home. It was early morning before I finally dropped off to sleep.

After being awakened, I still thought I'd dreamt I was going home. I was going home with half the original thirteen coming from 'D' Company, when we were first transferred to the Worcesters some twenty months earlier. I had only seen the others on such rare occasions, such as ration guards so to meet up again and travel home together would be a good feeling.

Sitting on empty crates the trucks left Niyor camp. For us it would be the last time. I tipped my hat in mocked salute, and said goodbye to Niyor for good. To wear a beret instead of a bush hat felt a little strange. I looked around and thought of the life I had led and was now leaving behind me and thanked God for allowing me to return home in one piece.

Instead of going to Singapore the train we boarded was going north to a place on the west coast, a transit camp called Swettenham. The train journey was painfully slow. On one occasion we stopped to reload wood from the trackside. Back home they used coal for fuel, but here there was a plentiful supply of wood. With the tender full again the train journey continued.

From time to time we saw patrols near rural villages. Regiments this far north would be the Green Howards, the Royal

Marines and the West Kents. The latter were constantly in the news suffering many casualties. The area was an old stamping ground of the Worcesters, and a Communist's dream with its valleys and hills.

Trying to get comfortable on the wooden slats of the coach's seats proved almost impossible on the crowded train. Three from our party were already utilising the luggage racks and, although cramped, they had fallen asleep. This brought giggles from the children onboard as the swaying train rocked, threatening to throw the sleepers from the narrow racks.

Arriving at the station at the end of the line we gathered our kitbags. Nick pocketed the playing cards we had been playing with for the last few hours. Those on the rack were now awake and were waiting to get down as the passengers left the train.

Outside the station, amid the comings and goings, stood the transport. The red flash of the crossed kukri and bayonet stood out on the cab door of the truck. Recognising us by our cap badges the driver stubbed out his cigarette then asked, 'Enjoy the journey, chaps?'

With a 'Not too bad' and a 'It was all right' coming from the lads we loaded the kitbags onto the lorry. After reporting to the office we were sent to tents that were bedded down away from the other platoon lines. We were separated by a football pitch and were left alone for the rest of the day. We went to dinner then settled down for an early night.

I woke in the night restless, wondering what was happening to me. Morning came and found me bathed in sweat. The bed was spinning and I found it hard to focus my eyes. I sat on the edge of the bed, trying to put my head together. The others by now had noticed my condition. Nick, in the bed nearest to me, leaned over and felt my forehead. Looking concerned he told me what I already knew.

'Ebee you are burning up. The best thing to do is report sick over at the medical tent.'

The rest went for breakfast, leaving me alone. I got to my feet and threw the bedclothes roughly across the bed. I then walked unsteadily into the blinding sunlight. I shielded my eyes with my hands and looked for the medical tent. It seemed far away. With eyes only partly open I crossed the empty playing field. The sky and the surrounding tents were swimming uncontrollably. The ground came up towards my eyes, then went down again under my feet. My head was pounding from a thousand hammers inside my skull. I felt like I was losing my mind as I lurched through the entrance of the medical tent.

Everything turned blurry and my body folded onto the floor. Then I could feel hands lifting me onto the bed. From somewhere inside my head a strange feeling of someone talking. The burbled words were lost as my whole body shook. I was shivering even with extra blankets placed over me by the medical orderly.

I drifted down into a deep abyss swirling faster and faster in a whirlpool of the past. Looming out of a grey fog, from the depths, came a man. He had a rifle, which he raised and pointed to the back of another man's head. A man in uniform, standing in a trench. At the sound of the gunshot the man turned to face the gunman. It was my own face.

The scene changed to a grass-covered courtyard. A cobra reared to strike a man also in the scene. He was moving towards two other men who were holding a third man. Hitting and punching him, he screamed out in silence. The man turned to see children playing with a dead snake. In this swirling nightmare world, a leering face suddenly confronted me. His hands held a gun. I saw the fingers tighten on the trigger, slowly cocking the gun. My hands were going out to stop him, but the finger completed the movement. And I saw the bullets emerge from the nozzle of the gun barrel. Getting closer and closer. Then gone.

I was climbing back up from the dark abyss drifting somewhere between darkness and consciousness. Tossing and turning, delirious and mumbling, the fever gradually subsided.

I felt terrible. My mouth was cracked and dry. My whole body was too weak to move. Slowly my eyes opened. Through the half-opened lids I could see a stranger standing beside me wearing a white coat. Seeing me awake he spoke for the first time.

'Glad to see you with us again. For a while there you had us worried.'

He saw that I was a bit confused and bewildered, so he calmed me down by telling me what I was doing there. My memory was a complete blank from the day of our arrival.

'It's all right calm down. You are safe in hospital and recuperating from a bad case of malaria. You want a drink?'

Nodding back yes the orderly lifted my head and held the glass to my lips. I drank deeply. The cool water took away the dryness of my throat. I lay back and closed my eyes and slept a much calmer and peaceful sleep.

I came out of my fever later that day and found out from the orderly I'd been laid low by the malaria bug for the last four days. My recollections were of ghostly figures of hell and earth. Visions of the subconscious mind, which flitted through my head from time to time.

During the next day or so my strength returned and I learned that the troopship we had been waiting for had beached on some North African shoreline. It had been burnt out although everyone was saved.

I left the hospital tent on unsteady legs and crossed the football field which I had previously stumbled across in a dream-like state. All that was a blank to me now. I joined the lads in packing the rest of my gear. Then shouldering our kitbags we left for the station in a fifteen hundredweight truck. We showed our travelling vouchers to the Sikh in the ticket office. Then we found the station had a bar, which made the waiting for the next train more congenial.

The clanking and hissing, mixed with the hub-bub of the jostling crowd made us reluctant to leave our favourite pastime. Once onboard though we hardly noticed it pull away from the now deserted platform.

On through the dark night the train thundered, the searchlight flashing as it swept the track. Fed with logs, the open fire could be seen glowing on sweeping bends while sparks flew from the smokestack. The Sikh fireman kept a good head of steam.

From the lit nameplates on the passing platforms I knew we were approaching the state of Johore Baru, the place I thought I would never see again. Beyond lay the station halt of Niyor. My thoughts turned to the many times I had seen this same train pass by in the night. I had a weird feeling as I thought of the searchlight passing over our heads knowing that if we'd been seen, the withering fire of the armoured car's twin guns could be brought down on us. Were those same watching eyes of 10 Platoon watching us now? I couldn't help but give out a faint sigh.

Yawning from a fitful sleep and my cramped position I opened my eyes and saw the hawker on the station selling tea to the crowd on Singapore station.

'What time is it Nick?' I asked.

He glanced at his watch and replied, 'It's just turned seven. Anyway, why ask me? You've got your own watch.'

I felt stiff from sitting for hours on the wooden bench seat. I grabbed my kitbag from the overhead rack and followed behind the others who dismounted on the concrete platform. We kept together as we pushed through the crowds, and made for the buffet bar. By now we had little money left in our pockets. Sitting round two tables we pooled our money and found we had enough for a cup of tea apiece. Finding myself chosen to order the tea I stood next to the counter and opening my hand I let the loose change and a low denomination note fall onto the counter. The onlooking Chinese counter hand was wide eyed as I asked for, 'Thirteen cups of tea if you please.'

I wiped my nose with the back of my hand and turned to look at the others, who were laughing and grinning. I walked over with the laden tray and placed it on the table. Everyone picked up a cup and sipped the strong tea as they smoked.

Among the early travellers were infantry reinforcements going northwards for the first time. They were looking forward to their forthcoming adventure. Their enthusiasm would be smashed within a few days of their arrival. What makes a man want to be a hero? It was hard to believe I was like them once.

We were unaware of the door to the buffet bar swinging open, until a Corporal shouted above the noise of the crowd.

'Any of you lot, from up country from the Worcesters? Come down from Port Swettenham to go home?'

'Over here,' we replied from round the table.

He looked across to where the chorus came from and answered, 'Right, there's a truck laid on to take you to Nee-Soon outside the station. Be on it in five minutes.'

With that he left and the door swung shut again. We gulped

down the tea and got to our feet. With kitbags on our shoulders yet again we followed each other through the station.

Outside alongside the station façade was a line of parked army vehicles. We walked down the line and stopped when we came to the lorry bearing the brigade flash. Recognising the Corporal behind the wheel, we threw in our kitbags and climbed on. We joined the mad rush and blaring horns as in and out the traffic we drove. Arguing taxi drivers leaned out of their windows. There was one scene with an upended cart where the porter struggled to get the bullock to its feet, while an angry taxi driver pointed to the cargo strewn across the highway.

Once we arrived at Nee-Soon we were taken to report to the armoury where we handed in our rifles and ammunition. It was like saying goodbye to an old friend. One more link with the platoon had been broken. We reported to the officer who dealt with the troops going home. He notified our group we would be driven down to the docks the next day where we would join the troopship *Dilwara* on her way home from Hong Kong. That afternoon we received our last pay before joining the ship.

After dinner the group did its own thing. Some went down the NAAFI for the last night while others went strolling around the camp. Myself, I took a leisurely walk into Nee-Soon. Like most towns and villages the shops stayed open. Having had pay that afternoon I had a few spare dollars in my pocket so I bought the odd souvenir or two.

I stood on the sidewalk. The streets were no different from any other apart from the out of bounds signs which were noticeable in any town with a barracks. Beyond the signs dark alleys led to the brothel houses where a whore could be bought for a few dollars, aged from ten upwards. I felt glad to be leaving to where a cool drink of clear water could be had without fear of disease. That place was home.

Next morning we stood at the foot of the gangplank as the naval purser checked our boarding documents for clearance. He handed the papers back to us, and we climbed onboard to the upper decks.

Through the open stairway the Chinese and Tamil dockers could be seen crossing the loading ramp from the dock to the open door in the side of the ship's hull, pushing sack trucks and manhandling fresh supplies through the open watertight doors. Their bodies glistened with sweat as they laboured. Inside the ship's bowels bangs and muffled shouts echoed as the freight was unloaded.

After being given our berthing accommodation we made our way below decks. We found the sleeping quarters somewhat cramped housing up to fifty men in banks of three high bunks. The air was stuffy, as the air-conditioning wasn't switched on until we put to sea so we stowed away our gear and took ourselves topside.

The gentle breeze made the open much more pleasant than below decks. From the high deck rail, above the warehouses alongside the quayside we could see the skyline of one of the world's busiest ports dominated by the white buildings of the Cathay Cinema, and the Christian church. A heat haze shimmered over the sprawling capital, known as the Gateway to the East. It was the last port before heading northwards into the China seas or southwards to the continent of Australia.

Below us the red-roofed warehouses, with their peeling paint, showed large quantities of rubber through the open doors. Some of the bales were stacked along the quay where huge cranes hoisted them onboard docked freighters. There were ships here from every seafaring nation.

Below our feet the loading ramp had been removed. Then a dull thunder followed as the loading doors were closed tight. The quayside, which had been teeming with life only a little earlier, was now almost quiet and only about a dozen labourers remained.

Above us the red and black funnel blew a long blast releasing a jet of steam into the sky. This reminded non-passengers to leave the ship, as we were about to sail. Down the gangway they went turning to wave and tearfully blow kisses to friends and relatives and saying their last goodbyes. They were still waving as the bullhorn blasted and the gangplank was raised. The labourers on the dockside lifted the heavy mooring ropes from the bollards struggling to send them splashing into the water. The forward and stern capstans then wound the dripping ropes aboard. Through the soles of our feet we could feel the gentle vibrations from the ship's engines.

Slowly the ship manoeuvred into position into the harbour, before moving into the open sea channels. The ship's screws then churned the sea into foam and in a little while the wake stretched out for miles behind the ship.

I stayed on top deck long after the others had gone below. The horizon was now just sea and sky. The prospect of going home was only marred by having to leave so many friends behind. Home was somewhere I had left as a boy, and would be returning to as a man. I had seen the best of men and had witnessed the very worst. Life would never be the same again.

The Last Thought

I have no drums to beat or flags to fly
My duty done I here now lie.
They said I was too young to sin, but not to die.
For someone so young I lost so much,
A lover's kiss and that mother's touch,
I walked alone amidst a hundred men
Though I lost my life but not my soul,
With outstretched hands I met my God
My death came quick.
Don't leave me here
In this imprisoned land,
My land is free
So take me there,
Where the drums beat
And my flag flies free.

No future left, nowhere to turn,
Just lying here, with vision blurred,
Knowing not if day or night,
Like moving shadows.
Through the mist they came,
My pain now gone,
Just a lifeless form they had won,
I could hear the drums,
And see the flags,
My other life had now begun.